Metacognitive and Cognitive Strategy Use in Reading Comprehension

Limei Zhang

Metacognitive and Cognitive Strategy Use in Reading Comprehension

A Structural Equation Modelling Approach

 Springer

Limei Zhang
Nanyang Technological University
Singapore
Singapore

ISBN 978-981-10-6324-4   ISBN 978-981-10-6325-1   (eBook)
https://doi.org/10.1007/978-981-10-6325-1

Library of Congress Control Number: 2017952908

Printed on acid-free paper

This Springer imprint is published by Springer Nature
The registered company is Springer Nature Singapore Pte Ltd.
The registered company address is: 152 Beach Road, #21-01/04 Gateway East, Singapore 189721, Singapore

Preface

This study is a revised version of my Ph.D. dissertation submitted to the National Institute of Education, Nanyang Technological University, in July 2013. It concerns the investigation of the relationships between Chinese college test takers' strategy use and reading test performance.

There are five main objectives in this study: (a) examining and identifying the patterns of Chinese college test takers' strategy use for the reading comprehension test; (b) exploring the factorial structure of EFL reading test performance as measured by the retired College English Test Band 4 (CET-4) Reading subtest; (c) investigating the relationships between test takers' strategy use and reading test performance; (d) examining the relationships between metacognitive and cognitive strategy use in test situations; and (e) investigating gender differences in strategy use and reading test performance.

In writing the book, I wish to express my sincere gratitude to Prof. Christine Goh for her invaluable and sustained support, enlightening guidance, and most importantly, for her insightful comments throughout the manuscript. It is my great honor to have had the opportunity to work with such an amazing and considerate professor.

I also wish to express my heartfelt appreciation to Prof. Antony Kunnan for giving me enlightening suggestions about structural equation modeling and for his ongoing technical advice; Prof. Lawrence Jun Zhang for his insightful comments, warm encouragement, and unyielding support during my study; and especially to Prof. Scott Paris, without whom it would not have been possible for me to start this fruitful journey and choose the appropriate research direction.

My heartfelt thanks go to Prof. Guangwei Hu, Prof. Yan Wang, and Prof. Yongbing Liu for their generous help toward the completion of the project, all the students involved in the study for their contribution of time, cooperation, and assistance, and other colleagues and researchers who were often the best critics.

Finally, I am greatly obliged to my family for their unwavering support, encouragement, and unconditional love in the course of my research.

Singapore, Singapore   Limei Zhang

Contents

List of Figures

List of Tables

Chapter 1
Introduction

Abstract This chapter starts with a presentation of the problem for this study. It then describes the context of the study by introducing the history, development, and recent reform of College English teaching and the College English Test in China. It moves on to discuss the rationale behind the study and its purpose. In the section that follows, research questions this study aims to address are presented. Important concepts and terms pertinent to this study are then defined and operationalized. Significance of the study is discussed at the end of this chapter.

1.1 Statement of the Problem

Researchers have shown considerable interest in studying individual characteristics in second language (L2) learners[1] (Cohen & Macaro, 2007) in the past decades. In particular, one individual difference variable, learning strategy, has gained much attention among researchers (e.g., O'Malley & Chamot, 1990; Oxford, 1990; Phakiti, 2003, 2008b; Politzer & McGroarty, 1985; Purpura, 1997, 1999; Wen & Johnson, 1997; Zhang, 2016a, b; Zhang, Chin, Gong, Min, & Tay, 2016; Zhang, Goh, & Kunnan, 2014; Zhang & Zhang, 2013). For example, a considerable number of studies have been conducted to investigate what proficient readers typically do while reading, especially through identifying the strategies they employ (e.g., Block, 1986, 1992; Kern, 1989; Macaro & Erler, 2008; Zhang, 2010).

In the same vein, language testing researchers have shown growing interest in the identification and characterization of individual characteristics that influence performance on language tests (Kunnan, 1995; Purpura, 1999). Bachman and Palmer (2010) argued that language knowledge is directed by a set of strategies which determine how language is realized in actual use situations. However, from the perspective of language assessment, test takers' strategy use has not been given sufficient attention, though research in this area could contribute to test score

---

[1]In line with common practice (e.g., Ellis, 1984; Hu, 1999; Mokhtari & Sheorey, 2008), *second language* (L2) is used throughout this study as a superordinate term referring to any language learned after the first language.

© Springer Nature Singapore Pte Ltd. 2018
L. Zhang, *Metacognitive and Cognitive Strategy Use in Reading Comprehension*,
https://doi.org/10.1007/978-981-10-6325-1_1

interpretation and construct validation (Bachman, 1990; Cohen, 2006; Messick, 1989). The goal of this study, therefore, is to investigate the relationships between Chinese college test takers' strategy use and test performance on the College English Test Band 4 Reading subtest.

Originally designed as a test to provide an objective assessment of students' overall English proficiency in tertiary institutions, the College English Test (CET), which is composes of College English Test Band 4 (CET-4) and College English Test Band 6 (CET-6), has an enormous impact on English as Foreign Language (EFL) teaching at the tertiary level in China. In addition, due to the increasing recognition of the test by institutions and society, the CET certificate has become a nationally recognized credential for the employment of college and university graduates, which can determine whether they are able to find a good job in the competitive job market in China. Therefore, Jin (2008) pointed out that the CET has "become a test of extremely high stakes" (p. 5).

Due to its wide influence and high stakes, more and more studies have been conducted on the CET in recent years. For example, Yang and Weir (1998) conducted the first validation study of the CET and provided comprehensive evidence for its validity. Jin and Wu (1998) presented further validity evidence of the CET through a verbal protocol study on test takers' reported use of skills on the test. Song and Cheng (2006) investigated the relationship between test takers' reported use of strategies and test performance on the CET-4 which showed that metacognitive strategies appeared to be more important to students than cognitive strategies. Xie (2013) examined the test preparation pattern for the CET-4 and its implication for the score validity.

However, since the introduction of the new CET-4, no study has been carried out to investigate its Reading subtest (i.e., the section of reading comprehension and the cloze) which is 45% of the total score. Zheng and Cheng (2008) argued that more research to validate the new CET-4 is seriously needed. This study is, therefore, designed to investigate Chinese college test takers' metacognitive and cognitive strategy use on a new version of the CET-4 Reading subtest and meanwhile examine the factorial structure of the test.

1.2   Context of the Study

This section introduces the history, development, and recent reform of Chinese College English teaching and the CET.

1.2.1   Chinese College English Teaching and Its Reform

Chinese College English teaching (CCET) refers to the teaching of English to undergraduates at Chinese colleges and universities who major in any discipline other than English. In almost all Chinese colleges and universities, College English is a compulsory course in the first two academic years for all non-English majors, hence making it one of the most important fundamental courses for almost every college student.

In contrast to the 60 founding years of the People's Republic of China, Chinese College English teaching has only 40 years of history from the end of the 1970s to the present day. During the period from 1949 to the early 1960s, due to China's close relations with the former Soviet Union, Russian was the second language taught in Chinese colleges and universities (Lofstedt, 1980). Thus, little encouragement to learn English was witnessed. However, from the mid-1960s onward, as a result of the worsened relations between the two countries, English began to dominate second language teaching in colleges and universities, with the exception of the 10-year period of the Cultural Revolution from 1966 to 1976, which virtually brought a halt to regular academic study in almost all Chinese colleges and universities (Deng & Treiman, 1997; Huang, 2005).

In 1977, the restoration of the National Tertiary Matriculation Examination (NTME) initiated the restoration of College English teaching. At that time, College English teaching was described as merely memorizing grammar rules and facts. Students' learning purpose was to understand the morphology and syntax of English (Richards & Rodgers, 2001). In the early 1980s, despite the serious shortage of qualified English teachers and decent learning facilities, College English teaching began to develop steadily when the Central Government implemented the opening-up policy (Hu & McKay, 2012; Wei & Fei, 2003). From the late 1980s to the mid-1990s, Chinese College English teaching experienced a period of rapid development which Zhang and Daun (2010) summarize as follows:

> During the late 1980s and the first half of the 1990s, a large quantity of qualified English-major graduates and post-graduates were produced.... Meanwhile, China's rapid economic growth made it possible to provide better facilities for higher education. ... Although college English was still conducted in traditional ways, there were few complaints. Both students and society were so excited with the progress and achievements China had made during the period that they failed to notice the problems and weaknesses of the College English Teaching. In short, together with the country's prompt economic growth, CCET also experienced a short-term prosperity during this phase. (pp. 169–170)

However, due to the traditional teacher-centered method, almost no progress was witnessed in College English teaching from the late 1990s to 2003 (Zhang & Daun, 2010). Even worse, due to the washback effect of the CET, many College English teachers taught nothing but test-taking techniques in the classrooms. Students, who were required to get the CET certificate for their exit from college, learned College English for the mere purpose of passing the CET (Jin, 2008). This practice of teaching and learning English posed serious problems as it could not meet the needs of the Chinese society in terms of its high demand for talents with excellent English proficiency in the increasingly globalized world. This pointed to the necessity of a thorough reform (Jin & Jin, 2008; Zhang & Daun, 2010).

Under these circumstances, a nation-wide College English teaching reform was initiated in 2004 under the leadership and support of the Chinese Ministry of Education. The initiation of the Chinese College English Teaching Reform was marked by a national video conference conducted by the Chinese Ministry of Education, which was attended by presidents from 180 universities. It was agreed at this conference that the Chinese College English Teaching Reform would be composed of three parts: the reform of teaching curriculum, the reform of teaching modes and approaches, and the reform of the assessment system, especially the CET-4 and CET-6.

1.2.2 The College English Test

Launched in 1987, the CET-4 and CET-6 are national standardized tests administered by the Chinese Ministry of Education in collaboration with the National College English Testing Committee (NCETC) and the National Education Examinations Authority (NEEA) twice a year in June and December. It is the largest English as a Second Language (ESL) test in the world in terms of the number of test takers involved (Jin, 2005; Zheng & Cheng, 2008). Before the adoption of the new version of the CET in 2006, almost all Chinese non-English-major undergraduates were required to sit for the test as the CET-4 certificate had a close link to students' undergraduate degree. After the test reform, the CET-4 certificate is no longer a prerequisite for obtaining the undergraduate degrees in many universities; however, most students still choose to sit for it because "CET certificates have become a nationally recognized credential for employment of college and university graduates" (Jin, 2008, p. 4).

As the third nationwide College English curriculum, the national College English Curriculum Requirement provides the national guidelines for English instructions to non-English-major students at the tertiary level in China (Ministry of Education, 2004, 2007). According to the Curriculum Requirement, English teaching has three types of requirements at the tertiary level: basic, intermediate, and advanced. The CET-4 and CET-6 are designed to measure students' mastery of English according to the basic and intermediate requirement, respectively. Based on the amended testing syllabus, the CET-4 and CET-6 play an important role in realizing the objective of College English teaching as they aim at measuring college students' comprehensive employment of English accurately (National College English Testing Committee, 2006).

During its more than 20-year history, the CET has undergone three important phases of development (Zheng & Cheng, 2008). In the first phase from 1987 to 1997, the main components of the test were designed. At this stage, 85% of the items on the CET-4 were multiple-choice questions (MCQs). Essay writing, the only component assessing test takers' productive skills, contributed to the remaining 15% (Jin, 2008). The reporting system had a total of 100 marks ($M = 72$; $SD = 12$) (Jin & Yang, 2006; Zheng & Cheng, 2008).

The second phase, which lasted from 1997 to 2005, focused on the changes to test formats in order to "rectify inadequate assessment of students' productive skills resulting from a heavy reliance on objective test formats" (Jin, 2008, p. 5). Newly introduced constructed response formats at the time included short answer questions, compound dictation (i.e., dictation of words, phrases, or sentences in one task), and English-to-Chinese translation tasks. In 1999, the CET Spoken English Test (CET-SET) was introduced as an optional component of the CET test battery to evaluate students' speaking ability.

From 2005 onward, in accordance with the newly enacted National College English Curriculum Requirement (Ministry of Education, 2004), new test formats and a new scoring system were introduced and piloted. In 2006, a new version of the CET was introduced nationwide. In the new version of the CET-4, an array of changes was made regarding the allocation of percentage of marks to each section, test formats, and reporting system. For example, the percentage of scores for listening was increased from 20 to 35%. In addition, the vocabulary and structure section was removed and new test formats were introduced, such as banked cloze, and Skimming and Scanning. Further, the new scoring system had a total of 710 marks ($M = 500$; $SD = 70$) (National College English Testing Committee, 2006). The following section gives an in-depth description of the current version of the CET.

Each of the new CET-4, which takes 125 min to complete, comprises four parts: listening comprehension, reading comprehension, cloze or error correction, and writing and translation (see Table 1.1 for brief information of the CET-4). A more detailed introduction to each part is provided in the following section.

Listening comprehension. The section of listening comprehension, accounting for 35% of the total score, assesses students' ability to understand dialogs and passage reading in standard British or American English at a speed of 130 words per minute (wpm) for the CET-4. It comprises two parts: conversations (15%) and passage reading (20%). In the conversations part, there are seven to eight short conversations and two long conversations. The response format is MCQ. The passage reading section includes three passages followed by MCQs and one passage with compound dictation in which some words and sentences are left out for students to fill in after listening to the passage. The students are required to complete this part within 35 min.

Table 1.1 Content, item types, and score value on the CET-4

	Content	Item type	Score (%)	Value (%)
Listening comprehension	Dialog	Multiple-choice	15	35
	Passage	Multiple-choice and compound dictation	20	
Reading comprehension	Reading in Depth	Banked cloze	5	35
		Multiple-choice	20	
	Skimming and Scanning	Multiple-choice	10	
Cloze	Cloze	Multiple-choice	10	10
Writing and translation	Writing	Short essay writing	15	20
	Translation	Chinese–English translation	5	

Reading comprehension. The CET-4 reading comprehension test is designed to measure and assess students' ability to grasp written information through reading which consists of understanding main ideas, important facts, and details, comprehending implied meanings of the texts, and inferring authors' views and attitudes. Three main types of specific skills are assumed to be assessed in the reading comprehension part:

(1) skills of distinguishing and understanding main ideas and important details, which can be subdivided into, and delineated as including: (a) understanding explicitly conveyed concepts or details; (b) comprehending implicitly conveyed concepts and details; (c) understanding the meaning of the passage by judging communicative functions of the sentences; (d) understanding main ideas of the passage; and (e) inferring the authors' views and attitudes;
(2) skills of understanding passages by means of language skills, which can be subdivided into (a) understanding the meaning of words based on the information given in the context; (b) knowing the relationships between sentences; and (c) understanding the relationships between different parts of the passage; and
(3) special reading skills, which comprise skimming the passage to get the main idea and scanning the passage to get particular information (National College English Testing Committee, 2006).

The CET-4 reading comprehension part, which contributes 35% to the total score, comprises two sections: Skimming and Scanning (10%), and Reading in Depth (25%). According to the National College English Testing Committee (2006), skimming assesses students' ability to get the main idea, whereas scanning evaluates students' ability to obtain particular information through fast reading. For Skimming and Scanning, students will read one or two long passages (1000 words for the CET-4). The response formats for this section include MCQ, sentence completion, and true or false questions.

The part of Reading in Depth has two sections: banked cloze and passage reading. Banked cloze assesses students' ability to understand and use words in actual contexts in which students are asked to read one passage with 200–250 words and to choose one word for each of the ten blanks from a bank of 15 words. The part of passage reading includes three 300–350-word passages which assess students' ability to obtain main ideas, important facts, and make inferences about word meanings from the context. The response format for this part is MCQ.

Test takers are required to complete this part within 40 min: 15 min for Skimming and Scanning and 25 min for Reading in Depth.

Cloze. Designed to assess students' ability to understand and infer meanings from the contexts of the passage, the Cloze section contributes 10% of the total score (National College English Testing Committee, 2006). In this part of the CET-4, students are asked to read one passage (220–250 words) and answer 20 multiple-choice cloze questions. The section takes 15 min to complete.

In addition, aiming to test students' comprehension skills from the lexico-grammatical perspective, cloze is designed to assess students' ability to understand and use English at the basic level. In this study, both sections of reading comprehension and cloze are included in investigating the relationships between college test takers' strategy use and test performance on the CET-4 Reading subtest.

Writing and translation. The section of writing and translation assesses students' ability to express and communicate their ideas in written English. It accounts for 20% of the total score: translation constituting 5% and essay writing 15%. In the translation part, students are required to complete five sentences by translating the given Chinese sentences into English. For the section of writing, students are required to write a composition of approximately 120 words for the CET-4 based on the "given topics, outlines, pictures, or graphs" (National College English Testing Committee, 2006, p. 4). Test takers are required to finish the essay writing in 30 min and translation in five minutes.

After the latest reform, five scores are reported in the report card for the CET-4: an overall score out of a total of 710 points, a score for listening comprehension (249 points, 35%), a score for reading comprehension (249 points, 35%), a score for cloze (70 points, 10%), and a score for writing and translation (142 points, 20%).

As the CET has become a test of extremely high stakes due to the increasing recognition and use of its certificate (Jin, 2008), more attention has been given to the processes that test takers involve in taking the CET. The popular myth is that test takers' enhanced performance is closely linked to practice-only test preparation methods and use of testwiseness strategies. Thus, to dispel the myth and enhance students' test performance on the CET-4, it is imperative and timely to link their strategy use and test performance. It is hoped that practice-only test preparation methods will give way to more beneficial and useful methods of reading instruction and test preparation.

1.3   Purpose of the Study

As discussed in the sections above, due to the important role test takers' strategy use plays in test performance interpretation and construct validation, researchers have been interested in examining how test takers' strategy use is related to their test performance. In spite of the studies conducted in this field (e.g., Cohen, 2006, 2013; Cohen & Upton, 2006; Phakiti, 2008a, b; Purpura, 1997; Song & Cheng, 2006), the review of relevant literature revealed that the following gaps have not been thoroughly addressed and investigated, suggesting a need for further research in this area.

First, L2 reading researchers developed a few instruments to elicit students' strategy use in the process of reading comprehension (e.g., Carrell, 1989; Mokhtari, Sheorey, & Reichard, 2008; Phakiti, 2003, 2008b), but few of them provided a link between strategy use and reading comprehension tests. Additionally, few were grounded in reading theories and the framework of test-taking strategies. As such, it is imperative to design a questionnaire for the calibration of test takers' metacognitive awareness and strategy use in the context of reading comprehension tests. It is believed that such a questionnaire can help students become more strategic readers and test takers. In addition, it could also help with test validation and reading instructions. Therefore, as an important part of the study, the Reading Test Strategy Use Questionnaire (ReTSUQ) was developed and validated for this study and wider use.

Second, in spite of the consensus that metacognitive and cognitive strategies are very important in language use situations, the relationships between metacognitive and cognitive strategy use have not been examined empirically. For example, some researchers pointed out that the distinction between metacognitive and cognitive strategies is "fuzzy" (Baker, 1991; Chapelle, Grabe, & Berns, 1997) and "difficult to demarcate" (Paris, Wasik, & Turner, 1991, p. 610); other researchers have argued that language learner strategy use is substantiated by metacognitive and cognitive strategies among others (e.g., O'Malley & Chamot, 1990; Oxford, 1990). Yet others have demonstrated that metacognitive and cognitive strategies are correlated (e.g., Phakiti, 2003, 2008b; Purpura, 1997, 1998, 1999).

To conclude, three models (i.e., the unitary, higher-order, and correlated model) have emerged from the relevant literature, depicting the relationships between metacognitive and cognitive strategy use. This study was, therefore, to make an empirical investigation into the relationships between metacognitive and cognitive strategies in relation to language use, especially in the test context. Research in this area is expected to throw light on the construct of strategy use in specific language use contexts (Bachman & Palmer, 2010; Phakiti, 2003; Purpura, 1999).

Third, according to Bachman and Palmer (2010), factors that affect test takers' performance include their language ability (i.e., language knowledge and strategic competence), cognitive strategies, personal attributes, and topical knowledge.[2] Personal attributes refer to learners' age, gender, nationality, and level and type of education. Among the numerous studies conducted to address the gender differences in academic performance, a group of researchers investigated the differences in strategy use and reading performance between male and female students (e.g., Bügel & Buunk, 1996; Chavez, 2001; Phakiti, 2003; Sheorey & Mokhtari, 2001; Young & Oxford, 1997). It was pointed out that understanding strategic behaviors in reading comprehension across gender groups would contribute to the construction of reading theories, help raise instructors' awareness of gender differences in facilitating students' progress in reading comprehension, and accommodate individual students' personal needs to ensure equal opportunities for academic success (Chavez, 2001; Phakiti, 2003).

However, the paucity of studies in this area suggests that more research is needed to fill the gap revealed (Logan & Johnson, 2010; Phakiti, 2003). To this end, there is a need for continued, sufficient, and thorough examination of how male and

---

[2]Topical knowledge concerns content knowledge which is beyond the scope of this study.

female students are similar or different in their employment of different strategies when engaging in reading comprehension activities. Participants in this study share similar features in age, nationality, level of education. Gender is thus one of the personal features that distinguish this group of language learners. To provide a deeper understanding of test takers' strategy use and test performance, this study aims to investigate the relationships among test takers' gender, metacognitive and cognitive strategy use, and test performance.

Finally, with China's policy of further opening up, and extensive exchange and communication with western countries in commerce, culture, science, and technology, there is an increasing demand for a large number of competent English users in a variety of professions. Considerable attention has been drawn accordingly to the area of English teaching in mainland China. Consequently, a growing number of studies have been conducted on mainland Chinese EFL learners (e.g., Bedell & Oxford, 1996; Gan, Humphreys, & Hamp-Lyons, 2004; Gu & Johnson, 1996; Song & Cheng, 2006; Wen & Johnson, 1997; Zhang, 2002, 2010). However, few of these studies have investigated the CET-4 Reading subtest in China, which is 35% of the total score of the high-stakes CET-4. Therefore, it is necessary and timely that more research is carried out to investigate this influential test to provide useful information to instructors, test developers, and students.

As pointed out by Messick,

...different individuals performed the same tasks in different ways and that even the same individual might perform in a different manner across items or on different occasions. That is, individuals differ consistently in their strategies and styles of task performance. This has consequences for the nature and sequence of processes involved in item responses and, hence, for the constructs implicated in test scores. (1989, p. 54)

As an attempt to investigate test takers' test-taking processes, this study has theoretical, methodological, and practical implications for language assessment as well as ESL/EFL teaching and learning.

In summary, the purpose of this study is to explore and investigate the relationships between Chinese college test takers' metacognitive and cognitive strategy use, and test performance on the CET-4 Reading subtest. The specific purpose is to examine students' test-taking processes through the identification and characterization of their strategy use on the reading comprehension test and investigate how strategy use influences their reading test performance in general and across gender groups.

Three parts were designed in this study to enhance the understanding of the relationships between test takers' strategy use and reading test performance.

First, on the basis of relevant reading models, theories on metacognition and Cohen's framework of test-taking strategies, the ReTSUQ was developed and validated. As an important measurement tool of the participants' strategy use on the CET-4 Reading subtest, it was used in the following Study 1 and Study 2. In addition, it can be used to calibrate test takers' strategy use in similar reading test contexts.

Second, Study 1 investigates Chinese college test takers' strategy use and reading test performance from a general perspective. It addresses the question of how metacognitive and cognitive strategies are interrelated in test contexts and provide empirical answers to the factorial structure of the CET-4 Reading subtest as well as the relationships between test takers' strategy use and reading test performance.

Finally, Study 2 focuses on the investigation of gender differences in test takers' strategy use and reading test performance. This study aims to examine whether male and female students differ in their use of strategies on the reading comprehension test, as well as in their reading test performance.

1.4 Research Questions

This study addresses the following research questions:

Study 1: Chinese College Test Takers' Strategy Use and Reading Test Performance

1. What is the trait structure of Chinese college test takers' strategy use on the retired CET-4 Reading subtest as measured by the ReTSUQ?
2. What is the trait structure of the test takers' reading test performance as measured by the retired CET-4 Reading subtest?
3. What is the relationship between test takers' metacognitive and cognitive strategy use? In other words, of the three models—the unitary, higher-order, and correlated–which model of strategy use and reading test performance fits the data best?
4. What are the relationships between Chinese college test takers' metacognitive and cognitive strategy use and reading test performance? Specifically, is the factor structure of the relationships between Chinese college test takers' reading strategy use and reading test performance invariant across the two samples of similar characteristics?

Study 2: Gender Differences in Test Takers' Strategy Use and Reading Test Performance

1. Is the factorial structure of strategy use as measured by the ReTSUQ invariant across male and female students?
2. Is the factorial structure of the reading comprehension test performance as measured by the retired CET-4 Reading subtest invariant across male and female students?
3. Is the structure of the relationships between test takers' strategy use and reading test performance invariant across male and female students?

1.5 Key Terms

This section defines several key terms which are relevant to the study.

1.5.1 First Language (L1) Reading and Second Language (L2) Reading

According to Ellis (1984), the term second language (L2) refers to any language learned after the first language (L1) or the native language. Although some researchers tried to make a distinction between second and foreign language (see Richard, Platt, & Platt, 1992), second language (L2) is used as a cover term throughout this study to refer to any language other than L1 or native language.

Although the consensual view among researchers is that findings from studies on L1 reading are relevant to understanding L2 reading performance (e.g., Grabe, 2009; Koda, 2005), it is necessary to be aware of the various differences between them before applying the findings from L1 reading research to L2 reading research and instruction. According to Grabe (2009), the three main differences between L1 and L2 reading can be summarized as follows: (a) linguistic and processing differences; (b) developmental and educational difference; and (c) sociocultural and institutional differences. In other words, it is easily recognizable that compared with their L1 counterparts, L2 readers have fewer linguistic resources to support their comprehension. In addition, due to less processing practice and different systems of orthography and morphology of their L1 from L2, they may have slow word recognition, and syntactic and semantic processing which are of prime importance in comprehending L2 texts. From the developmental and educational perspectives, L2 readers would bring their L1 reading experiences and skills into L2 reading, which will have an impact on their L2 reading development.

1.5.2 Test Takers' Characteristics

According to Bachman (1990), Bachman and Palmer (2010), Kunnan (1995), and Purpura (1999), personal attributes that affect test performance can be categorized into four major types: (a) background or demographic characteristics such as a person's age, gender, and first language proficiency level; (b) sociopsychological characteristics such as his/her attitude and motivations; (c) personality characteristics including a person's level of self-esteem and anxiety; and (d) cognitive characteristics which refer to his/her aptitude and learning strategies. In the current study, the investigation of test takers' characteristics focuses on their strategy use on the CET-4 Reading subtest. Specifically, the focus of this study is on Chinese college test takers' metacognitive and cognitive strategy use on the CET-4 Reading comprehension test and how male and females students' strategy use affects their reading test performance, respectively.

1.5.3 Strategic Competence and Metacognitive and Cognitive Strategies

According to Bachman and Palmer (2010), language ability comprises language knowledge and strategic competence. Strategic competence is perceived as consisting of "higher-order metacognitive strategies that provide a management function in language use" (p. 48) which includes three components: goal setting, appraising, and planning. In other words, Bachman and Palmer (2010) argued that metacognitive strategies decide how language ability is actualized in language use (Bachman, 2013).

In the literature about the role of strategies in language use, metacognitive strategies are defined in different ways by a variety of researchers. For example, Purpura (1997) argued that metacognitive strategies are "a set of conscious or unconscious mental or behavioral activities which are directly or indirectly related to some specific stage of the overall process of language acquisition, use or testing" (p. 6). Having adopted Flavell's (1979) and O'Malley and Chamot's (1990) framework, Wenden (1998) argued that metacognitive strategies are the skills "through which learners manage, direct, regulate, guide their learning, i.e., planning, monitoring and evaluating" (p. 519). Phakiti (2008b) stated that "metacognitive strategies are conscious processes that regulate cognitive strategies, action and other processing" which consist of planning, monitoring, and evaluating strategies (p. 243). This conceptualization of metacognitive strategies is consistent with Brown's (1980) and Paris and Winograd's (1990) framework of metacognitive strategy use in reading comprehension.

In addition, Cohen (2006) argues that when completing the language tests, test takers have to "deal with both language issues and the item-response demands" (p. 308). As such, three types of strategies are involved in language tests: language learner strategies, test management strategies, and testwiseness strategies. Language learner strategies deal with language issues in tests—these strategies are equivalent to reading strategies in the current study; test management strategies provide meaningful responses to test items; and testwiseness strategies "circumvent the need to tap their actual language knowledge" (Cohen & Upton, 2006, p. 4). Thus, in this study, I propose that metacognitive strategies refer to test takers' *conscious and purposeful* cognitive activities of controlling their test-taking and reading processes which comprises planning, evaluating, and monitoring strategies (Cohen & Upton, 2006; Paris & Winograd, 1990).

In addition, in Bachman and Palmer's (2010) updated model of language use, cognitive strategies are defined as the strategies employed by language users when executing and actualizing their plans in language use. Although Bachman and Palmer (2010) consider them to be test takers' "peripheral" instead of "focal" attributes (p. 43), researchers have given much attention to investigating cognitive strategies in language use. For example, influenced by Anderson's (1982, 2010) cognitive theory of learning, O'Malley and Chamot (1990) defined cognitive strategies as behaviors that "involve mental manipulations or translations of materials or tasks" which improve "comprehension, acquisition, or retention" (p. 229). Wenden (1991) argued that cognitive strategies are "mental steps or operations that learners use to process both linguistic and sociolinguistic content" (p. 19). Finally, Purpura (1999) viewed cognitive strategies as "a set of conscious or unconscious mental or behavioral activities or operations which are directly or indirectly related in comprehending, storing, or retrieval of information" in language acquisition and use situations (p. 7). Since the current study focuses on test takers' reading comprehension performance, it is proposed that cognitive strategies are closely related to students' specific cognitive behavior of reading comprehension. In other words, cognitive strategies are viewed as the conscious mental behaviors or activities used by readers and test takers to actualize their plans in language use situations, especially in the reading comprehension test.

1.5.4 Reading Skills and Reading Strategies

In the literature on reading, the terms "skills" and "strategies" are used frequently. However, research shows that reading skills and reading strategies are different. According to Afflerbach, Pearson, and Paris (2008b), the key difference between skill and strategy is whether the operation is automatic or deliberately controlled. As such, they define reading strategies as "deliberate, goal-directed attempts to control and modify the reader's efforts to decode text, understand words, and construct meanings of text" (p. 386). In contrast, reading skills are "automatic actions that result in decoding and comprehension with speed, efficiency, and fluency and usually occur without awareness of the components or control involved" (p. 386). In other words, a reading strategy is characterized by the reader's deliberate control, goal-directedness, and awareness of his/her reading behaviors, whereas reading skills are deployed out of habit and function automatically without the reader's consciousness.

Although reading skills and strategies are different in terms of the intentionality and automaticity, they are related to each other as strategies may evolve into skills with frequent practice and successful use. For example, a student may slow down his/her reading speed and re-read the text to increase understanding if the text becomes difficult. This is a deliberate and conscious act prompted by the student's understanding that the meaning construction does not go very smoothly. If this strategy is successful, the student may use it continuously. With frequent practice, this strategy may require less and less effort and attention to such an extent that it becomes automatic and unconscious. In other words, the reading strategy becomes a reading skill that requires no effort.

To sum up, the difference between reading skills and strategies can be understood as distinguishing the automatic reading process from the deliberately controlled reading process. Research shows that with proper instruction on reading strategies, readers can become fluent and skilled readers (Afflerbach, Pearson, & Paris, 2008a; Paris, Wasik, & Turner, 1991).

1.5.5   Second Language Reading Test Performance

Bachman and Palmer's (2010) model of language ability was used to define second language reading test performance in this study. In this model, language ability comprises language knowledge and strategic competence. Language knowledge includes organizational knowledge and pragmatic knowledge. Organizational knowledge is about "how utterances or sentences and texts are organized" and pragmatic knowledge is "how utterances or sentences and texts are related to the communicative goals of the language users and to the features of the language use setting" (p. 45). Organizational knowledge can be further divided into grammatical knowledge (i.e., knowledge of vocabulary, syntax, and phonology/graphology) and textual knowledge (i.e., knowledge of cohesion and rhetorical or conversational organization). In this study, second language reading test performance is defined by knowledge of vocabulary, syntax, phonology/graphology, cohesion, rhetorical, or conventional organization and specific reading skills (i.e., Skimming and Scanning) which are measured by the retired CET-4 Reading subtest.

1.5.6   Exploratory Factor Analysis Versus Confirmatory Factor Analysis

Factor analysis is used to determine how the shared common variance–covariance characteristics of some observed variables define theoretical constructs or factors (i.e., latent variables) (Schumacker & Lomax, 2004).

In practice, there are two main types of factor analysis: exploratory factor analysis (EFA) and confirmatory factor analysis (CFA). In 1904, Spearman used the correlation procedure to develop a factor analysis procedure which has now come to be called exploratory factor analysis (Schumacker & Lomax, 2004; Thompson, 2004). In EFA, researchers do not expect a specific number of factors under analysis. Instead, they seek to explore and find a model that fits the data best and meanwhile has theoretical support.

CFA, on the other hand, was developed more recently (Jöreskog, 1969) in attempts to test the significance of a hypothesized factor model by examining whether the sample data confirm the proposed model. In other words, CFA requires the researcher to have an a priori-specified theoretical model or certain expectations regarding the number of factors, which factors are correlated, and which observed factors measure given factors (Thompson, 2004). Thus, researchers who aim to test theory-driven questions prefer CFA to EFA as CFA is a powerful way to test a theory and to evaluate the degree of model fit.

1.5.7   Structural Equation Modeling

Structural equation modeling (SEM) is a statistical technique for testing different theoretical models. It demonstrates how a set of observed variables define latent variables and the relationships among these variables (Schumacker & Lomax, 2004). Bentler (1995) argued that it is a useful methodology to specify, estimate, and test hypothesized relationships among variables statistically.

SEM is more powerful than other statistical procedures due to the fact that it examines the relationships between a variety of independent and dependent variables simultaneously. In addition, it allows for the possibility of examining the relationships among latent variables in order to explain patterns of behaviors. The measurement error can also be accounted for in the models.

Given the advantages of SEM methodology and increasing user-friendliness of commercial computer programs, SEM has become a popular method for testing or developing theories in non-experimental research (Byrne, 2006). Correlation, multiple regression, and analysis of variance (ANOVA) have been widely used to analyze reading tests and reading comprehension traditionally (Barnett, 1986; Clapham, 1998; Kobayashi, 2002; Koda, 1993; Leeser, 2007; Qian, 2002; Riley & Lee, 1996; Wolf, 1993). Although these statistical methods provide information about the relationships between observed variables, they cannot estimate the relationships between latent variables (Hoyle, 1995; Kline, 2011). To address this limitation, a growing number of studies in language testing have employed SEM as the primary statistical method (Kunnan, 1998). In'nami and Koizumi (2011) argued that it is the most often used procedure to investigate learners' strategy use and test structure. Thus, SEM is the primary statistical method used in this study to examine test takers' strategy use on the reading comprehension test.

1.5.8   Multi-sample/Multi-group   Structural Equation Modeling

Apart from the SEM analyses based on a single group, some analyses involve more than one group/sample in which researchers are interested in whether "components of the measurement model and/or the structural model are invariant (i.e., equivalent) across particular groups of interest" (Byrne, 2011, p. 193). This is the multi-sample or multi-group SEM analysis (Byrne, 2011; In'nami & Koizumi, 2011). Multi-sample SEM addresses the question of whether components of the measurement and structural model are invariant across samples (Byrne, 2011; Kline, 2011). In cross-validation studies, a series of competing models derived from theories and empirical studies are tested with both samples to identify a baseline model. After the baseline model is established, tests of invariance are to be conducted simultaneously across two samples (In'nami & Koizumi, 2011). While testing for invariance across different samples, cross-group equality constraints are placed on a set of parameters in an increasingly stringent manner (Byrne, 2001, 2011).

Several studies have tested the factorial invariance with multi-sample/multi-group analysis (i.e., Bae & Bachman, 1998; In'nami & Koizumi, 2011; Purpura, 1998). Among these studies, Purpura (1998) investigated how the relationships between metacognitive and cognitive strategy use and second language test performance varied among high- and low-proficiency groups in the First Certificate of English (FCE) Anchor test. However, to date, no studies have tested the invariance of the factor structure of the relationships between reading strategy use and reading test performance across samples of similar characteristics. Therefore, it is expected that the gap in literature will be bridged with the current study which examines whether the factor structure of the relationships between Chinese test takers' reading strategy use and reading test performance is generalizable across samples of similar characteristics as well as across gender groups.

1.5.9 Cross-Validation

Cross-validation is a statistical technique of using the results of the analysis from one sample to develop a theory and then assess how the results will generalize to another sample for the purpose of validating or testing the theory. Cross-validation is an important methodology to avoid circular reasoning in which the claimed effect depends on a cause which brings about the effect (Vogt, 2005). In this study, multi-samples of similar characteristics are used in Study 1 to investigate the relationships between Chinese college test takers' strategy use and reading test performance. In Study 2, multi-groups of male and female students are used to examine the gender differences in strategy use and reading test performance.

1.6 Significance of the Study

The investigation of test takers' metacognitive and cognitive strategy use and L2 reading test performance is expected to have theoretical, methodological, and practical implications for second language assessment and second language teaching and learning.

Theoretical implications. From the theoretical perspective, although L2 reading has been studied for more than 30 years, the construct of L2 reading ability is still a topic of heated debate that gives rise to the question of how to operationalize it in reading comprehension tests (Child, 1988; Liao, 2009). The current study makes an investigation into the factorial structure of the L2 reading test performance as measured by the CET-4 Reading subtest through the SEM approach. Expectedly, this study is to make contributions to the investigation of the construct of L2 reading ability in the test setting.

Second, language testing researchers have recently recognized that individual characteristics have influence on test takers' test performance (Bachman, 1990; Kunnan, 1995). In addition, the focus of attention in testing research has shifted from the content and product of the tests (i.e., the test scores), to the processes test takers may undertake during the test and how the processes relate to their test performance (Anderson, Bachman, Perkins, & Cohen, 1991). The current study was designed to examine how test takers' personal features, especially their strategy use and gender, are related to their reading test performance and the construct validity of the test. This will provide implications for language teachers, test developers, and students.

Third, according to Bachman and Palmer (2010), language users' focal attribute is language ability which comprises language knowledge and strategic competence. Strategic competence is perceived to be referring to metacognitive strategies; however, in addition, language users' peripheral attributes include personal attributes, topical knowledge, affective schemata, and cognitive strategies. In other words, both metacognitive and cognitive strategies are incorporated in this language use model. This study, though not designed to test all concerned variables in this model, investigates the relationships between test takers' metacognitive and cognitive strategy use in language use situation. Findings from this study are thus expected to provide validating information about Bachman and Palmers' (2010) model to some degree, especially with regard to how language users' metacognitive strategy use is related to their cognitive strategy use in actual use situations.

Methodological implications. From the methodological perspective, this study can provide implications for research conducted on the CET-4 Reading regarding the methods used in investigating the factor structure of the test as well as the relationships between Chinese test takers' strategy use and test performance.

This study first employs EFA to explore the underlying structure of the CET-4 Reading subtest and then uses CFA to confirm the factor models of the reading comprehension test based on relevant reading theories and the test specifications. In contrast to theory-generating EFA, CFA is considered as a theory-testing procedure (Stevens, 2002). It is based on the solid theoretical background that requires researchers to know (a) the number of factors, (b) how variables reflect factors, and (c) if factors are correlated (Thompson, 2004). The hypothesized factor structures will be tested and confirmed with data. Although previous studies have used this approach to examine the underpinning structure of other language tests (e.g., Liao, 2009; Purpura, 1999), no studies so far have investigated the underlying structure of the CET-4 Reading subtest using EFA and CFA.

Similarly, this study uses SEM to investigate the relationships between test takers' strategy use and their test performance on the CET-4 Reading subtest. As a powerful statistical technique that examines the relationships between latent and observed variables, SEM is being used in more and more studies regarding test takers' strategy use (In'nami & Koizumi, 2011). However, no studies have been conducted to examine Chinese test takers' strategy use and reading test performance on the CET-4 Reading subtest up to now. Given the widespread use and far-reaching influence of the test, this methodological attempt is especially meaningful to research conducted to the CET-4 test battery. In other words, this study is expected to give implications for the research methods used in studies in relation to the CET-4.

Practical implications. In addition to the theoretical and methodological implications mentioned above, this study can provide useful information for test developers, language instructors, and students. In this study, CFA was used to investigate the factorial structure of the ReTSUQ and test before the relationships between test takers' strategy use and reading test performance was examined through SEM. The information regarding the validity of the test will be very useful and beneficial for test developers to make improvements to this high-stakes test.

Additionally, as a national standardized test, the CET-4 has great impact on its stakeholders including test takers, language instructors, test users, and parents. For example, the widespread use of the CET-4 as a means of screening job applicants has exerted great pressure on students to achieve satisfactory scores in order to enhance their competitiveness in job hunting. Under these circumstances, a practice-only test preparation policy may have become popular among students as well as instructors. Therefore, the findings from this study are hopefully able to give instructors useful insights into how to help enhance students' reading ability and improve their test performance through effective use of reading strategies and test management strategies. Students will also be provided with useful information regarding how to employ effective strategies to enhance their reading test performance. It is expected that the practice-only test preparation method will give way to more beneficial and useful methods of reading instruction and test preparation.

In summary, this study is expected to make contributions to language assessment and L2 teaching and learning theoretically, methodologically, and practically.

References

Afflerbach, P., Pearson, P. D., & Paris, S. G. (2008a). Clarifying differences between reading skills and reading strategies. *The Reading Teacher, 61*(5), 363–373.

Afflerbach, P., Pearson, P. D., & Paris, S. G. (2008b). Skills and strategies: Their differences, their relationships, and why it matters. In K. Mokhtari & R. Sheorey (Eds.), *Reading strategies of first- and second-language learners*. Norwood, MA: Christopher-Gordon Publishers.

Anderson, J. R. (1982). Acquisition of cognitive skills. *Psychological Review, 89*, 369–406.

Anderson, J. R. (2010). *Cognitive psychology and its implications* (7th ed.). New York: Worth Publishers.

Anderson, N. J., Bachman, L., Perkins, K., & Cohen, A. (1991). An exploratory study into the construct validity of a reading comprehension test: Triangulation of data sources. *Language Testing, 8*(1), 41–66.

Bachman, L. F. (1990). *Fundamental consideration in language testing.* Oxford: Oxford University Press.

Bachman, L. F. (2013). Ongoing challenges in language assessment. In A. J. Kunnan (Ed.), *The companion to language assessment* (pp. 1586–1604). Hoboken, NJ: Wiley/Blackwell.

Bachman, L. F., & Palmer, A. S. (2010). *Language testing in practice.* Oxford: Oxford University Press.

Bae, J., & Bachman, L. F. (1998). A latent variable approach to listening and reading: Testing factorial invariance across two groups of children in the Korean/English two-way immersion program. *Language Testing, 15,* 380–414.

Baker, L. (1991). Metacognition, reading and science education. In C. M. Santa & D. E. Alvermann (Eds.), *Science learning* (pp. 2–13). Newark, DE: International Reading Association.

Barnett, M. A. (1986). Syntactic and lexical/semantic skill in foreign language reading: Importance and interaction. *Modern Language Journal, 70,* 343–349.

Bedell, D. A., & Oxford, R. L. (1996). Cross-cultural comparisons of language learning strategies in the People's Republic of China and other countries. In R. L. Oxford (Ed.), *Language learner strategies around the world: Cross cultural perspectives.* Honolulu: University of Hawai'i Press, Second Language Teaching & Curriculum Center.

Bentler, P. M. (1995). *EQA structural equations program manual.* Encino, CA: Multivariate Software.

Block, E. (1986). The comprehension strategies of second language readers. *TESOL Quarterly, 20* (3), 463–493.

Block, E. (1992). See how they read: Comprehension monitoring of L1 and L2 readers. *TESOL Quarterly, 26*(2), 319–343.

Brown, A. L. (1980). Metacognitive development and reading. In R. J. Spiro, B. C. Bruce, & W. F. Brewer (Eds.), *Theoretical issues in reading comprehension: Perspectives from psychology, linguistics, artificial intelligence and education* (pp. 453–482). Hillsdale, NJ: Erlbaum.

Bügel, K., & Buunk, B. P. (1996). Sex differences in foreign language text comprehension: The role of interests and prior knowledge. *Modern Language Journal, 80*(1), 15–31.

Byrne, B. M. (2001). *Structural equation modeling with AMOS: Basic concepts, applications, and programming.* Mahwah, NJ: Erlbaum.

Byrne, B. M. (2006). *Structural equation modeling with EQS: Basic concepts, applications, and programming* (2nd ed.). Mahwah, NJ: Lawrence Erlbaum Associates.

Byrne, B. M. (2011). *Structural equation modeling with Mplus: Basic concepts, applications, and programming.* New York: Routledge.

Carrell, P. L. (1989). SLA and classroom instruction: Reading. *Annual Review of Applied Linguistics, 9,* 223–242.

Chapelle, C., Grabe, W., & Berns, M. (1997). *Communicative language proficiency: Definitions and implications for TOEFL. TOEFL monograph series no. 10.* Princeton, NJ: Educational Testing Service.

Chavez, M. (2001). *Gender in the language classroom.* Boston: McGraw Hill.

Child, J. (1988). Reading proficiency assessment: Section 1: A framework for discussion. In P. Lowe Jr. & C. W. Stansfield (Eds.), *Second language proficiency assessment: Current issues* (pp. 125–135). Englewood Cliffs, NJ: Prentice Hall.

Clapham, C. (1998). The effect of language proficiency and background knowledge on EAP students' reading comprehension. In A. J. Kunnan (Ed.), *Validation in language assessment: Selected papers from the 17th language testing research colloquium, Long Beach* (pp. 141–168). Mahwah, NJ: Lawrence Erlbaum Associates.

Cohen, A. D. (2006). The coming age of research on test-taking strategies. *Language Assessment Quarterly, 3*(4), 307–331.

Cohen, A. D. (2013). Using test-wiseness strategy research in task development. In A. J. Kunnan (Ed.), *The companion to language assessment* (pp. 893–905). Hoboken, NJ: Wiley/Blackwell.

Cohen, A. D., & Macaro, E. (Eds.). (2007). *Language learner strategies: Thirty years of research and practice*. Oxford: Oxford University Press.

Cohen, A. D., & Upton, T. A. (2006). *Strategies in responding to the new TOEFL reading tasks (Monograph no. 33)*. Princeton, NJ: ETS. Retrieved from http://www.ets.org/Media/Research/pdf/RR-06-06.pdf.

Deng, Z., & Treiman, D. J. (1997). The impact of the cultural revolution on trends in the People's Republic of China. *American Journal of Sociology, 103*(2), 391–428.

Ellis, R. (1984). *Classroom second language development*. Oxford: Pergamon.

Flavell, J. H. (1979). Metacognition and cognitive monitoring: A new area of cognitive-developmental inquiry. *American Psychologist, 34*(10), 906–911.

Gan, Z., Humphreys, G., & Hamp-Lyons, L. (2004). Understanding successful and unsuccessful EFL students in Chinese universities. *Modern Language Journal, 88,* 229–244.

Grabe, W. (2009). *Reading in a second language: Moving from theory to practice*. Cambridge: Cambridge University Press.

Gu, Y., & Johnson, R. K. (1996). Vocabulary learning strategies and language learning outcomes. *Language Learning, 46*(4), 643–679.

Hoyle, R. H. (1995). The structural equation modeling approach: Basic concepts and fundamental issues. In R. H. Hoyle (Ed.), *Structural equation modeling: Concepts, issues, and applications* (pp. 1–15). London: SAGE Publications.

Hu, G. W. (1999). *Explicit metalinguistic knowledge at work: The case of spontaneous written production by formal adult Chinese of English*. Unpublished Ph.D. dissertation. Singapore: National Institute of Education/Nanyang Technological University.

Hu, G. W., & McKay, S. L. (2012). English language education in East Asia: Some recent developments. *Journal of Multilingual and Multicultural Development, 33*(4), 345–362.

Huang, L. (2005). *Elitism and equality in Chinese higher education: Studies of student socio-economic background, investment in education, and career aspiration*. Stockholm: Stockholm University.

In'nami, Y., & Koizumi, R. (2011). Factor structure of the revised TOEIC® test: A multiple-sample analysis. *Language Testing, 29*(1), 131–152.

Jin, Y. (2005). The national college english test. In L. Hamp-Lyons (Chair), *The big tests: Intentions and evidence. Symposium presented at the International Association of Applied Linguistics (AILA) 2005 Conference in Madison, WI.*

Jin, Y. (2008). Powerful tests, powerfulness test designers? Changes facing the College English Test. *CELEA Journal, 31,* 3–11.

Jin, Y., & Jin, G. (2008). Foreign language teaching reform and improvement of college English teaching quality. *Asian Social Science, 4*(4), 127–128.

Jin, Y., & Wu, J. (1998). A construct validation study of the CET reading subtests with introspection. *Foreign Language World, 70*(2), 47–52.

Jin, Y., & Yang, H. (2006). The English proficiency of college and university students in China: As reflected in the CET. *Language, Culture and Curriculum, 19*(1), 2006.

Jöreskog, K. G. (1969). A general approach to confirmatory maximum likelihood factor analysis. *Psychometrika, 34,* 183–202.

Kern, R. G. (1989). Second language reading strategy instruction: Its effects on comprehension and word inference ability. *Modern Language Journal, 73*(2), 135–149.

Kline, R. B. (2011). *Principles and practices of structural equation modeling* (2nd ed.). New York: Guilford.

Kobayashi, M. (2002). Method effects on reading comprehension test performance: Text organization and response format. *Language Testing, 19,* 193–220.

Koda, K. (1993). Transferred L1 strategies and L2 syntactic structure in L2 sentence comprehension. *Modern Language Journal, 77,* 490–500.

Koda, K. (2005). *Insights into second language reading*. New York: Cambridge University Press.

Kunnan, A. J. (1995). *Test taker characteristics and test performance: A structural modeling approach.* Cambridge: Cambridge University Press.

Kunnan, A. J. (1998). An introduction to structural equation modeling for language assessment research. *Language Testing, 15*(3), 295–332.

Leeser, M. J. (2007). Learner-based factors in L2 reading comprehension and processing grammatical form: Topic familiarity and working memory. *Language Learning, 57,* 229–270.

Liao, Y.-F. (2009). *A construct validation study of the GEPT reading and listening sections: Re-examining the model of L2 reading and listening abilities and their relations to lexico-grammatical knowledge.* Unpublished Ph.D. dissertation. USA: Columbia University.

Lofstedt, J.-I. (1980). *Chinese educational policy.* Atlantic Highlands, NJ: Humanities Press.

Logan, S., & Johnson, R. S. (2010). Investigating gender differences in reading. *Educational Review, 62*(2), 175–187.

Macaro, E., & Erler, L. (2008). Raising the achievement of young-beginner readers of French through strategy instruction. *Applied Linguistics, 29*(1), 90–119.

Messick, S. (1989). Validity. In R. L. Linn (Ed.), *Educational measurement* (pp. 13–103). New York: Macmillan.

Ministry of Education. (2004). *College english curriculum requirements (for trial implementation).* Shanghai: Shanghai Foreign Language Education Press.

Ministry of Education. (2007). *College English curriculum requirements.* Shanghai: Shanghai Foreign Language Education Press.

Mokhtari, K., & Sheorey, R. (2008). *Reading strategies of first- and second-language learners: See how they read.* Norwood, MA: Christopher-Gordon Publishers.

Mokhtari, K., Sheorey, R., & Reichard, C. A. (2008). Measuring the reading strategies of first and second language readers. In K. Mokhtari & R. Sheorey (Eds.), *Reading strategies of first- and second language learners.* Norwood, MA: Christopher-Gordon Publishers Inc.

National College English Testing Committee. (2006). *CET-4 test syllabus and sample test paper (2006 revised version).* Shanghai: Shanghai Foreign Language Education Press.

O'Malley, J. M., & Chamot, A. U. (1990). *Learning strategies in second language acquisition.* Cambridge: Cambridge University Press.

Oxford, R. L. (1990). *Language learning strategies: What every teacher should know.* New York: Newbury House.

Paris, S. G., Wasik, B., & Turner, J. (1991). The development of strategic readers. In R. Barr et al. (Eds.), *Handbook of reading research* (pp. 609–640). New York: Longman.

Paris, S. G., & Winograd, P. (1990). How metacognition can promote academic learning and instruction. In B. F. Jones & L. Idol (Eds.), *Dimensions of thinking and cognitive instruction* (pp. 15–51). Hillsdale, NJ: Erlbaum.

Phakiti, A. (2003). A closer look at gender differences in strategy use in L2 reading. *Language Learning, 53*(4), 649–702.

Phakiti, A. (2008a). Strategic competence as a fourth-order factor model: A structural equation modelling approach. *Language Assessment Quarterly, 5*(1), 20–42.

Phakiti, A. (2008b). Construct validation of Bachman and Palmer's (1996) strategic competence model over time in EFL reading tests. *Language Testing, 25*(2), 237–272.

Politzer, R., & McGroarty, M. (1985). An exploratory study of learning behaviors and their relationship to gains in linguistic and communicative competence. *TESOL Quarterly, 19,* 103–124.

Purpura, J. E. (1997). An analysis of the relationships between test takers' cognitive and metacognitive strategy use and second language test performance. *Language Learning, 47,* 289–325.

Purpura, J. E. (1998). Investigating the effects of strategy use and second language test performance with high- and low-ability test takers: A structural equation modeling approach. *Language Testing, 15,* 333–379.

Purpura, J. E. (1999). *Learner strategy use and performance on language tests: A structural equation modeling approach.* Cambridge: Cambridge University Press.

Qian, D. D. (2002). Investigating the relationship between vocabulary knowledge and academic reading performance: An assessment perspective. *Language Learning, 52,* 513–536.

Richard, J. C., Platt, J., & Platt, H. (1992). *Dictionary of language teaching and applied linguistics*. Essex: Longman.

Richards, J., & Rodgers, T. (2001). *Approaches and methods in language teaching* (2nd ed.). Cambridge: Cambridge University Press.

Riley, G. L., & Lee, J. F. (1996). A comparison of recall and summary protocols as measures of second language reading comprehension. *Language Testing, 13,* 173–189.

Schumacker, R. E., & Lomax, R. G. (2004). *A beginner's guide to structural equation modeling* (2nd ed.). Mahwah, NJ: Lawrence Erlbaum Associates.

Sheorey, R., & Mokhtari, K. (2001). Coping with academic materials: Differences in the reading strategies of native and non-native readers. *System: An International Journal of Educational Technology and Applied Linguistics, 29,* 431–449.

Song, X., & Cheng, L. (2006). Language learner strategy use and test performance of Chinese learners of English. *Language Assessment Quarterly, 3*(3), 243–266.

Stevens, J. P. (2002). *Applied multivariate statistics for the social science* (4th ed.). Mahwah, NJ: Lawrence Erlbaum Association.

Thompson, B. (2004). *Exploratory and confirmatory factor analysis: Understanding concepts and applications*. Washington, DC: American Psychological Association.

Vogt, W. P. (2005). *Dictionary of statistics and methodology: A nontechnical guide for the social sciences*. Thousand Oaks: Sage Publications.

Wei, Y., & Fei, J. (2003). Using English in China. *English Today, 19*(4), 42–47.

Wen, Q., & Johnson, R. (1997). L2 learner variables and English achievement: A study of tertiary-level English majors in China. *Applied Linguistics, 18,* 27–48.

Wenden, A. L. (1991). *Learner strategies for learner autonomy*. London: Prentice-Hall.

Wenden, A. L. (1998). Metacognitive knowledge and language learning. *Applied Linguistics, 19* (4), 515–537.

Wolf, D. (1993). A comparison of assessment tasks used to measure FL reading comprehension. *Modern Language Journal, 77,* 473–489.

Xie, Q. (2013). Does test preparation work? Implications for score validity. *Language Assessment Quarterly, 10*(2), 196–218.

Yang, H. Z., & Weir, C. J. (1998). *Validation study of the National College English test*. Shanghai: Shanghai Foreign Language Education Press.

Young, D. J., & Oxford, R. (1997). A gender-related analysis of strategies used to process written input in the native language and a foreign language. *Applied Language Learning, 8,* 43–73.

Zhang, L. J. (2002). Exploring EFL reading as a metacognitive experience: Reader awareness and reading performance. *Asian Journal of English Language Teaching, 12,* 65–90.

Zhang, L. J. (2010). A dynamic metacognitive systems account of Chinese university students' knowledge about EFL reading. *TESOL Quarterly, 44,* 320–353.

Zhang, L. M. (2016a). Chinese college test takers' individual differences and reading test performance: A structural equation modelling approach. *Perceptual and Motor Skills.* doi:10.1177/0031512516648131.

Zhang, L. M. (2016b). Investigating the relationships between test takers' cognitive and metacognitive strategy use and EFL reading test performance. In V. Aryadoust & J. Fox (Eds.), *Current trends in language testing in the Pacific Rim and the Middle East: Policies, analyses, and diagnoses*. Newcastle: Cambridge Scholars Publishing (CSP).

Zhang, L. M., Chin, C. K., Gong, C., Min, Y., & Tay, B. P. (2016). Investigating the relationship between Singapore lower secondary students' strategy use and Chinese writing performance: A mixed method approach. *Journal of Chinese Language Education, 14*(1), 19–32.

Zhang, X., & Daun, H. (2010). The reform of Chinese college english teaching (CCET) in the context of globalization. In J. Zajda & M. A. Geo-JaJa (Eds.), *Globalisation, comparative education and policy research* (pp. 165–181). Heidelberg: Springer.

Zhang, L. M., Goh, C., & Kunnan, A. (2014). Analysis of test takers' metacognitive and cognitive strategy use and EFL reading test performance: A multi-sample SEM approach. *Language Assessment Quarterly, 11*(1), 76–120.

Zhang, L. M., & Zhang, L. J. (2013). Relationships between Chinese college test takers strategy use and EFL reading test performance: A structural equation modelling approach. *RELC Journal, 44*(1), 35–57.

Zheng, Y., & Cheng, L. (2008). Test review: College English test (CET) in China. *Language Testing, 25*(3), 408–417.

Chapter 2
Development of the Framework
of Language Use

Abstract The purpose of this chapter is to situate the study within the context of currently existent theoretical framework in relation to the assessment of reading comprehension and investigation of the relationships between strategy use and reading test performance. The review of theoretical studies comprises five sections. The first section introduces Hymes' (1967, 1972) theory of communicative competence. This is followed by Canale and Swain's (1980) and Canale's (1983a) model of communicative competence. Next, Bachman's (1990) framework of communicative language ability is presented. Finally, Bachman and Palmer's (1996, 2010) most recent framework of language use is introduced and reviewed. This chapter ends with a discussion of the relevance of the aforementioned theoretical studies to the current study.

The primary purpose of language testing is to make inferences and draw conclusions about test takers' language ability. Arguably, the development and use of any language test should be informed by the consideration of the totality of language ability (Bachman & Palmer, 1996). As such, language ability needs to be defined in sufficiently precise and accurate terms (Bachman, 1990). In the part that follows, the historical development of the framework of language and communication ability in relation to second language teaching, learning, and testing will be reviewed and discussed with a focus on two aspects: (1) development of the dimensions of language and communication ability, and (2) development of the framework of strategic competence.

Influenced by the structuralist theory of language, Lado (1961) proposed his skills and component model in which language was viewed as consisting of independent elements such as pronunciation, morphology, syntax, and lexis. The elements of language were related to each other and integrated the skills of speaking, listening, reading, and writing. Lado advocated discrete-point testing in language elements measurement.

Drawing on Lado's (1961) concept of language proficiency, Carroll (1968) put forth his definition of language competence in terms of independent elements (i.e., phonology, orthography, grammar, and the lexis). However, Carroll argued that test

© Springer Nature Singapore Pte Ltd. 2018

L. Zhang, *Metacognitive and Cognitive Strategy Use in Reading Comprehension*,
https://doi.org/10.1007/978-981-10-6325-1_2

tasks should be designed with the aim of predicting language use that test takers may encounter in real-life situations (Purpura 2004). Thus, Carroll (1961) proposed using integrative tasks to complement discrete-point approaches to measuring learners' ability to use language knowledge. However, Lado's (1961) and Carroll's (1968) models did not indicate how skills and language knowledge are related (Bachman, 1990). It was not clear whether different skills are simply language elements in different modalities or totally different from each other in quality.

2.1 Hymes' (1967, 1972) Theory of Communicative Competence

One of the most influential discussions of language performance in applied linguistics is Hymes' (1967, 1972) theory of communicative competence (McNamara, 1996). Hymes proposed his concept of communicative competence in reaction to Chomsky's (1965) distinction between language competence and performance (Widdowson, 1989).

Chomsky's view of underlying language competence and performance engendered much discussion and even controversy though his seminal work *Syntactic Structure* is widely recognized as one of the most important publications in twentieth-century linguistics. For example, Campbell and Wales (1970) pointed out that Chomsky's restricted view of competence omitted by far the most important linguistic ability, which is "the ability to produce or understand utterances which are not so much grammatical but, more important, appropriate to the context in which they are made" (p. 247). Hymes (1972) concurred with Campbell and Wales and asserted that there was a major gap in Chomsky's definition due to his ignorance of the issue of appropriateness.

On this basis, Hymes defined communicative competence as a person's capabilities which are dependent on both his tacit knowledge and ability for use (Hymes, 1972). In other words, for Chomsky, competence is knowledge, but for Hymes, competence is knowledge and ability. In addition, Hymes identified four parameters of communicative competence—possibility, feasibility, appropriateness, and performance—which are delineated as follows (p. 281):

1. Whether (and to what degree) something is formally possible;
2. Whether (and to what degree) something is feasible in virtue of the means of implementation available;
3. Whether (and to what degree) something is appropriate (adequate, happy, successful) in relation to a context in which it is used and evaluated;
4. Whether (and to what degree) something is in fact done, actually performed, and what its doing entails.

According to Widdowson (1989), Hymes extends Chomsky's concept of competence in two ways. First, he includes aspects of knowledge other than grammar (i.e., the knowledge of what is feasible, appropriate, and actually performed). The first parameter can be perceived as grammatical competence, while the other three can be considered as pragmatic competence. Second, Hymes includes the dimension of ability for use, indicating there are two components in Hymes' competence: knowledge and ability. Additionally, the two components are related to the four parameters of knowledge (possibility, feasibility, appropriateness, and performance), respectively, which boils down to eight elements in contrast to Chomsky's two elements model.

In summary, Hymes's theory of communicative competence broadened the scope of Chomsky's model. Therefore, it provided an important theoretical foundation for the subsequent development of theory of communicative competence for second language teaching, learning, and testing.

2.2 Canale and Swain's (1980) and Canale's (1983a) Model of Communicative Competence

Motivated by Hymes (1967, 1972) and other linguists' work (e.g., Allan & Widdowson, 1975; Munby, 1978; Savignon, 1972), Canale and Swain (1980) proposed their influential theory of communicative competence which was refined by Canale (1983a, b). In their initial framework, there were three components of communicative competence: (1) grammatical competence, which includes knowledge of lexical items and of rules of morphology, syntax, sentence-grammar semantics, and phonology; (2) sociolinguistic competence, which is made up of two sets of rules: sociocultural rules of use and rules of discourse; and (3) strategic competence, which includes verbal and non-verbal communication strategies that may be called into action to compensate for breakdowns in communication. Notably, strategic competence comprises two main types: the strategies related to grammatical competence and those associated with sociolinguistic competence (Canale & Swain, 1980). Canale and Swain (1980) also asserted that certain strategies were expected to change with age and second language proficiency. Stern (1978) believed that as coping strategies, they were more likely to be acquired through experience in real-life situations instead of through classroom practice.

Subsequently, Canale (1983a, b) revised the model and added another component (i.e., discourse competence) to distinguish it from sociocultural competence. Discourse competence refers to the knowledge of the connections among utterances in a text to form a meaningful whole. Canale (1983b) extended the definition of strategic competence to include both compensatory and enhancement functions of production strategies. In other words, strategies play the roles of compensating for breakdowns in communication due to lack of language competence and enhancing the effect of communication.

In summary, it is generally acknowledged that Canale and Swain's (1980) and Canale's (1983a, b) models of communicative competence have broadened our view of language and provided the main theoretical framework for communicative language teaching and testing. Building on Hymes' (1972) model, Canale and Swain incorporated grammatical competence, sociolinguistic competence, and strategic competence into the model of language knowledge. In addition, they introduced the notion of discourse competence. However, the problem with this model is that it fails to point out how its various components interact with each other and with the context in which language use happens. This problem is addressed in Bachman's (1990) model of communicative language ability which is discussed below.

2.3 Bachman's (1990) Framework of Communicative Language Ability

Inspired by Canale and Swain (1980), Canale (1983a, b), and many others' work, Bachman (1990) proposed his multi-componential model of communicative language ability (CLA). Bachman's (1990) CLA model comprises three components: language competence, strategic competence, and psychophysiological mechanisms.

According to Bachman's (1990) model, language competence consists of a set of specific knowledge components employed in communication. It can be subdivided into organizational competence and pragmatic competence. There are two components in organizational competence: grammatical competence and textual competence. Grammatical competence refers to the competencies in language use which comprise some independent knowledge such as knowledge of vocabulary, morphology, syntax, and phonology/graphology. Textual competence involves knowledge of the conventions for joining sentences together to form a text of two or more sentences structured by rules of cohesion and rhetorical organization. Pragmatic competence includes two components: illocutionary competence and sociolinguistic competence. Illocutionary competence pertains to knowledge of the pragmatic conventions for performing acceptable language functions, whereas sociolinguistic competence includes knowledge of the sociolinguistic conventions for performing language functions appropriately in a given context.

In addition, strategic competence comprises three components: assessment, planning, and execution. Assessment enables us to (1) identify the information needed for the realization of the communication goal; (2) determine our language resources available in achieving the communicative goal; (3) make sure that the abilities and knowledge are shared by our interlocutor; and (4) evaluate how well the communicative goal has been achieved. Planning helps retrieve relevant knowledge from language users and formulates a plan to realize the communicative goal.

Drawing on the relevant psychophysiological mechanisms, execution implements the plan "in the modality and channel appropriate to the communicative goal and the context" (Bachman, 1990, p. 103). Psychophysiological mechanisms are the neurological and physiological processes in the execution of language use (Bachman, 1990). In addition, knowledge structure, which is part of the proposed model, refers to language users' topical knowledge about the world, and the context of situation concerns the situations characteristic of the language use.

Further, Bachman (1990) elaborates on strategic competence as follows:

> The interpretation of discourse, in other words, requires the ability to utilize available language competencies to assess the context for relevant information and then match this information to information in the discourse. It is the function of strategic competence to match the new information to be processed with relevant information that is available (including presuppositional and real-world knowledge) and map this onto the maximally efficient use of existing language abilities. (p. 102)

To summarize, Bachman's (1990) model of communicative language ability is multi-componential and shares the same essential components as Canale and Swain's (1980). The significant feature of Bachman's model is that it separates strategic competence (i.e., more general skills in language use) from language competence (i.e., knowledge of and about language), indicating that strategic competence is not part of language competence (McNamara, 1996). According to Bachman (1990), strategic competence is defined as "a general ability, which enables an individual to make the most effective use of available abilities in carrying out a given task" (p. 106). In other words, strategic competence, which includes assessing, planning, and executing, is better understood as ability or capacity rather than an area of knowledge.

The separation of strategic competence from language knowledge is especially significant and relevant to the present study. As stated by Messick (1989), validity is "an integrated evaluative judgment of the degree to which empirical evidence and theoretical rationales support the adequacy and appropriateness of inferences and actions on test scores" (p. 13). Bachman's model, to some degree, provides the theoretical rationale for such inferences about test takers' ability on the basis of their test performance. In addition, Bachman's model helps recognize the role of strategic competence in the test-taking situation. This provides the theoretical support for the investigation of test takers' strategy use in reading comprehension tests in the present study.

2.4 Bachman and Palmer's (1996, 2010) Framework for Language Use

Bachman and Palmer (1996) elaborated on this model further. They made three main types of changes to Bachman's (1990) model:

(a) There is an explicit modeling of the role of non-cognitive factors, including affective schemata and personal characteristics.
(b) Strategic competence has been conceived as a set of metacognitive strategies.
(c) There are some nominal changes. For example, knowledge structures are termed topical knowledge, etc.

First of all, Bachman and Palmer (1996) claimed that personal characteristics such as age, sex, nationality, and level and type of education are not part of test takers' language ability. These individual attributes are supposed to influence their performance on language tests. Affective schemata were thought of as "the affective or emotional correlates of topical knowledge" (p. 65) which provide the basis for language users to assess the characteristics of the language use task and its environment in terms of past emotional experiences in similar contexts.

In addition, similar to Bachman (1990), Bachman and Palmer (1996) propose that language knowledge comprises two broad categories: organizational and pragmatic knowledge. Organizational knowledge is subdivided into grammatical knowledge and textual knowledge. Pragmatic knowledge includes two areas of knowledge: functional knowledge and sociolinguistic knowledge. Functional knowledge is concerned with individuals' "ability to interpret relationships between utterances or sentences and texts and the intentions of language users" (p. 69). It includes knowledge of ideational, manipulative, heuristic, and imaginative functions. Sociolinguistic knowledge refers to language users' knowledge to create or interpret language appropriate to a particular language use setting. It includes knowledge of dialects/varieties, registers, natural or idiomatic expressions, cultural references, and figures of speech. In conclusion, organizational and pragmatic competences are two important components of individuals' language competence. In this study, organizational competence is operationalized by students' performance on the CET-4 Reading subtest. However, pragmatic competence is excluded from the present study due to the limitations of the study scope.

Strategic competence is viewed as "a set of metacognitive components or strategies" which "provide a cognitive management function in language use" (Bachman, 1990, p. 70). It comprises three components as follows:

(1) goal setting, which involves deciding what the language user is going to do when facing language use or test tasks;
(2) assessment, through which the individual associates his/her topical knowledge and language knowledge with the language use setting and tasks; and
(3) planning, which concerns the individual's decision of how to use language knowledge, topical knowledge, and affective schemata to complete the tasks successfully.

Bachman and Palmer (2010) updated the framework of language use and incorporated cognitive strategies into it. According to them, language users/test takers' focal attributes are still part of language ability which comprises language knowledge and strategic competence. The peripheral attributes of language users include personal attributes, topical knowledge, affective schemata, and cognitive strategies. They argued that cognitive strategies are "what language users employ when they execute plans" in actual language use situations (p. 43). Thus, in Bachman and Palmer's (2010) model, both metacognitive and cognitive strategies are included. As the core of strategic competence, metacognitive strategies are part of the test takers' focal attributes while cognitive strategies are perceived as test takers' peripheral features.

The following example of reading tests illustrates the interactions among test takers' language knowledge and their metacognitive and cognitive strategy use. When learners take a reading test, they demonstrate their ability in using the target language through their response to test items by tapping into their knowledge in vocabulary, morphology, syntax, and phonology. In addition, their textual competence is tested while they tackle the items examining their text comprehension ability. In responding to the reading test items, learners appear to make different evaluations of what are required for accomplishing the task and of their own language resources. On this basis, they formulate a plan to complete the test. For example, they may decide to use more inference-making strategies in reading the text and responding to the items if they have sufficient knowledge in morphology. In addition, if they find that they do not have the required lexical knowledge, they may formulate plans to skip items for the purpose of better time management. In this study, analysis of empirical data would shed light on the relationships between metacognition, cognitive strategies, and students' test performance.

2.5 Relevance to the Study

The previous section reviews the historical development of the framework of language and communication ability in relation to second language teaching, learning, and testing by focusing and elaborating on the influential perspectives and models in this field. Among them, Bachman and Palmer's (1996, 2010) multi-componential view of language ability has provided a particularly productive and comprehensive theoretical framework for both research and practice of second language acquisition and testing (Bachman & Cohen, 1998; Purpura 2004).

Bachman and Palmer's model has been widely accepted as a more useful and complete model of language ability than earlier ones (Chapelle, Grabe, & Berns, 1997). For example, this model incorporates the effects of personal characteristics, topical knowledge, and affective schemata into the framework. In other words, it takes into consideration how individuals' attributes interact with one another as well as how these attributes interact with the characteristics of the target language use contexts (Liao, 2009). In addition, strategic competence, which is defined as "a set of metacognitive strategies" (Bachman & Palmer, 1996, p. 70), is perceived as providing a cognitive management function in language use which links an individual's characteristics within and with those of language use tasks and settings. Thus, this model provides a general theoretical background for the investigation of test takers' strategy use and test performance in this study.

From the perspective of language knowledge, this study examines Bachman and Palmer's (2010) notion of organizational knowledge measured by the CET-4 Reading subtest by means of morphology, syntax, lexis, cohesion, and coherence, etc. In addition, this study also attempts to investigate Bachman and Palmer's (2010) definition of strategic competence, especially regarding the relationships between metacognitive and cognitive strategies, and reading test performance. Finally, their model provides the general background for the ReTSUQ which was developed and used in this study.

In summary, the review of the frameworks of language and communication ability provides historical and developmental perspectives on how language ability is defined and operationalized. In the following section, relevant literature on reading comprehension assessment will be reviewed and introduced.

References

Allan, J. P. B., & Widdowson, H. G. (1975). Grammar and language teaching. In J. P. B. Allan & S. P. Corder (Eds.), *Paper in applied linguistics* (pp. 45–97). London: Oxford University Press.

Bachman, L. F. (1990). *Fundamental consideration in language testing*. Oxford: Oxford University Press.

Bachman, L. F., & Cohen, A. D. (1998). *Interface between second language acquisition and language testing research*. Cambridge: Cambridge University Press.

Bachman, L. F., & Palmer, A. S. (1996). *Language testing in practice*. Oxford: Oxford University Press.

Bachman, L. F., & Palmer, A. S. (2010). *Language testing in practice*. Oxford: Oxford University Press.

Campbell, R., & Wales, R. (1970). The study of language acquisition. In J. Lyons (Ed.), *New horizons in linguistics* (pp. 242–260). Harmondsworth: Penguin Books.

Canale, M. (1983a). From communicative competence to communicative language pedagogy. In J. C. Richards & R. W. Schmidt (Eds.), *Language and communication* (pp. 2–27). London: Longman.

Canale, M. (1983b). On some dimensions of language proficiency. In J. W. Oller Jr. (Ed.), *Issues in language testing research* (pp. 333–342). Rowley, MA: Newbury House Publishers.

Canale, M., & Swain, M. (1980). Theoretical bases of communicative approaches to second language teaching and testing. *Applied Linguistics, 1*, 1–47.

Carroll, J. B. (1961). Fundamental consideration in testing for English proficiency for foreign students. In *Testing the English proficiency of foreign students* (pp. 31–40). Washington, DC: Center for Applied Linguistics.

Carroll, J. B. (1968). The psychology of language testing. In A. Davies (Ed.), *Language testing symposium: A psycholinguistic approach* (pp. 46–69). London: Oxford University Press.

Chapelle, C., Grabe, W., & Berns, M. (1997). *Communicative language proficiency: Definitions and implications for TOEFL 2000. TOEFL monograph series no. 10*. Princeton, NJ: Educational Testing Service.

Chomsky, N. (1965). *Aspects of the theory of syntax*. Cambridge, MA: MIT Press.

Hymes, D. (1967). Models of the interaction of language and social setting. *Journal of Social Issues, 23*(2), 8–38.

Hymes, D. (1972). On communicative competence. In J. B. Pride & J. Holmes (Eds.), *Sociolinguistics* (pp. 269–293). Harmondsworth: Penguin.

Lado, R. (1961). *Language testing: The construction and use of foreign language tests*. New York: Longman.

Liao, Y.-F. (2009). *A construct validation study of the GEPT reading and listening sections: Re-examining the model of L2 reading and listening abilities and their relations to lexico-grammatical knowledge*. Unpublished Ph.D. dissertation. USA: Columbia University.

McNamara, T. (1996). *Measuring second language performance*. London and New York: Longman.

Messick, S. (1989). Validity. In R. L. Linn (Ed.), *Educational measurement* (pp. 13–103). New York: Macmillan.

Munby, J. (1978). *Communicative syllabus design*. Cambridge: Cambridge University.

Purpura, J. E. (2004). *Assessing grammar*. Cambridge, UK: Cambridge University Press.

Savignon, S. J. (1972). *Communicative competence: An experiment in foreign language teaching*. Philadelphia: The Center for Curriculum Development.

Stern, H. H. (1978). *The formal-functional distinction in language pedagogy: A conceptual clarification*. Paper read at the 5th AILA Congress, Montreal, August.

Widdowson, H. G. (1989). Knowledge of language and ability for use. *Applied Linguistics, 10*(2), 128–137.

Chapter 3
Reading Comprehension and Strategy Use

Abstract This chapter focuses on reading comprehension and strategy use. The first part defines reading comprehension based on extant voluminous literature. Relevant reading models are then reviewed and discussed. Next, relevant empirical studies on reading comprehension and strategy use are introduced. Theory of metacognition and its application to reading comprehension are presented first, followed by studies on the relationship between strategy use and language performance, test-taking strategies, gender differences in strategy use and language performance, and Chinese college students' strategy use and language performance. On this basis, hypothesized models are postulated for testing and investigation in the following parts of the study.

As discussed in the previous part, the framework of language and communication ability has evolved and the perspectives on language ability have been developed and clarified over time. In relation to the current study, the following section reviews the relevant literature about assessing reading comprehension.

As a core function of literacy, effective reading with appropriate speed and comprehension enables people to communicate messages and create new ideas (Paris & Hamilton, 2009). Researchers have come to the consensus that reading is probably one of the most important skills for L2 learners in academic contexts (Carrell, 1989a; Grabe, 1991; Lynch & Hudson, 1991). Since English has become the primary language of global commerce and communication, and of science and technology in the modern world, researchers have devoted much time and efforts to studying different aspects of L1 and L2 reading (Sheorey & Mokhtari, 2008). Although reading research has expanded considerably in recent years (Grabe, 2009), it seems to be difficult to capture the definition of reading comprehension with one single statement due to its complex nature (Alderson, 2000). The following section discusses how different researchers define reading comprehension in a variety of ways.

© Springer Nature Singapore Pte Ltd. 2018
L. Zhang, *Metacognitive and Cognitive Strategy Use in Reading Comprehension*,
https://doi.org/10.1007/978-981-10-6325-1_3

3.1 Research About Reading Comprehension

From the early focus on thinking and reasoning (Paris & Hamilton, 2009; Thorndike, 1917), to the recent ten adjectives used to delineate reading comprehension (Grabe, 2009), researchers have tried to define reading comprehension in various ways.

Different definitions of reading comprehension. Urquhart and Weir (1998, p. 22), for example, defined reading comprehension as "the process of receiving and interpreting information encoded in language form via the medium of print."

Koda (2005) argued that "comprehension occurs when the reader extracts and integrates various kinds of information from the text and combines it with what is already known" (p. 4).

Paris and Hamilton (2009, p. 32) believed that "reading comprehension is only a subset of an ill-defined larger set of knowledge that reflects the communicative interactions among the intentions of the author, the content of the text/message, the abilities and purpose of the reader, and the context/situation of the interaction (p. 32)."

Grabe (2009, p. 14) used ten adjectives to define reading comprehension as a "complex combination of processes": a rapid, efficient, comprehending, interactive, strategic, flexible, purposeful, evaluative, learning, and linguistic process which delineates what fluent readers do when processing texts.

Based on the definition of the Reading Framework for the 2009 National Assessment of Educational Progress (National Assessment Governing Board, 2008), reading comprehension is "an active and complex process that involves understanding written text, developing and interpreting meaning, and using meaning as appropriate to type of text, purpose and situation" (p. 2).

Reading for Understanding: Toward an R&D Program in Reading Comprehension (RAND Reading Study Group, 2002, p. 11), often referred to as the RAND Report, defined reading comprehension as "the process of simultaneously extracting and constructing meaning through interaction and involvement with written language. It consists of three elements: the reader, the text and the purpose of reading."

The different definitions of reading comprehension have shown us diverse and rich perspectives on reading comprehension. In this study, reading comprehension is perceived as a constructive process in which the text, the reader, and the context interact. This concept of constructive and interactive reading includes key principles of the top-down processing model of reading reflected in schema theory (Anderson & Pearson, 1984), bottom-up text-processing strategies emphasized by van Dijk and Kintsch (1983), and comprehension monitoring processes advocated by several notable researchers (e.g., Baker & Brown, 1984; Garner, 1987; Paris & Winograd, 1990). Before further discussion on issues regarding reading comprehension, it is necessary to examine the major differences between L1 and L2 reading in order to have an accurate understanding of how the findings from L1 reading research can be applied to L2 reading studies.

Differences between L1 and L2 reading. There are many differences between L1 and L2 reading which include linguistic and processing differences, developmental and educational differences, and sociocultural and institutional differences. (Grabe, 2009), though it is generally acknowledged that many findings from L1 reading research are relevant to understanding phenomena in L2 reading studies (Buck, Tatsuoka, & Kostin, 1997). This section outlines two major differences between L1 and L2 reading which are most relevant to the focus of the study: linguistic and processing differences.

Linguistic differences. It is well understood that L2 readers begin their reading process with very different linguistic resources from L1 readers. According to research and estimates, L1 children normally know 5000–8000 words orally at six years old when their reading instruction begin. Upon this age, they would have stored very good implicit knowledge of morphology, syntactic structure of the language, as well as knowledge of text structure. However, L2 readers with a knowledge bank of 5000–8000 words are considered advanced readers. In addition, to develop good knowledge of morphology and syntax will take L2 readers several years. Thus, it is argued that L2 readers are assumed to have to develop their linguistic resources and reading comprehension skills simultaneously (Grabe, 2009).

Second, transfer effects between L1 and L2 will facilitate or interfere with L2 reading. Koda (2007) states:

> unlike first language reading, second language reading involves two languages. The dual language involvement implies continual interaction between the two languages as well as incessant adjustments in accommodating the disparate demands each language imposes. For this reason, L2 reading is cross-linguistic, and thus, inherently more complex than L1 reading. (p. 1)

The commonly held view is that students' false cognates or near cognates influence their vocabulary recognition. In addition, linguistic differences at orthographic, syntactic, and discourse levels can also mislead L2 readers, especially at the beginning stage. Although it is a basic fact that L2 readers have resources of two languages and advanced L2 readers can develop good metalinguistic awareness (i.e., the ability to reflect on the nature of languages consciously) in L2 reading comprehension, less successful L2 readers may not have the requisite metalinguistic knowledge which supports their L2 reading comprehension. Thus, less successful L2 readers' L1 knowledge may only interfere with their L2 reading performance (Koda, 2007).

Processing differences. In addition to linguistic differences, there are also processing differences between L1 and L2 readers. Due to various reasons, L2 readers are slow in word recognition and less accurate in word recognition processing which leads to a slow reading rate. Perfetti (1992, 2007) argued that the fact that L2 readers have less complete lexical representations for most words may contribute to their slow word recognition, and syntactic and semantic processing. However, compared with L1 readers, L2 readers also have some advantages (Grabe, 1991). For example, most L2 learners are older than L1 learners, suggesting that by their age, L2 learners would have developed their conceptual sense of the world well. Thus, it is more likely that they can make sound and logical inferences from the text which is a cognitively indispensable component of reading comprehension.

In summary, while L2 readers are limited in linguistic resources and their experience with their native language may interfere with L2 reading processing, they enjoy the advantage over L1 readers in terms of experience with their native language and the world, as most L2 readers are older in age than L1 readers. Reading researchers are, therefore, suggested to conduct studies examining the differences and similarities between L1 and L2 reading processes which will inform classroom instruction in reading comprehension. In addition, given linguistic, processing, educational, developmental, and sociocultural differences between L1 reading and L2 reading, it is recommended that findings and implications from L1 reading research be examined carefully before its application to L2 reading research and instruction (Grabe, 2009).

3.2 Relevant Models of Reading Comprehension

Reading models provide specific descriptions and representations of reading theories which interpret what reading involves and how reading comprehension works. Most of these models are generally based on empirical studies on reading comprehension which help to explain the nature of reading abilities and make predictions about future research in relevant areas.

Researchers on reading comprehension have different ways of presenting models of reading (Alderson, 2000; Barnett, 1989; Grabe, 2009; Hudson, 2007; Urquhart & Weir, 1998). For example, Urquhart and Weir (1998) identified two different classes of reading models in the literature of reading comprehension: process models and componential models. Process models concern the actual process of reading, as well as how the factors involved interact with one another, whereas componential models are about the components involved in the reading process. Paris and Hamilton (2009) reviewed six prominent views of reading comprehension which include information processing models, the Simple View of Reading, Kintsch's (1998) construction–integration model, comprehension as envisionment through stances, stage models, and multi-component models of comprehension. In this section, several reading models pertinent to this study will be reviewed. They are multi-component models, information processing models, the Simple View of Reading, Anderson and Pearson's (1984) schema theory, Kintsch's (1998) construction and integration model, and Pressley and Afflerbach's (1995) constructively responsive reading model. LaBerge and Samuels' (1974) model, Stanovich's (1980) interactive compensatory model, and Rumelhart's (1994) model will be discussed in the elaboration of information processing models.

3.2.1 Multi-component Models

Instead of describing the actual process of reading comprehension, multi-component models examine the areas of skills or knowledge involved in the process. In other words, multi-componential models attempt to describe reading ability rather than the reading process. Thus, they perceive reading as isolable components which are distinct in theory (Hoover & Tunmer, 1993).

A review of literature on reading shows that researchers have provided different taxonomies of skills about reading comprehension based on their own empirical studies and research. For example, Davis (1968) postulated that there are four categories of reading skills: identifying word meanings, drawing inferences, identifying writer's technique and recognizing the mood of the passage, and finding answers to questions.

Lunzer, Waite, and Dolan's (1979) taxonomy included the following component skills which were arranged from lower to higher levels: word meaning, words in contexts, literal comprehension, drawing inferences from single strings, drawing inference from multiple strings, interpretation of metaphors, finding salient or main ideas, and forming judgments.

Munby (1978) came up with an even longer list of reading skills including recognizing the script of a language, deducing the meaning and use of unfamiliar lexical items, understanding explicitly stated information, understanding information when not explicitly stated, understanding conceptual meaning, understanding the communicative value of sentences, understanding the relations within the sentence, understanding the relations between parts of text through lexical cohesion devices, interpreting text by going outside it, recognizing indicators in discourse, identifying the main point of information in discourse, distinguishing the main idea from supporting details, extracting salient points to summarize the text, selective extraction of relevant points from a text, basic reference skills, Skimming and Scanning to locate specifically required information, and transcoding information to diagrammatic display.

Perfetti (1985), on the other hand, concluded that there are three main skills in reading comprehension: having lexical access, assembling and integrating propositions in working memory, and applying background knowledge to comprehension.

As an L2 reading model, Coady's (1979) psycholinguistic model included three components: conceptual ability, process strategies, and background knowledge. Conceptual ability refers to intellectual capacity; process strategies comprise both knowledge system and the ability to use the knowledge, and background knowledge is considered as an actual component instead of an addition to comprehension (Urquhart & Weir, 1998).

Grabe (1991) proposed six general component skills and knowledge areas which comprise automatic recognition skills, vocabulary and structural knowledge, formal discourse structure knowledge, content/world background knowledge, synthesis and evaluation skills/strategies, and metacognitive knowledge and skills monitoring.

To sum up, the foregoing multi-component models of reading provide a rich description of the component skills essential to reading comprehension. The review of these models leads to the general consensus about the vital component skills of reading including word recognition, syntactic knowledge, discourse structure, background knowledge, metacognitive knowledge, and strategy use (Grabe, 1991, 2009; Urquhart & Weir, 1998).

Word recognition. Researchers have come to the consensus that word recognition is critical to fluent reading (Adam, 1990; Grabe, 1991, 2009; Perfetti, 1999, 2007; Rayner & Pollatsek, 1989; Stanovich, 2000). Perfetti and Hart (2001) and Perfetti (2007) suggested that word recognition is the interaction of activated orthographic, phonological, semantic, and syntactic processes. Grabe (2009) argued that "fast and automatic word recognition occurs when visual input from the word on the page activates lexical entries in the readers' lexicon that have well-represented information of four types: orthographic, phonological, semantic and syntactic" (p. 23). Thus, automaticity in word identification skills is critical to fluent reading. Automaticity is distinguished from speed in that the former involves unawareness of the process (Grabe, 2009).

In addition to automaticity, accurate recognition processes and well-developed lexical entries are required in word recognition (Perfetti, 1992, 2007; Perfetti & Hart, 2001).

Syntactic knowledge. Research showed that there is a strong relation between syntax and reading comprehension. In other words, syntactic knowledge appears to be an important contributor to reading comprehension ability (Alderson, 1993; Enright et al., 2002; Nagy, 2007; Snow, Griffin, & Burns, 2005; van Gelderen et al., 2004). For example, van Gelderen et al. (2004) found the correlation between L2 grammar and reading is as strong as 0.80. Alderson's (1993) study about IELTS reading showed the correlation between reading and grammar is also as high as 0.80, and Enright et al.'s (2002) study indicated a robust correlation of 0.91 between the structure knowledge and reading comprehension of the Computer-Based Test of English as a Foreign Language (TOEFL CBT).

Thus, it appears that syntactic knowledge facilitates the construction of text comprehension with ongoing instructions (Grabe, 2009). In other words, readers need to process syntax to derive meaning from the recognized words (Urquhart & Weir, 1998). This concurs with the argument that semantic proposition units "cannot be formed without the syntactic parsing of clauses or sentences" (Grabe, 2009, p. 30).

Discourse structure. Discourse structure is related to the understanding of the relations among concepts in the text (Buck et al., 1997). Research on reading comprehension has shown that knowledge of how a text is organized influences its comprehension (Alderson, 2000; Grabe, 1991; Koda, 2005). In other words, readers need to be aware of how the cohesive devices are structured in order to construct meaning from the text (Hudson, 2007).

Halliday and Hasan (1976) defined cohesive ties as reference, substitution, ellipsis, conjunction, and lexical cohesion (i.e., repetition and collocation). Studies showed that text coherence increases readers' understanding of the text

(McNamara, Kintsch, Songer, & Kintsch 1996) and is important to readers' development of a coherent representation of the message in the text (Halliday & Hasan, 1976; Hudson, 2007; Moe & Irwin, 1986). This is because cohesive devices provide readers with knowledge about the relations between the elements of information presented by the author (Frederiksen, 1977; Hudson, 2007).

Background knowledge. Considerable research has shown that background knowledge is a contributing factor in reading comprehension (Adam, Bell, & Perfetti, 1995; Anderson & Pearson, 1984; Long, Johns, & Morris, 2006; Perfetti, Marron, & Foltz, 1996; Stanovich, 2000; Zwaan & Rapp, 2006).

For example, Anderson and Pearson (1984) believed that comprehension comes from the interaction of new information with old knowledge. Kintsch (1998) believed that the construction of an elaborated situation model depends on the reader's ability to make inferences beyond the literal text and to make the connection between the text and his/her previous experience and background knowledge. Koda (2007) stated explicitly that "successful comprehension is achieved through the integrative interaction of extracted text information and a reader's prior knowledge" (p. 4). Grabe (2009) argued that background knowledge is essential considering the fact that reading comprehension combines text input, cognitive processes, and the information we have known. Thus, the consensual view among researchers is that background knowledge is an important and central component in reading comprehension (Grabe, 2009; Hudson, 2007).

Metacognitive knowledge and strategy use. Metacognitive knowledge is widely recognized as a critical component of skilled reading (Anderson, 1991, 2005; Brown, Armbruster, & Baker, 1986; Flavell, Miller, & Miller, 2002; Grabe, 1991, 2009; Hudson 2007; Phakiti, 2003, 2008a). Based on the metacognitive framework proposed by Vandergrift and Goh (2012), metacognitive awareness is "a state of consciousness of our own thoughts as we focus on a particular cognitive or learning situation" (p. 84). Metacognitive awareness is demonstrated in three ways: metacognitive knowledge, metacognitive experience, and strategy use. While metacognitive experience involves involuntary fleeting sensations of thoughts about one's thinking, metacognitive knowledge and strategy use are demonstrations of individuals' multifaceted understanding of themselves as learners, and the tasks and actions needed to assist language use. Collectively, they form an individual's metacognitive awareness (Goh & Zhang, 2013).

Flavell (1979) argued that metacognitive knowledge includes learners' knowledge of person, tasks, and strategies. Research showed that metacognitive knowledge concerns executive cognition which underpins two important functions of metacognition: knowledge about cognition and regulation of cognition (Baker & Brown, 1984; Bialystok, 2001; Brown, 1980; Brown et al., 1986; Flavell, 1979). According to Paris and Winograd (1990), metacognitive knowledge "captures two essential features of metacognition (i.e., self-appraisal and self-management)" (p. 17). Self-appraisal refers to personal reflections on one's own knowledge and abilities, as well as making judgments about task and strategy factors affecting performance. On the other hand, self-management is "metacognition in action," which helps the individual "orchestrate cognitive aspects of problem solving"

(p. 17). In other words, self-appraisal is about "knowing" which is learners' self-evaluation of their own person, tasks, and strategy knowledge, while self-management is about "doing," which demonstrates learners' strategy use in a specific language use or language learning situation (Vandergrift & Goh, 2012).

Learners' self-appraisal affects their use of strategies. In other words, their use of strategy builds on their metacognitive knowledge. In the present study, the focus is on test takers' strategy use which falls into the commonly used distinctions of metacognitive and cognitive strategies. Metacognitive strategies are operationalized by planning, evaluating, and monitoring strategies (Brown, 1980; O'Malley and Chamot, 1990; Paris & Jacobs, 1984; Wenden, 1998), and cognitive strategies refer to specific learner strategies (i.e., reading strategies in this study) (Cohen, 2006; Vandergrift & Goh, 2012).

Reading researchers have come to a consensus that good readers demonstrate the ability to use reading strategies more effectively than poor readers. They believe that strategic reading is a critical feature of expert readers (Paris, Wasik, & Turner, 1991). Researchers have conducted countless studies compiling lists of strategies used, improving readers' strategy use through direct training, and instructions with the aim of enhancing their reading comprehension (e.g., Anderson, 1991; Barnett, 1989; Cohen, 1990; Zhang, 2010; Zhang, Goh, & Kunnan, 2014).

3.2.2   Information Processing Models

Information processing models provide descriptions of the mental operations readers engage in during text comprehension (Paris & Hamilton, 2009). Generally, the process models can be categorized into three approaches: bottom-up, top-down, and interactive approaches. In bottom-up approaches (Gough, 1972; LaBerge & Samuels, 1974; Samuels & LaBerge, 1983), readers begin with the text. They absorb and analyze small chunks of text in a linear information processing fashion and then add them to the next chunks until meaning is constructed from the text. However, researchers found that bottom-up approaches are not adequate for the interpretation of text comprehension. In top-down approaches (Goodman, 1967, 1986, 1994, 1996; Smith, 1971, 1983), readers generate a series of expectations (or guesses) about the incoming text based on their prior knowledge or particular context clues and then sample a minimal part of the text to confirm or reject their expectations and then make new predictions. Inference-making and readers' background knowledge are important features of top-down models. However, the past 20 years' research on reading comprehension has proved that such a top-down approach to reading seems to exist only in researchers' imagination (Gough & Wren, 1999; Grabe, 1991, 2000, 2009; Perfetti, 1985, 1994; Pressley, 2006; Rayner & Pollatsek, 1989; Urquhart & Weir, 1998). In actual fact, top-down models appear to be ineffective in interpreting the process of reading comprehension.

In the interactive approach (Kintsch, 1988, 1998; Kintsch & van Dijk, 1978; Rumelhart, 1977, 2004; Stanovich, 1980, 1986, 2000; van Dijk & Kintsch, 1983), no regular sequences exist in the bottom-up or top-down approaches. Instead, textual information and readers' mental activities simultaneously impact readers' comprehension. In other words, the useful elements from both bottom-up and top-down approaches can be combined in the interactive approach. Although current theories on reading are all interactive in nature (Urquhart & Weir, 1998) and most teachers have accepted interactive approaches to reading comprehension (Hudson, 2007), many current discussions of views on reading avoid the three categories of approaches in order to keep away from the danger of overgeneralization and simplification. Instead, they present specific models of reading and explanations of prevailing views (Grabe, 2009). The following section introduces LaBerge and Samuels' (1974) model, Stanovich's (1980) interactive compensatory model, and Rumelhart's (1994) model as they are representative of information processing models.

LaBerge and Samuels' (1974) and Samuels and LaBerge's (1983) model. The original LaBerge and Samuels' (1974) model was often cited as a bottom-up view of reading. However, after several revisions, the addition of the feedback loops in its later version which allows later processing stages to influence the earlier ones (i.e., Samuels, 1977; Samuels & LaBerge, 1983) makes it fall into the category of the interactive approach to reading comprehension (Barnett, 1989). According to LaBerge and Samuels (1974) and Samuels and LaBerge (1983), automaticity and attention are two important elements in reading comprehension. A skill or subskill is viewed as automatic when a person can finish the complete process with his attention directed somewhere else. For example, only when readers achieve automaticity in word recognition, can they use more attention for meaning construction. They believe that readers can only attend to one thing at a time when reading. However, as long as only one thing requires attention, they can process many things concurrently.

For Samuels and LaBerge (1983), reading comprehension is composed of two tasks: decoding and comprehension. Decoding refers to transferring printed words to articulatory or phonological representation, whereas comprehension involves constructing meaning from the decoded materials. In this model, there are five components in the processing system (i.e., visual memory, phonological memory, semantic memory, episodic memory, and attention) and the feedback loops. In other words, if the reader can decode textual information automatically, he/she is able to direct more attention to comprehension, which is important to fluent reading. Since comprehension is derived from word recognition, developing automatic word recognition and decoding are primarily important. Decoding abilities and reading comprehension have been found to be closely related to each other, and the correlations between them vary from 0.30 to 0.70 (Juel, Griffith, & Gough, 1986; Yuill & Oakhill, 1991).

Rumelhart's model. As a response to the view of linear processing in reading comprehension presumed by the bottom-up model, Rumelhart (1977) argued that reading comprehension is a perceptual and cognitive process. By this, Rumelhart meant that syntactic, semantic, lexical, and orthographic information has an influence on text processing. According to Rumelhart, readers extract words and spelling that are recorded in a mental system, which is termed visual information score (VIS). VIS is a feature extraction device responsible for interpreting the critical features of the words and moving them into a certain pattern synthesizer. The pattern synthesizer plays the role of synthesizing and interpreting what the readers have read based on their previous knowledge about spelling, patterns, syntax, vocabulary, semantics, and context of the language in order to construct meaning from the text. As Rumelhart (1977) stated:

> ...all of the various sources of knowledge, both sensory and nonsensory, come together at one place and the reading process is the product of the simultaneous joint application of all the knowledge sources" (p. 588).

In summary, a hierarchy of knowledge structure exists in Rumelhart's model. In other words, based on this model, understanding of knowledge at each level is influenced by a higher level of analysis (Barnett, 1989). For example, at the letter cluster level, readers seek information about the letter sequence that forms units in the target language and make hypotheses from the lexical level, whereas at the lexical and syntactic level, the quality of the hypotheses is decided by the quality of evidence on which they are based. In addition, the hypotheses synthesize top-down and bottom-up approaches and reinforce both.

The implication of this model for second language readers lies in that these adult readers will bring their experience and knowledge of first language structure and semantics to the text of the target language. In other words, the interaction of a variety of knowledge helps these readers construct meanings from multiple sources. In particular, it is argued that adult readers would employ strategies to compensate for their lack of language proficiency in the process of reading comprehension in the test (Zhang & Zhang, 2013).

Stanovich's (1980) interactive compensatory model. First proposed in 1980, the interactive compensatory model views reading as involving many efficient and automatic processes, and employing information simultaneously from readers' sources of knowledge such as orthographic, vocabulary, syntactic, semantic, and background knowledge (Grabe, 2009; Hudson, 2007; Stanovich, 1980, 1986, 2000). The interactive nature of the reading process shows that a deficit in one skill may be compensated for by another present skill. In other words, when one process in reading becomes less efficient, other processes will provide compensatory support to allow comprehension to continue. The model assumes that all processes in reading comprehension will interact and support one another potentially.

According to Stanovich (1980),

> Interactive models assume that a pattern is synthesized based on information provided simultaneously from several knowledge sources. The compensatory assumption states that a deficit in any knowledge source results in a heavier reliance on other knowledge sources, regardless of their level in their processing hierarchy (p. 63).

Thus, Stanovich's model is useful to explain how efficient L2 readers use their first-language skills and strategies to compensate for their linguistic weakness in the second language (Barnett, 1989).

3.2.3 The Simple View of Reading

Suggested by Gough and Tunmer (1986), the Simple View of Reading is based on the idea that reading is a combination of word decoding abilities (D) and comprehension ability (C). The model can be expressed in an equation: $R = D \times C$, suggesting that reading (R) is the product (or interaction) of decoding abilities (D) and comprehension abilities (C), the former being bottom-up processing and the latter being top-down processing (Adolf, Catts, & Little, 2006; Chen & Vellutino, 1997; Gough, Hoover, & Peterson, 1996; Gough, Juel, & Griffith, 1992; Grabe, 2009; Hoover & Gough, 1990; Hoover & Tunmer, 1993)

This model indicates that when decoding ability is not adequate, reading comprehension suffers as the reader does not have enough attention and cognitive resources to focus on comprehension. When decoding becomes automatic and accurate, comprehension becomes easier and more efficient.

The Simple View of Reading is an extension of the model proposed by LaBerge and Samuels (1974). This mode is powerful in that it is theoretically parsimonious and comprehensive in isolating the decoding skills from the comprehension skills. Advocates of this model may expect that reading comprehension is affected by many other factors, but the central point is that comprehension is primarily viewed as decoding abilities multiplied by comprehension ability.

According to Grabe (2009), the implications of this model for L1 and L2 readers are different. As L1 readers, they have good comprehension ability even at early reading levels, although their decoding ability is not sufficiently efficient and accurate. Thus, when they become skillful at decoding by fourth grade (as typical good L1 readers), their comprehension ability becomes very strong. In contrast, its implication for L2 readers' development of comprehension ability is not as obvious as they seldom achieve the same word recognition fluency as good L1 readers. However, similar to LaBerge and Samuels' (1974) and Samuels and LaBerge's (1983) models, the Simple View of Reading shows that word recognition plays a very crucial role in reading comprehension.

3.2.4 Schema Theory

Anderson and Pearson (1984) argued that comprehension comes from the interaction of new information with old knowledge. Their schema-theoretic view of reading does not present a model of the entire reading process. Instead, it focuses on the role of readers' schemata, the knowledge already stored in memory in the process of comprehension. In other words, Anderson and Pearson's schema theory focuses on how schemata "function in the process of interpreting new information and allowing it to enter and become a part of the knowledge store" (p. 255).

Anderson and Pearson used the schema of ship christening as an example:

> Queen Elizabeth participated in a long-delayed ceremony in Clydebank, Scotland, yesterday. While there is still bitterness here following the protracted strike, on this occasion a crowd of shipyard workers numbering in the hundreds joined dignitaries in cheering as the HMS Pinafore shipped into the water (p. 260).

Although ship christening does not appear in this paragraph, the mention that the Queen is attending a ceremony which leads to a ship slipping into the water matches the ship christening schema. In other words, readers' stored knowledge about ship christening provides clues about the comprehension of the text.

Moreover, they acknowledge the pivotal role of reference-making in the process of schemata activation occurring either when text information is input in the initial process of decoding, or when it is retrieved from memory. Reference-making is involved in four situations: (1) deciding what schema should be activated in comprehending the text; (2) deciding whether a particular contextual character or item fits a specific schema slot; (3) filling a particular schema slot by assigning default values when there is lack of concrete information in the text; and (4) drawing conclusions in the absence of knowledge within a schema. They concluded that inference-making, which contributes to a coherent understanding of the text, is made at the time when the text is read. In addition, other inference-drawing processes will follow if circumstances require. Further, Anderson and Pearson (1984) pointed out that readers most likely learn and remember important text elements, as compared to less important ones by selective attention. This is called the selective-attention hypothesis. Anderson and Pearson argued that this hypothesis is effective in interpreting positive effects of equipping readers with instructional objectives and questions.

To summarize, in Anderson and Pearson's schema theory, the reader is perceived as an active participant. In other words, readers' world knowledge, previous experience, and ability to infer play very important roles in their reading comprehension. The implication of this model for L2 reading lies in that L2 readers engaging in academic reading typically have a rich store of world knowledge and experience with L1 reading that involves much higher-level language processing (Grabe, 2009). Therefore, these L2 readers would bring their knowledge and experience of L1 reading practice into their L2 reading comprehension. In this sense, this model is especially important to L2 adult readers who possess rich knowledge and experience of L1 reading practice.

3.2.5 Construction–Integration Model

Proposed by Kintsch (1998), the construction–integration model is regarded as the most popular model of adult reading comprehension (Paris & Hamilton, 2009). Kintsch argued that while engaging in reading comprehension, readers construct two models simultaneously: a model of the literal text and a model of the situation implied by the text. The text model is based on readers' understanding of information directly from the text, whereas the situation model involves readers' integration of the information from the text and their prior knowledge. In this process, reference-making plays a very important role. The two models reinforce each other when readers involve in the process of re-reading and thinking about meaning derived from the text in iterative ways. In other words, as a situation model, the construction–integration model combines a construction process with an integration phase. In the construction process, a text base is constructed from the linguistic input as well as from the reader's general knowledge, while in the integration process, the text base is integrated into a coherent whole. For example, a causal link may be inferred from the proposition "Jane could not find the vegetable and the fruit she was looking for." and "She became upset." in the sense that one may become upset because of not finding something he/she is looking for, thus forming a situation model (see Kintsch, 1988, p. 106).

It is argued in this model that text comprehension involves several processes: (1) the microprocessing of the meaningful elements to organize them into a coherent piece; (2) text reduction to condense the full meaning of the text into a gist; and (3) generation of new text based on the information received in the comprehension processes. The semantic relations among the ideas conveyed may be explicitly expressed in the surface structure or implicitly inferred in the process of text interpretation with the help of contextual and background knowledge.

In addition, the semantic structure of a text is considered in terms of two levels: microstructure and macrostructure. Microstructure refers to the local level of the discourse, meaning the structure of individual propositions and their relations, whereas macrostructure indicates the global nature of the discourse as a whole. The two levels are related by a set of semantic mapping rules called macrorules. Text base is an abstract term for coherent and structured units in the semantic structure. The coherence of a discourse is defined by the notion that the respective sentences and propositions are connected and these propositions are organized globally at the macrostructure level. The first step to form a coherent text base is examining its referential coherence. Reference coherence is the linguistic criterion for semantic coherence of a text base which corresponds to argument overlap among propositions. If there is argument overlap among all the propositions, the new proposition is considered to be accepted and further processing will continue; if gaps are found, inference processes will start to add more propositions to the text base to fill the gap in order to make it coherent. Kintsch (1998) pointed out that the distinction between micro- and macrostructure is orthogonal to that of the distinction between the text and situation models which constitute the construction–integration model. As the local structure of the text, microstructure is the sentence-by-sentence information which is integrated with reader's knowledge and experience. The macrostructure, which represents the text structure globally as a series of propositions organized in a hierarchical order, is derived from the microstructure inferred by the reader.

According to this model, there are three kinds of information in discourse processing: information from the text itself, information from the situation or context, and information from the cognitive presuppositions which refer to the reader's internal cognitive information such as his/her general knowledge, beliefs, opinions, or attitudes in general, and motivations, goals, or specific tasks in the specific processing of text. The reader may have the ability to use the various kinds of information flexibly, and the information may be processed in different possible orders. Therefore, Paris and Hamilton (2009) argued that the construction–integration model is bottom-up and top-down. It is bottom-up because it incorporates the construction of a text base process which starts with decoding the linguistic input, and it is also top-down as the construction of the situation model depends on readers' general knowledge about language and the world. In reading comprehension, the two processes constrain each other to come up with the cohesive interpretation of the text.

3.2.6 Constructively Responsive Reading Model

As one of the most comprehensive works on specific strategies employed by readers in reading comprehension, Pressley and Afflerbach's (1995) *Verbal Protocols of Reading: The Nature of Constructively Responsive Reading* analyzed 38 primary research studies of reading strategy use using think-aloud protocol. Based on their analysis, they found that skilled and responsive readers use a number of strategies which contribute to effective and successful reading. Further, they integrated several reading theories (e.g., Anderson & Pearson, 1984; Rosenblatt, 1978; van Dijk & Kintsch, 1983) and developed a prominent framework termed constructively responsive reading, which gives a rich description of reading comprehension.

They argued that three interplaying activities are performed during reading comprehension: comprehending, evaluating, and monitoring, which characterize meaning construction before, during, and after reading. In addition, readers are not presumed to simply dive into a text. Instead, they make plans to fulfill task demands. This framework is consistent with the established theories of metacognition about reading (Baker & Brown, 1984; Paris & Winograd, 1990) and the three-dimension concept of metacognitive awareness: planning, evaluating, and monitoring (Brown, 1980; Garner, 1987).

Additionally, Pressley and Afflerbach (1995) argued that the cognitive process of reading comprehension (i.e., comprehending) comprises five phases: general progression, identifying important information, inference-making, integrating different parts of the text, and interpreting, which are explicated in details as follows:

(a) General progression refers to the general progression followed by readers from the beginning to the end of the text which often comes after "before-reading overviewing" (p. 37). Pressley and Afflerbach argued that this phase of reading is normally not strategic but involves automatic decoding of the text and smooth comprehension of the text without taking much effort (Johnson & Afflerbach, 1985).

(b) Identifying important information is the process in which readers refine their understanding of the text constantly when the new input is not consistent with their initial hypotheses (Pressley & Afflerbach, 1995).

(c) Inference-making refers to the process of reading in which readers "go beyond the information given in the text" (p. 46) through implication in order to "fill in meaning gaps in text" (p. 49).

(d) Integrating different parts of the text is when readers manipulate the text to fit the information across the text based on their understanding of the text as well as their prior knowledge and experience of the world (see Kintsch & van Dijk, 1978).

(e) Interpreting refers to the interpretive processes in reading which involves making text more concrete (e.g., the instantiation of schemata and generalization of the visual images).

To sum up, Pressley and Afflerbach's constructively responsive reading model gives a rich description of the process of reading comprehension which comprises general progression or initial reading of the text, identifying important information, inference-making, integrating different parts of the text, and interpreting. In addition, it provides a comprehensive study of reading strategies used in the process of reading comprehension. In the present study, the ReTSUQ was developed based on their framework, especially the cognitive strategies included in the questionnaire.

3.2.7 Relevance to the Study

The reviewed literature about reading comprehension has important implications for the current study.

First, the primary goal of an assessment task is "to collect relevant information for purposes of making inferences or decisions about individuals" (Alderson, 2000, p. 203). This can be achieved by characterizing the construct of reading accurately and eliminating irrelevant factors in choosing text materials and test methods (Urquhart & Weir, 1998). With a detailed introduction on how reading comprehension is defined and how several relevant reading models interpret and describe the process of reading comprehension, the construct definition of reading comprehension in relation to this study is in order.

In the present study, reading comprehension is viewed as a constructive process in which the text, the reader, and the context interact with one another (Grabe, 2009; Kintsch, 1988; Pressley & Afflerbach, 1995). In this process, both top-down processing and bottom-up processing are involved in which the former can be reflected through readers' integration of their background knowledge and prior experience into their reading comprehension, whereas the latter is mainly demonstrated through readers' decoding of the text at the word level using their lexico-grammatical knowledge (Gough & Tunmer, 1986; Kintsch, 1988; Samuels & LaBerge, 1983). Meanwhile, comprehension monitoring with its toolbox of strategies comes into play when readers fail to construct meaning from the text successfully (Baker & Brown, 1984; Paris & Winograd, 1990; Pearson, 2009). To sum up, the component skills which ensure successful comprehension in reading comprise lexico-grammatical knowledge, background knowledge, and metacognitive knowledge. In the present study, the focus is on EFL readers' lexico-grammatical knowledge and metacognitive knowledge.

Second, the review of the reading models situates the study within the context of theories in relation to reading comprehension. For example, based on Kintsch's (1988) construction–integration model, readers are seen as active agents of reading comprehension, which points to the conclusion that readers' knowledge and previous experiences play a vital role in reading comprehension. In other words, the readers' active role in meaning construction in the reading process demonstrates that reading is a constructive process in which the text, the reader, and the context interact (Carrell, 1989b; Paris & Hamilton, 2009). The reader reconstructs the text information based on his/her word processing knowledge (i.e., lexico-grammatical knowledge) (e.g., Gough & Tunmer, 1986; LaBerge & Samuels, 1974) and his/her knowledge about the world or schemata (e.g., Anderson & Pearson, 1984). In this process, the role of inference-making, an integral part of the models of Kintsch (1988) and Anderson and Pearson (1984), has gained more and more attention from researchers.

Third, the reviewed models provide the basis for a better understanding of the participants in this study as second language or foreign language readers in terms of the cognitive processes they go through while engaging in reading texts in English. According to the multi-component models, word recognition, syntactic knowledge, discourse structure, background knowledge, and metacognitive knowledge and strategy use are important component skills of reading comprehension. In addition, LaBerge and Samuel's (1974) and Samuels and LaBerge's (1983) models and Gough and Tunmer's (1986) Simple View of Reading showed that the combination of readers' automaticity in word recognition (i.e., the core of decoding abilities) and their comprehension abilities leads to reading comprehension. This provides the theoretical basis for the model hypothesized in the later part of this study. Furthermore, Rumelhart's (2004) and Stanovich's (1980) interactive compensatory models argued that if readers do not know much vocabulary, fail to achieve reading automaticity, or do not have adequate language proficiency, they could seek other sources to understand the text. In other words, second and foreign language readers who have few cognitive resources in vocabulary and language proficiency may use knowledge of the text and topic to understand or rely on inference-making more than first language readers in reading comprehension. More importantly, they may use more strategies than first language readers to glean meaning from text (Pearson & Tierney, 1984; Stanovich, 1980).

Fourth, as one of the most comprehensive and influential models on strategy use in reading comprehension, Pressley and Afflerbach's (1995) constructively responsive reading model provides the theoretical basis for the ReTSUQ. According to this model, comprehension comprises five phases: general progression or initial reading of the text, identifying important information, inference-making, integrating different parts of the text, and interpreting. The cognitive strategies on the ReTSUQ are based on this framework.

To sum up, the reviewed literature on reading comprehension provides significant implications for investigating Chinese college readers' processes of reading comprehension, especially in the situation of taking the CET-4 Reading subtest.

The next section focuses on the theory of metacognition and strategy use in reading comprehension, which is another important dimension of this study.

3.3 Theory of Metacognition and Its Application to Reading Comprehension

Metacognition, which is perceived as thinking about thinking or cognition about cognition, plays a vital role in many cognitive activities in relation to L2 learning (Flavell, 1979). As the focal theme in the current study is to investigate test takers' strategy use in the context of a reading comprehension test, this section reviews relevant literature about the theory of metacognition and its application to reading comprehension research as well as methods of eliciting strategy use.

3.3.1 Definition of Metacognition

Metacognition is "knowledge and cognition about cognitive phenomena" (Flavell, 1979, p. 906). In other words, metacognition refers to knowledge of cognitive processes and products and includes reflecting on one's own thoughts or cognition about cognition. In addition, Anderson (2005) believed that metacognition is closely related to critical reflection and evaluation of one's own thinking which can bring about specific changes in how to learn.

Flavell's model of metacognition incorporated metacognitive knowledge and metacognitive experiences. Metacognitive knowledge comprises knowledge or beliefs about learners' person, task, and strategy variables, which are the factors affecting the course and outcome of cognitive activities. Metacognitive experiences pertain to cognitive or affective experiences in relation to intellectual activities which are consciously activated metacognitive knowledge in practice.

Wenden (1998) further explicated the function of metacognitive knowledge in language learning. In her extended explanation, person knowledge pertains to learners' general knowledge about "human factors that facilitate or inhibit learning" (p. 518). It consists of four categories of knowledge or beliefs: (1) the cognitive and affective factors that influence language acquisition such as age, language aptitude, and motivation; (2) learners' specific knowledge about how the above factors apply in their language learning experiences; (3) learners' self-efficacy belief; and (4) learners' belief about their ability to attain specific learning goals. According to Wenden (1998), task knowledge refers to learners' knowledge about the purpose of the task and how it is related to their language learning needs. Task knowledge also includes information regarding the nature and demand of the task. Strategic knowledge pertains to general knowledge about strategies and specific knowledge about when and how to use them.

Further, Wenden (1998) defined metacognitive strategies as the general skills "through which learners manage, direct, regulate, guide their learning" which comprise planning, evaluating, and monitoring (p. 519). This categorization of metacognitive strategies is based on Brown, Bransford, Ferrara, and Campione (1983). In addition, O'Malley and Chamot (1990) also adopted the three strategies (i.e., planning, evaluating, and monitoring) in their taxonomy of language learning strategies. To summarize, Wenden's article pointed to the importance of metacognitive knowledge in language learning, which is a prerequisite for appropriate deployment of metacognitive strategies.

In addition, Flavell (1979) believed that metacognitive knowledge plays an important role in many cognitive activities in relation to language use such as listening comprehension (e.g., Goh, 1998, 2008; Vandergrift, Goh, Mareschal, & Tafaghodtari, 2006), reading comprehension (e.g., Baker & Brown, 1984; Brown, 1980; Paris & Jacobs, 1984; Paris, Lipson, & Wixson, 1983; Paris & Winograd, 1990), and writing (e.g., Zimmerman & Bandura, 1994). Based on previous studies (e.g., Baker & Brown, 1984; Brown, Bransford, Ferrara, & Campione, 1983) and their own seminal work (e.g., Paris & Jacobs, 1984; Paris et al., 1983) with regard to the function of metacognition in reading comprehension, Paris & Winograd (1990) argued that metacognition in reading comprises *self-appraisal* and *self-management*. Self-appraisal refers to personal reflections on one's own knowledge and abilities as well as making judgments about task and strategy factors affecting performance. On the other hand, self-management is "metacognition in action," which helps individuals "orchestrate cognitive aspects of problem solving" (Paris & Winograd, 1990, p. 17), and includes planning, evaluation, and regulation. In the planning stage, readers adjust their rate and standard of comprehension to the required purposes of the tasks; in the evaluation stage, readers assess their own comprehension; and in the regulation stage, they monitor their reading processes and consequent revisions of reading plans and strategies (Jacobs & Paris, 1987).

To sum up, Paris and Winograd's (1990) types of strategies of planning, evaluation, and regulation are equivalent to Wenden's (1998) planning, evaluating, and monitoring framework (see Wenden, 1998; O'Malley & Chamot, 1990, for similar frameworks). This framework provides the specific theoretical framework for this study. In other words, the development of the metacognitive strategy use questionnaire used in the current study is grounded in this framework of metacognition.

In addition, literature on reading research showed that the relationship between metacognition and reading comprehension has long been established (see Brown, 1980; Carrell, 1989a; Paris & Jacobs, 1984; Phakiti, 2003; Pressley & Afflerbach, 1995; Sheorey & Mokhtari, 2001; Zhang, 2010). For example, Pearson (2009) pointed out that in this meaning-constructing process of comprehension, metacognition plays the role of a fixer or problem solver, maximizing comprehension of the text and repairing comprehension failure by using a toolbox of strategies. Brown (1980) postulated that L1 readers' metacognition is closely related to their reading performance. Paris and Jacobs' (1984) study revealed a significant relation between children's reading awareness (i.e., metacognition) and comprehension skills. For L2 reading, Carrell's (1989a) research showed the close relationships between readers' metacognitive awareness and their reading ability in both their L1 and L2. Zhang (2010) reported that Chinese EFL readers' metacognitive awareness had links to their EFL reading proficiency. In conclusion, general findings are that expert readers may control their reading processes by utilizing a repertoire of appropriate strategies through their use of metacognitive knowledge and monitoring. In other words, skilled readers are distinguished from unskilled readers by their conscious awareness of the strategic reading processes and the actual use of reading strategies (Macaro & Erler, 2008).

Further research into metacognition and reading comprehension attempted to address the causal relationships between them. For example, Roeschl-Heils, Schneider, and van Kraayenoord (2003) showed that metacognitive knowledge explained approximately 25% of the variance in reading comprehension. Similarly, Phakiti (2003) concluded that strategy use accounted for 15–22% of the observed variance in a reading comprehension test. Finally, Cain, Oakhill, and Bryant's (2004) longitudinal study suggested that monitoring comprehension was a significant predictor of comprehension. In all, the consensual view among researchers is that metacognition is an important contributor to reading comprehension performance.

3.3.2   Methods of Eliciting Strategy Use

Students' metacognition about strategic reading can be observed externally when they underline some parts of the text, take notes, or look forward and backward across pages. However, most reading strategies concern internal thinking during reading (Paris & Flukes, 2005). Therefore, the measurement of students' strategic reading is often inferred from what they say about their reading process. There are three frequently used methods to elicit information about students' metacognition about strategic reading: self-report during reading, interview after reading, and survey of readers' thinking in the process of reading.

Self-report during reading. When assessing metacognitive aspects of strategic reading with self-report, researchers normally require readers to think aloud during reading by raising questions periodically about what they were thinking about at specific points during their reading. Ericsson (2002) argued that when subjects are instructed to verbalize their ongoing thoughts while focusing on a task, researchers can get the closest connection between their thinking processes and the verbal report (Dörnyei, 2007). For example, to date, the most comprehensive research on reading strategy through the use of think-aloud protocols was completed by Pressley and Afflerbach (1995), who analyzed 38 research studies of reading strategy use by employing think-aloud protocols. Although the use of think-aloud protocols can reveal how students plan and regulate their reading comprehension, some researchers suspect that verbal reports of cognitive processes are not always accurate due to the following two reasons: (1) The quality of the verbal report is subject to variability if the prompts are vague, and (2) the content of the verbal report may be distorted because the participants are likely to aim to please the examiner or try to appear smart (Paris & Flukes, 2005).

Interview after reading. Interview is regarded as the most frequently used method in qualitative inquiries (Dörnyei, 2007). In the field of reading comprehension, interviews may include open-ended questions about various aspects of reading (Paris & Flukes, 2005). For example, Myers and Paris (1978) carried out the first metacognitive study about reading by employing interviews with second and sixth graders about how task, person, and strategy variables influence reading. They identified developmental improvement in children's strategy awareness and variables that make reading easy or difficult. In addition, interviews can also be used to assess what students gain from classroom instruction. For example, Paris and Jacobs (1984) used interviews to evaluate third and fifth graders' strategy knowledge gained from a classroom intervention. Their findings revealed that those who participated in the intervention program gained more strategy awareness than the control group. Paris and Flukes (2005) argued that interviews can also be used to diagnose students' awareness of reading strategies and assess the relative value and frequency of different strategy use. Paris and Myers (1981) conducted research by creating interviews to ask children to judge the value of different types of reading strategies and the frequency of using them.

In addition, researchers have come to the consensus that interviews can be used widely with readers of different ages, cultures, and languages to reveal readers' metacognitive aspect of strategic reading (e.g., Paris & Flukes, 2005; Wagner, Spratt, Gal, & Paris, 1989). A recent example of using interviews to investigate L2 readers' strategy use was conducted by Zhang (2010) who employed semi-structured interviews to study 20 Chinese college students' reading experiences within the framework of a dynamic metacognitive systems perspective. The finding indicates that there is strong relationship between metacognition and successful EFL reading comprehension. In addition, it is also suggested that successful L2 readers can be distinguished from less successful ones by the amount and quality of the metacognitive knowledge they possess.

Surveys and questionnaires. Although self-reports and interviews provide rich and in-depth data about readers' metacognitive aspect of strategic reading, they are to be administered individually, which requires much time. Therefore, many researchers use the alternative method of surveys and questionnaires because they can be administered more efficiently in groups to elicit information about reading strategy use. Both L1 and L2 reading researchers have developed questionnaires and administered them among readers of different age, culture, and language groups to elicit readers' reading strategy use (e.g., Carrell, 1989b; Jacobs & Paris, 1987; Mokhtari & Reichard, 2002; Mokhtari, Sheorey, & Reichard, 2008; Phakiti, 2003, 2008b; Schmitt, 1990).

Jacobs and Paris (1987) created the Index of Reading Awareness (IRA) out of Paris and Jacobs' (1984) open-ended interview method. The IRA is composed of 20 items grouped into four subscales of evaluation, planning, regulation, and conditional knowledge used to assess children's knowledge about reading strategies. The items are multiple-choice questions. Each of the three choices is judged to be worth zero, one, or two points, and the total score ranges from 0 to 40 points. With this instrument, Jacobs and Paris (1987) found that older children had more knowledge of reading strategies than younger children; girls had more strategic knowledge than boys, and those with strategy instruction had more knowledge than those with no instruction. However, as demonstrated by Jacobs and Paris, the IRA was primarily a survey designed for young L1 readers.

Schmitt (1990) created a variation of the IRA which was termed the Metacomprehension Strategy Index (MSI). The MSI consists of 25 items which measures middle and upper elementary school students' strategic awareness. Good internal reliability was reported about the MSI. In addition, it was correlated with the IRA closely, indicating that the two instruments measure similar constructs (Paris & Flukes, 2005). In addition, it was found that the experimental group scored significantly higher than the control group, suggesting the sensitivity of the MSI to the treatment effects.

Based on reading strategies identified by Pressley and Afflerbach (1995), Mokhtari and Reichard (2002) developed the Metacognitive Awareness of Reading Strategies Index (MARSI). The MARSI is a 30-item Likert survey on a five-point scale (i.e., 1 = "I never or almost never do this," and 5 = "I always or almost always do this") designed to assess adolescent and adult readers' metacognition. There are three subscales in the MARSI: global reading strategies, problem-solving strategies, and support reading strategies. The reported subscale internal reliability ranged from 0.86 to 0.93 (Cronbach's alpha, α). One major difference of this measure from the previous two instruments is that the MARSI was designed for measuring adolescent and adult readers' metacognition, whereas the previous ones were meant for younger readers.

In L2 reading, Carrell (1989a) created the Metacognitive Awareness Questionnaire (MAQ) to investigate L1 and L2 readers' metacognitive awareness and strategy use. The MAQ is a 36-item survey on a five-point Likert scale (i.e., 1 = strongly agree, and 5 = strongly disagree) which are categorized into four types: confidence (6 items), repair (5 items), effective (17 items), and difficulty

(8 items). The MAQ proved to be an effective measure of readers' metacognitive awareness in reading comprehension, but no internal consistency estimates were reported in Carrell's study.

As a variant of the MARSI, the survey of reading strategy (SORS) was designed to measure the type and frequency of reading strategies used by adolescent and adult ESL students while reading academic materials in English (Mokhtari et al., 2008). The SORS is composed of 30 items using a five-point Likert (i.e., 1 = "I never or almost never do this," and 5 = "I always or almost always do this"). It was reported that the overall reliability of the SORS was 0.89 (Cronbach's α). Like the MARSI, the SORS measures three subcategories of reading strategy: global reading strategy (13 items), problem-solving strategies (9 items), and support strategies (8 items). The SORS was used in a series of studies to investigate the relationships between readers' strategy use and reading performance (e.g., Sheorey & Mokhtari, 2008). In other words, the SORS was mainly used to gauge readers' metacognitive awareness in non-test contexts.

Phakiti (2003) developed a 35-item cognitive and metacognitive questionnaire to examine the relationships between test takers' strategy use and reading test performance. Similar to Purpura (1999) in the item contents but adjusted to the context of the reading test, his questionnaire included two categories: cognitive and metacognitive strategies. The cognitive strategies comprise two subscales: comprehending and retrieval, while metacognitive strategies have two subscales as well: planning and monitoring. The reported reliability estimate was 0.879 (Cronbach's α). The results showed that both cognitive and metacognitive strategies had a positive relationship with reading performance. In addition, metacognitive strategies were positively related to cognitive strategies with the correction-for-attenuation correlation coefficient of 0.76 (Cronbach's α).

Further, Phakiti (2008b) developed a 30-item strategy use questionnaire to validate Bachman and Palmer's (1996) theory of strategic competence and examine the relationships between test takers' strategy use and reading test performance. Based on the theory of human information processing theory (Gagnè, Yekovich, & Yekovich, 1993) and relevant literature, his questionnaire comprised 13 items of cognitive strategies and 17 items of metacognitive strategies, with six subscales: comprehending, memory, retrieval, planning, monitoring, and evaluating. The overall reliability estimate was reported as 0.95 (Cronbach's α). His study showed that metacognitive strategies were closely related to cognitive strategies. Phakiti's two questionnaires proved to be effective and useful instruments in measuring test takers' reading strategies and test management strategies (e.g., Phakiti, 2003, 2008b; Zhang & Zhang, 2013); however, as measures of metacognitive awareness during reading comprehension, the instruments were not grounded in established reading theories which gave specific descriptions to reading comprehension processes, indicating that further research is needed for developing questionnaires which are not only measures of strategy use on the reading comprehension test, but also based on relevant reading theories and studies.

In summary, the review of literature about methods of eliciting strategy use shows that the above-mentioned methods are useful means of assessing readers' processes of strategic reading in constructing meaning in reading comprehension. It is commonly recognized that these methods can also be combined and adapted to assess different readers' metacognition in different contexts (Paris & Flukes, 2005). The following section presents empirical studies related to strategy use and reading test performance.

3.3.3 Empirical Studies on Strategy Use and Reading Test Performance

Since Rubin's (1975) first study on good language learners, extensive research has endeavored to define learner strategies, analyze their type and frequency, and devise taxonomies.

Oxford's (1990) definition of learner strategies is "specific actions taken by the learner to make learning easier, more enjoyable, more self-directed, more effective and more transferrable to new situations" (p. 8), which suggests consciousness common to all strategy use. She divided learner strategies into two main types: direct and indirect strategies. Direct strategies are further divided into three categories: memory, cognitive, and comprehension strategies, whereas indirect strategies are subdivided into metacognitive, affective, and social strategies.

In addition, O'Malley and Chamot (1990) defined strategies as "the special thoughts or behaviors that individuals use to help them comprehend, learn, or retain new information" (p. 1). They divided language learner strategies into three categories: metacognitive, cognitive, and social/affective strategies. Metacognitive strategies are perceived as higher-order executive skills which provide managing functions in controlling individuals' learning through planning, monitoring, and evaluating. Cognitive strategies are problem-solving strategies which include rehearsal, inference-making, summarizing, deducing, transferring, and elaboration strategies. They help facilitate learners' acquisition of knowledge and skills. Social/affective strategies refer to the strategies that help induce positive emotional reaction toward language learning, such as cooperation, or self-talk strategies. Based on various definitions and categories of learner strategies, a considerable number of studies have investigated the relationships between strategy use and language performance. The following sections focus on empirical studies which are pertinent to this study.

Studies on relationships between strategy use and language performance. In this section, several relevant studies on language strategy use and language performance are reviewed first, followed by the review of studies on reading strategy use and reading comprehension performance in both non-test and test contexts.

Politzer and McGroarty (1985) conducted one of the earliest studies which examined the relationships between learning strategies and language proficiency using a questionnaire. In this study, they examined the strategy use and language performance of 37 Asian and Hispanic Americans who were involved in an eight-week intensive ESL course. The students in the course were pre- and post-tested with three language proficiency tests which were meant to measure their gains in listening comprehension, grammar skill, and communicative ability. The questionnaire used in their study is termed the Behavior Questionnaire which included three parts: classroom behaviors, learning behavior during individual study, and interacting with others outside the classroom. The effect size of their t-test analysis indicated the different effects of learning strategies on students with different ethnic backgrounds. In addition, their study is exploratory in nature with regard to the investigation of the relationships between learning strategies and language proficiency by means of questionnaires.

Among the studies using questionnaires, Purpura's (1999) work is different from the previous ones in the sense that it was not only rooted in human information processing theory (Gagnè et al., 1993), but has also investigated the psychometric characteristics of the questionnaire thoroughly. In the human information processing theory, Gagnè, Yekovich, and Yekovich (1993) argued that four stages are involved in the process of human learning: selecting, comprehending, storing/memorizing, and retrieving. On the basis of this framework, Purpura (1999) developed his strategy use questionnaire and used SEM to examine the relationships between test takers' strategy use and test performance on the University of Cambridge's FCE Anchor Test with 1382 EFL participants. His 40-item cognitive questionnaire included eleven strategy-type variables representing three underlying processing variables: comprehending, memory, and retrieval which reflected the stages of human learning processes. In the comprehending stage, learners hold the new information in their working memory long enough to transform it into meaningful symbols; in the memory stage, they reflect on the information to make connections and recognize patterns for the storage of the information in their long-term memory; and in the retrieval stage, learners withdraw the information from their long-term memory for use. The 40-item metacognitive questionnaire involved four strategy-type variables (i.e., assessing the situation, monitoring, self-evaluating, and self-testing) and two underlying process type variables (i.e., online and post-assessment processes). As shown in the study, two underlying factors explained the second language test performance: reading ability and grammar ability. Purpura's (1997) study showed that metacognitive strategy use had no direct effect on language performance, but it was closely related to and exerted an executive function over cognitive strategy use.

Song (2005) abridged Purpura's (1999) questionnaire into a 43-item questionnaire (i.e., 27 cognitive strategy and 16 metacognitive strategy use items) and administered it to 161 test takers taking the MELAB. The result showed that MELAB test takers' use of cognitive strategies comprises six categories: repeating/confirming information strategies, writing strategies, practicing strategies, generating strategies, applying rules strategies, and linking with prior knowledge strategies, whereas metacognitive strategies have three categories: evaluating, monitoring, and assessing strategies. Regarding the relationships between strategy use and test performance, this study showed that repeating/confirming information strategies had a significant and negative effect, while linking with prior knowledge had a significant positive effect on test performance. In addition, it was found that monitoring strategy was a strong and positive predictor of the MELAB GCVR (grammar, cloze, vocabulary, and reading) sections' scores and the MELAB total score.

A generalized conclusion from these studies is that more advanced or proficient language learners use strategies more frequently, flexibly, and appropriately (e.g., O'Malley & Chamot, 1990; Vann & Abraham, 1990).

Similarly, L1 and L2 reading researchers have long been interested in understanding what proficient readers typically do and what strategies they use while reading (Brown, 1980; Carrell, 1989b; Kern, 1989; Mokhtari & Sheorey, 2002; Mokhtari et al., 2008; Paris et al., 1983; Pressley, 2006; Pressley & Afflerbach, 1995; Zhang, 2010). It has been generally acknowledged that readers' strategic behaviors have close relationships with their reading comprehension performance. For example, Brown (1980) argued that L1 readers' metacognition is closely related to their reading performance, and Paris and Jacobs' (1984) study revealed significant relationships between children's metacognition and comprehension skills. In L2 reading, Carrell's (1989a) research similarly showed a close relationship between readers' metacognitive awareness and their L1 and L2 reading ability. Zhang (2002, 2010) reported that Chinese EFL readers' metacognitive awareness had links with their reading proficiency.

Extant literature shows that researchers have employed a variety of methods to examine the relationship between readers' strategy use and their reading comprehension performance, such as interview (see Paris & Jacobs, 1984; Zhang, 2010), verbal report (see Block, 1986, 1992; Cohen & Upton, 2006), and questionnaire (e.g., Carrell, 1989a; Jacobs & Paris, 1987; Mokhtari & Reichard, 2002; Phakiti, 2003, 2008b; Sheorey & Mokhtari, 2001). The studies using questionnaires have addressed the correlational or causal relationship between readers' strategy use and reading performance.

To investigate L1 and L2 readers' metacognitive awareness and strategy use, Carrell (1989a) used the MAQ to investigate the relationships between 45 Spanish native speakers' and 75 English native speakers' metacognitive awareness and their reading ability in both their L1 and L2. Two texts with multiple-choice questions were used as the instruments to gauge subjects' reading ability in both L1 and L2. The questionnaire used in this study was a 36-item survey on a five-point Likert scale (1 = strongly agree, and 5 = strongly disagree) with four subscales: confidence, repair, effective, and difficulty strategies. Confidence strategies provided a measure of readers' confidence in their L1 or L2; repair strategies measured readers' awareness of repair strategies; effective strategies tapped into subjects' perception of effective/efficient strategies; and difficulty strategies examined the aspects of reading which made readers feel difficulty. The researcher regressed subjects' reading proficiency in their L1 and L2 on the four subscales of MAQ. Her findings demonstrated that readers' metacognitive awareness is closely related to their reading ability.

Mokhtari and Reichard (2002) developed the 30-item MARSI to assess adolescent and adult readers' metacognition. Grounded in Pressley and Afflerbach's

(1995) constructively responsive reading model, this instrument produced three subscales after EFA: global reading strategies, problem-solving strategies, and support reading strategies on a five-point scale (i.e., 1 = "I never or almost never do this," and 5 = "I always or almost always do this"). The internal reliability of the subscales ranged from 0.86 to 0.93 (Cronbach's α). Further, the authors correlated 443 students' self-reported reading ability with the MARSI. Results showed that readers who rated themselves as excellent readers used significantly more global and problem-solving strategies than those who reported themselves as average or below average readers.

Sheorey and Mokhtari (2001) examined the relationships between 150 US native English students' and 152 ESL students' reported use of reading strategies and their self-perceived reading ability in English. The data collection instrument was the 30-item SORS adapted from the MARSI to assist ESL students to enhance their metacognitive awareness. It was designed to measure the type and frequency of reading strategies used by adolescent and adult ESL students while reading academic materials in English (Mokhtari et al., 2008). The overall internal reliability is 0.89 (Cronbach's α). The SORS has three factors: metacognitive strategies, cognitive strategies, and support strategies, which have been renamed by Mokhtari, Sheorey, and Reichard (2008) as global strategies (13 items), problem-solving strategies (9 items), and support strategies (8 items) as they synthesized their research on the development of the two instruments (i.e., MARSI and SORS). One of their major findings was that both ESL and US high-reading-ability students reported using more cognitive and metacognitive reading strategies than lower-reading-ability students.

Phakiti (2003) developed a 35-item strategy use questionnaire to examine the relationships between 384 Thai test takers' strategy use and reading test performance. Based on the theory of human information processing (Gagnè et al., 1993), his questionnaire included two categories: cognitive and metacognitive strategies. The cognitive strategies comprised two subscales: comprehending and retrieval, and metacognitive strategies comprised two subscales: planning and monitoring. He found that the use of cognitive and metacognitive strategies, which explained 15–22% of the test score variance, had a positive relationship to the reading performance, and in addition, metacognitive strategies were positively related to cognitive strategies (i.e., $r = 0.76$).

Phakiti (2008a) conducted an additional study to test a fourth-order factor model of strategic competence that underlines both strategic knowledge (i.e., trait strategy use) and strategic regulation (i.e., state strategy use) through the use of the SEM approach. In psychology, traits refer to individuals' stable attributes, whereas states are transitory and unstable attributes. According to Phakiti (2008a), the review of literature indicated the gap of the investigation of both the state and trait strategic constructs over time. This fourth-order model was hypothesized to test the strategic competence underlying state and trait cognitive and metacognitive strategy use over time. 561 Thai university students answered a trait strategic knowledge questionnaire before the midterm and final reading achievement tests over a period of two months. After each test, they also answered a state strategic regulation questionnaire. The study found that (1) strategic competence directly affected trait metacognitive strategy use and (2) trait metacognitive strategy use directly influenced state cognitive strategy use and state metacognitive strategy use. In addition, it was found that state metacognitive strategy use directly affected state cognitive strategy use. These findings indicated that strategic competence is a highly complex, multifaceted, and subtle construct.

Building on his research, Phakiti (2008b) attempted to validate Bachman and Palmer's (1996) theory of strategic competence with the 30-item strategy use questionnaire and an EFL reading test answered by 561 Thai university students. His questionnaire items were chosen based on the theory of human information processing theory (Gagnè et al., 1993) and relevant literature which comprised 13 items of cognitive strategies and 17 items of metacognitive strategies with six subscales: comprehending, memory, retrieval, planning, monitoring, and evaluating. His SEM analyses indicated the two underlying factors of the EFL reading test were lexico-grammatical reading ability (LEX_GR) and text comprehension reading ability (TxtCOM). LEX_GR affected TxtCOM directly and significantly. In addition, he found that cognitive strategies explained 16–30% of the lexico-grammatical performance variance and that metacognitive strategies were closely related to cognitive strategies. The findings of this study corroborated Purpura's research (1997, 1999) in that it also concluded that metacognitive strategy use had a direct effect on cognitive strategy use.

To summarize, the review of the relevant literature showed that language learner strategy use is closely related to their language performance. Further, readers' strategy use affects their performance of reading comprehension in both test and non-test contexts. In other words, the consensual view among researchers is that expert readers can control their reading processes effectively by utilizing a repertoire of appropriate strategies.

In addition, although the reading strategy questionnaires used in the previous studies have played an important role in measuring readers' strategy use in the process of reading comprehension and have significantly influenced the theory and practice of reading research, most of them are concerned with reading strategies in the non-test context. According to Cohen (1998), language learner strategies are generally categorized into two types: language learning and language use strategies. Language learning strategies are general strategies which are purposefully employed by language learners to continuously enhance their language learning; in contrast, language use strategies are specific strategies which are employed by language users to improve language performance in specific situations (Phakiti, 2003). For example, as one type of language use strategy, test management strategies in the test context are particularly important to test takers because they need to demonstrate their language proficiency within the limited assessment time (Cohen, 2006). Given the significance of test management strategies in explaining language test performance and validity studies (Bachman, 1990; Cohen, 2006; Messick, 1989), incorporating test management strategies in the instrument to measure strategy use in the test context is timely and necessary.

On the other hand, the few questionnaires designed to measure test takers' strategy use in reading tests were not based upon reading theories (e.g., Phakiti, 2003, 2008b). Therefore, these instruments seem to be unable to capture test takers' specific process of reading comprehension effectively. Additionally, extensive research into the complex processes involved in reading comprehension has resulted in theories and notions which can delineate and interpret test takers' reading comprehension processes more convincingly and precisely. For example, Rosenblatt (1978) conceptualized reading comprehension as a transaction between readers and text. Accordingly, the interactive meaning-making processes are made possible when readers apply their prior knowledge, inference-making ability, and comprehension monitoring skills, which is one important dimension of metacognition (see Anderson & Pearson, 1984; Carrell, 1989a; Kintsch & van Dijk, 1978). This is consistent with Pressley and Afflerbach's (1995) notion of constructively responsive reading. The current study draws on Pressley and Afflerbach's (1995) framework, relevant theories on metacognition (Paris & Winograd, 1990; Wenden, 1998), Bachman and Palmer's (2010) model, and Cohen and Upton's (2006) framework to develop the ReTSUQ which measures test takers' strategy use in reading comprehension tests.

Studies on test-taking strategies. The previous section reviewed the relevant studies on relationships between strategy use and language performance, especially reading test performance. Since this study was designed to investigate the relationships between test takers' strategy use on a reading comprehension test, a review of literature on test-taking strategies would be necessary and pertinent to this study. Thus, this section is devoted to the review of relevant and important literature in this regard.

Defining test-taking strategies. According to Cohen (1998), test-taking strategies are variants of language use strategies which are applied to tasks in language tests. Test-taking strategies can be defined as "those test-taking processes that the respondents have selected and are conscious of" (Cohen & Upton, 2006, p. 4). In other words, the test-taking processes that are consciously selected by test takers in language assessment contexts are called test-taking strategies (Cohen, 2013). Similar to all language use strategies, test-taking strategies contain the elements of selection and flexibility.

In addition, Cohen and Upton (2006) noted that test takers draw on three main types of strategies as follows:

(a) language learner strategies, which deal with language issues in the tests and are equivalent to reading strategies in the current study;
(b) test management strategies, which provide meaningful responses to test tasks and items; and
(c) test-wiseness strategies, which "circumvent the need to tap their actual language knowledge" (p. 4).

To sum up, based on this taxonomy, test-taking strategies comprise test management strategies and test-wiseness strategies although three types of strategies call into play in test takers' responding to language test items and tasks (Cohen, 2013).

Test management strategies help test takers cope effectively and meaningfully with different test formats and facilitate test performance (Cohen, 1998; Nevo, 1989). These are the strategies test takers use to deal with logistic issues such as budgeting time on the test and deciding where to find the appropriate answers. With regard to test-wiseness strategies, Allan (1992) argued that test-wiseness strategies refer to how test takers "use test-taking strategies to select the correct response... without necessarily knowing the content or using the skills that are being tested" (p. 102). In other words, test takers may use test-wise techniques to obtain correct answers without fully or even partially understanding the text, suggesting that they do not provide responses to the test items and tasks via the text but rather, around it (Cohen, 1998; Fransson, 1984). Therefore, test-wiseness strategy use is a source of test invalidity, which suggests that it is important to investigate it carefully in order to eliminate it and ensure the construction of valid language tests. However, due to the limited scope of the investigation, this study focuses on test takers' language learning strategies (i.e., reading strategies in this study) and test management strategies.

The following section reviews several influential studies on test-taking strategies, especially in the area of second language reading assessment, which are pertinent to the current study. To provide a complete picture of the studies on test takers' strategy use, the review will include studies on test management strategies as well as test-wiseness strategies.

Empirical studies on test-taking strategies. Since the late 1970s, there has been a growing interest among language testing researchers in investigating the strategies used by test takers in the process of taking tests (Allan, 1992; Anderson, 1989; Anderson, Bachman, Perkins, & Cohen, 1991; Cohen, 1984, 1998, 2006, 2013; Cohen & Aphek, 1979; Cohen & Upton, 2006; Farr, Pritchard, & Smitten, 1990; Gordon, 1987; Homberg & Spaan, 1981; MacLean and d'Anglejan, 1986; Nevo, 1989; Phakiti, 2003, 2006, 2008a, b; Purpura, 1997, 1998; Rupp, Ferne, & Choi, 2006; Song, 2005; Song & Cheng, 2006; Zhang, 2014; Zhang, Aryadoust, & Zhang, 2013; Zhang & Zhang, 2013) as they increasingly realize that test-taking strategies play an important role in interpreting test performance and providing implications for test construct validity (Allan, 1992). A spectrum of research methods was employed in the studies regarding test-taking strategies. This includes verbal reports (e.g., Cohen, 1984, 1998; Cohen & Upton, 2006; Nevo, 1989), questionnaires (e.g., Purpura, 1997; Phakiti, 2008b; Zhang & Zhang, 2013), and interviews (Rupp et al., 2006). The following section gives an in-depth review of several studies mentioned above which used different research methods and are most pertinent to this study.

Nevo (1989) provided both introspective and retrospective verbal report data about test-taking strategies of 42 tenth-grade students of French with Hebrew as their first language who took a multiple-choice reading comprehension test given in both languages. In this study, she first administered a multiple-choice reading comprehension test in both Hebrew and French. After each question, she required the test takers to indicate the primary and secondary instrumental strategies they employed to arrive at each answer through a checklist which was administered to test takers alongside the test paper. The responses were anonymous in order to encourage the students to report what they really did instead of what should be done.

Nevo's pilot study indicated that it was necessary to provide test takers with the list of strategies. She therefore employed an innovative test format which allowed test takers to report their strategy use after finishing each item, which ensured that test takers gave feedback immediately after the process. Nevo's checklist consisted of 15 strategies. The primary finding of this study was that it was indeed possible to get feedback from test takers after they had answered each item on the test while providing them with a strategy checklist. In addition, the participants reported to have benefited from the opportunity to become aware of the process of how they took reading tests.

Recognizing the importance of gathering information on test-taking processes as a part of construct validation, Anderson, Bachman, Perkins, and Cohen (1991) conducted a study to investigate the relationship among test-taking strategies, item content, and item performance from think-aloud protocols. Twenty-eight (28) Spanish-speaking students took part in the Descriptive Test of Language Skill (DTLS) Forms A and B. In order to preserve the integrity of the timing of the testing condition and at the same time let the test takers think aloud the strategies they used during the examination, the test conditions were modified in that participants were first told to spend 30 min to complete as much of the test as possible and then were required to describe the reading and test-taking strategies they had used, during which the examination time was suspended. After the retrospective think-aloud session, test takers would resume the test. The researchers extracted 47 processing strategies from the verbal protocols which were categorized into five groups: strategies for supervising strategy use, support strategies, paraphrase strategies, strategies for establishing coherence in text, and test-taking strategies. Their study also used different types of data including verbal reports of strategy use, content analyses of test tasks, and indices of item difficulty and discrimination to validate the construct.

Cohen and Upton (2006) conducted a study which provided descriptions of reading and test-taking strategies used by test takers in the reading section of LanguEdge courseware (Educational Testing Service, 2002) which was used to introduce the design of the new TOEFL. The primary goal of this research was to examine whether test takers' strategy use varied when they answered the two types of items: single-selection MCQ questions in Basic Comprehension and Inferencing sections and the selected-response Reading to Learn. Thirty-two (32) students of four language groups (i.e., Chinese, Japanese, Korean, and other) participated in this study and provided their verbal report data. Results showed that test takers were required to use their academic reading skills to give responses to the reading section of the new TOEFL, although they were found to use an array of test-taking strategies. In addition, they found that these test-taking strategies were mainly test management strategies, and not test-wiseness strategies. Further, they found that the different sections of the LanguEdge prototypical tests "assess similar components of academic reading, as well as test-taking ability" (p. 118).

The previous studies investigated test-taking strategies primarily through qualitative research methods (i.e., verbal report protocols), which was the research method frequently employed in similar studies in the 1970s and 1980s. In addition, researchers also used questionnaires to examine issues regarding test-taking strategies. For example, Purpura (1997) investigated the relationships between test takers' strategy use and second language test performance through the use of a cognitive and metacognitive questionnaire and a language proficiency test. By using EFA, CFA, and SEM, this study examined how test takers' reported cognitive and metacognitive strategy use might affect their second language test performance. The participants were 1382 test takers from 17 test centers in Spain, Turkey, and the Czech Republic who sat for the University of Cambridge's FCE Anchor Test. The two instruments used in this study were a questionnaire of test takers' reported cognitive and metacognitive strategy use and a proficiency test. The 40-item cognitive questionnaire representing ten strategy-type variables was based on Gagnè et al.'s (1993) model of human information processing. The 40-item metacognitive questionnaire representing four strategy-type variables and two underlying process type variables was based on Bachman, Crushing, and Purpura (1993) 68-item metacognitive strategy questionnaire. The FCE Anchor Test developed by the University of Cambridge Local Examinations Syndicate was used to assess the EFL students' language ability. One version of the test was used to measure the students' second language test performance which consisted of two general sections with 70 items. Subjects used one hour to complete the 80-item combined cognitive and metacognitive strategy use questionnaire and 90 min for the 70-item FCE Anchor Test. The results showed that metacognitive strategy use had a significant and direct impact on cognitive strategy use. In addition, strategy use had no direct effect on reading ability but had indirect influence on reading ability through lexico-grammatical ability.

Based on Purpura's (1997) baseline model, Purpura (1998) reexamined the model of strategy use and second language test performance with high- and low-ability test takers. The strategy questionnaire and language test used in Purpura (1997) were administered to 1382 test takers. First, separate baseline models of strategy use and second language test performance were established. Then, the baseline models were estimated simultaneously with constraints imposed across high- and low-ability groups. The results indicated that metacognitive strategy use and second language test performance models produced almost the same factorial structure for each group. However, the models for cognitive strategy use were different across the groups in that the model for the low-ability group was much less complex than that of the high-ability group, indicating that the high-ability group achieved automaticity in activating and retrieving information from long-term memory, while the low-ability group seemed to have difficulty in information activation and retrieval in the test-taking process (Purpura, 2013). Thus, it was found that some evidence of cross-group invariance was observed, but the cross-group tests of invariance were partially supported by the data. Further, he concluded that test takers' use of retrieval strategies and metacognitive strategies jointly accounted for their variation in lexico-grammatical and reading ability.

Apart from verbal reports and questionnaire procedures, studies on test-taking strategies have also exploited the richness of interview data to inform these research issues. For example, Rupp, Ferne, and Choi (2006) conducted their research on test-taking strategies from the qualitative data obtained from ten semi-structured interviews with non-native adult English readers who were given three passages with some multiple-choice questions from a large-scale test in Canada, the CanTEST. Their research showed that test takers selected a variety of unconditional and conditional response strategies in selecting their answers. According to Rupp et al. (2006), the unconditional strategies were the major strategy types that test takers employed and relied on "in order to have a good sense of what the text and questions were about before they responded to individual items" (p. 461), whereas conditional strategies were employed based on test takers' perceptions of the characteristics of the passage and the questions. Additionally, they classified test-taking strategies into three categories: general strategies, text-based strategies, and item-related strategies. In addition, they found that completing multiple-choice questions was viewed as a problem-solving task instead of a comprehension task. Furthermore, they found that the analysis of the characteristics of the items showed that the construct of reading comprehension had multiple different representations.

In summary, the aforementioned studies on test-taking strategies have provided empirical, methodological, and theoretical implications for further research in this field. However, the review of literature revealed gaps in this field. For example, although researchers employed questionnaires to investigate the relationships between test takers' strategy use and reading test performance, no instruments have been developed based on the theoretical frameworks of reading comprehension and test-taking strategies. Given the rich and enlightening information provided by the literature in reading comprehension and test-taking strategies, it is necessary and imperative to develop a reading test strategy use questionnaire to measure learners' strategy use on the reading comprehension tests. Therefore, this study aimed to develop such a questionnaire to gain a better understanding of test takers' strategy use in reading comprehension tests.

Studies on Chinese learners' strategy use and language performance. The previous section reviews the literature about reading comprehension and strategy use including models of reading comprehension, theories on metacognition, and relevant research on strategy use and reading test performance. On top of that, researchers have also conducted studies to specifically investigate Chinese EFL/ESL learners' strategy use and language performance.

With China's policy of opening up and extensive communication with Western countries in commerce, technology, and culture, there is now an increasing demand for a large number of competent English users in a variety of professions. Accordingly, considerable attention has been drawn to the field of ESL in mainland China. In recent years, more studies have been conducted on mainland Chinese ESL learners (e.g., Gan, Humphreys, & Hamp-Lyons, 2004; Gu & Johnson, 1996; Wen & Johnson, 1997; Zhang, 2010, 2014; Zhang & Zhang, 2013). This section reviews the studies on Chinese learners' strategy use and language performance which are very relevant to the current study.

Wen and Johnson (1997) investigated the relationships between 242 Chinese L2 learners' learner variables and their English language proficiency through the use of a questionnaire and a nationwide standardized English proficiency test (i.e., the Graded Test for English Majors Band 4 or GEM-4). They identified 16 learner variables including gender, L1 and L2 language proficiency, learning purpose, belief, effort, and strategy use. The mixed method study showed that gender, and L1 and L2 proficiency had direct effects on English achievement. In addition, they found that strategies relating to vocabulary learning and tolerating ambiguity (risk-taking or inference-making) had direct and positive effects on their English test performance. Furthermore, their study indicated that female students' average score for reading was superior to that of male students in a standardized nationwide proficiency test. Additionally, female students attached more importance to metacognitive strategies and inference-making strategies than male students.

Song and Cheng (2006) investigated the relationships between students' language learner strategy use and their language test performance. They employed a revised version of Purpura's (1999) questionnaire which consisted of 34 items of cognitive and 30 items of metacognitive strategies. They assigned it to 121 Chinese college test takers taking the CET-4. Their study showed that CET-4 test takers used more metacognitive strategies than cognitive strategies. The most frequently reported strategy was inference-making strategy. Additionally, they found that the best predictors of the CET performance were strategies of inference-making and practicing naturalistically.

Zhang (2010) investigated Chinese EFL students' metacognitive knowledge systems in relation to their EFL reading experience framed within a dynamic perspective of metacognitive system which includes not only cognitive, but also socioaffective and sociocultural dimensions. 20 Chinese EFL students participated in semi-structured interviews after they had finished reading two texts of about 500 words each. The study indicated that metacognition is closely related to the EFL students' reading comprehension performance. In addition, it was found that successful EFL readers could be distinguished from less successful readers by the amount and quality of the metacognitive knowledge they possess.

Zhang and Zhang (2013) investigated the relationships between test takers' strategy use and test performance on the CET Reading subtest. 209 Chinese college students were invited to participate in a reading comprehension test and answer a 30-item strategy use questionnaire (Phakiti, 2008b). Results showed that two factors underlay test takers' reading test performance: lexico-grammatical reading ability (LEX_GR) and text comprehension reading ability (TxtCOM). In addition, metacognitive strategy use had a significant and direct effect on cognitive strategy use, implying that the former performed an executive function over the latter. Monitoring strategies were found to have a significant effect on LEX_GR, while evaluating strategies significantly affected TxtCOM, suggesting that metacognitive strategy use played an important role on the reading test.

In summary, researchers are paying growing attention to the investigation of Chinese English learners' strategy use and language performance. However, as indicated in the previous review, no studies have examined the underlying structure of the CET-4 Reading subtest and the relationships between its test takers' strategy use and test performance, with the exception of Zhang and Zhang (2013). In their study, however, Zhang and Zhang (2013) employed Phakiti's (2008a) questionnaire as a measure of test takers' strategy use in the reading comprehension test, which is based on the general human information processing theory (Gagnè et al., 1993), instead of specific reading theories. Different from Zhang and Zhang (2013), the ReTSUQ, a reading strategy questionnaire based on reading theories and empirical studies, is developed in the current study to investigate the relationships between test takers' strategy use and reading test performance.

3.4   Studies on Gender Differences in Strategy Use and Reading Test Performance

Researchers have long been intrigued by the topic of whether male and female students differ in their test performance. For example, Kunnan (1990) conducted gender analysis on the performance of 844 non-native-speaking students on the ESL placement examination at the University of California, Los Angeles (UCLA). It was found that 20 items, which were related to the topics of business, culture/anthropology, and aerospace engineering, favored the male groups. In addition, Walstad and Robson (1997) argued that both genders might go through different cognitive processes based on their finding that MCQs favor male test takers in economics tests. More recently, Aryadoust, Goh, and Lee (2011) investigated the different performances of gender groups on the MELAB listening test and found that several test items favor low-ability male test takers. To sum up, this line of research examined how different test items function differently on males and females.

In addition, a growing number of studies have been conducted to investigate the differences in reading achievement across gender groups in recent years. However, the extant literature showed that the findings from these studies are not consistent. Some studies identified significant gender differences in reading performance. For example, based on the data from 43 countries, Chiu and McBride-Chang (2006) showed that girls outperformed boys in reading skills. Logan and Johnson (2009) found that female students had better reading ability compared with male students, although the differences were of small magnitude. However, Bügel and Buunk (1996) found that male students generally had a higher text comprehension level than female students in a study involving 2980 secondary school students. In contrast, some studies did not detect any male and female differences in reading performance. For example, drawing on his study on 384 Thai university students' performance on a MCQ reading comprehension test, Phakiti (2003) found that there was no significant difference in male and female students' reading comprehension performance. In addition, McGeown, Goodwin, Henderson, and Wright (2012) also concluded that gender differences in reading skills were not found in their study. To sum up, the divergence and inconsistency in the previous findings indicated that the complex relationships between gender differences and reading performance are not revealed sufficiently, indicating the importance of identifying the possible causes of the conflicting findings and investigating these potential causes in well-controlled studies.

The review of literature showed that gender differences have been examined from such diverse perspectives as attitudes (e.g., Griffin, MacKewn, Moster, & Van Vuren, 2012), motivations (e.g., Logan & Medford, 2011; McGeown, Goodwin, Henderson, & Wright, 2012), and strategy use (e.g., Phakiti, 2003). Although researchers have explored gender differences in general learning strategies (e.g., Green & Oxford, 1995; Oxford & Nyikos, 1989; Oxford, Park-Oh, Ito, & Sumrall, 1993) and listening strategies (Vandergrift, 1997), few studies have investigated whether reading strategies are employed differently across gender groups.

Among the studies is one conducted by Young and Oxford (1997) who investigated 23 male and 26 female students' different strategy use in reading English (L1) and Spanish (L2) texts through the use of verbal recall protocols. The subjects were also required to report their comprehension level and their use of background knowledge. It was found that male and female students did not differ significantly in their reading ability and overall strategy use. However, male students were found to employ more monitoring strategies in terms of their reading pace, strategy use, etc., as well as paraphrasing strategies, than their female counterparts.

Sheorey and Mokhtari (2001) examined 302 native ($N = 150$; 73 males and 77 females) and non-native ($N = 152$; 92 males and 60 females) college students' differences in the reported use of reading strategies through the SORS. Participants were invited to complete a survey of reading strategies which was designed to differentiate readers in their strategies used while coping with academic tasks. They found that both native and ESL students showed awareness of almost all the strategies included in the questionnaire. In addition, the two groups demonstrated no differences in the order of importance they attributed to categories of reading strategies in the study. Furthermore, in the native speaker group, female students reported higher frequency of reading strategy use, indicating their greater awareness of strategic behaviors in reading comprehension.

Phakiti (2003) investigated gender differences in reading strategy use among 384 Thai college students (173 males and 211 females) by using a cognitive and metacognitive strategy questionnaire and a reading comprehension test. The participants were required to take the multiple-choice reading comprehension test and answer the questionnaire on their strategy use. The data were analyzed through multivariate analysis of variance. He found that male and female students did not show any differences in their reading comprehension performance and use of cognitive strategy use, but male students' use of metacognitive strategy was significantly higher than female students. It was concluded that gender differences seemed to play a role in strategy use which resulted in differences, though statistically insignificant, in their reading comprehension performance.

As suggested in the review of relevant literature, in the studies regarding gender differences in reading comprehension and strategy use, the frequently used statistical methods include frequency counts, ANOVA, t-tests, or multivariate analysis of variance (MANOVA) (e.g., McGeown et al., 2012; Phakiti, 2003; Sheorey & Mokhtari, 2001). To date, no studies have employed multi-group SEM to investigate gender differences in strategy use and reading comprehension performance. The advantage of SEM over other statistical methods is that it can be used to examine the relationships between observed and latent variables. In addition, it accounts for the measurement errors in the model explicitly which allows for a more accurate evaluation of the relationships under study. In multi-group SEM, researchers can test the invariance of measurement and structural models across two or more groups. Thus, this statistical method is used in this study to investigate the relationships between strategy use and reading test performance across male and female Chinese college test takers, the results of which are covered later in Chap. 6.

To sum up, as suggested by Logan and Johnson (2010), the paucity of studies in gender differences in reading strategy use suggests that more research is needed in this area to fill the gap revealed in the review of literature. Thus, Chap. 6 is devoted to investigating gender differences in strategy use and reading test performance among Chinese college students.

3.5 Relevance to the Study

The empirical studies and theoretical frameworks discussed above have important implications for the present study. Based on them, hypothesized models were formulated for empirical testing and investigation in this study.

The hypothesized strategy use model. Test takers' metacognition was hypothesized to be substantiated by the metacognitive and cognitive strategies they use in the test context. Test takers control their reading and test-taking processes with their metacognitive and cognitive strategies including planning strategies, evaluating strategies, monitoring strategies, strategies for general progression, strategies for identifying important information, inference-making strategies, integrating strategies, and interpreting strategies (Cohen & Upton, 2006; Paris & Winograd, 1990).

Informed by Pressley and Afflerbach's (1995) constructively responsive reading model, the theory of metacognition (e.g., Baker & Brown, 1984; Paris & Winograd, 1990; Wenden, 1998), and Bachman and Palmer's (2010) framework for language use, the current study proposes that metacognition refers to test takers' *purposeful* cognitive activities for controlling their reading and test-taking processes (Cohen & Upton, 2006; Paris & Winograd, 1990). This comprises eight constituent elements (i.e., eight types of strategies): planning strategies, evaluating strategies, monitoring strategies, strategies for general progression, strategies for identifying important information, inference-making strategies, integrating strategies, and interpreting strategies, which are delineated as follows:

(a) **Planning strategies** help test takers achieve their pre-established goals. For example, before completing reading tasks, test takers identify and assess the characteristics of reading tasks and formulate their plans. They adapt their reading activities to their plans and test demands (Cohen & Upton, 2006; Jacobs & Paris, 1987; Wenden, 1998).

(b) **Evaluating strategies** refer to the cognitive processes that test takers apply to assess tasks and their own personal cognitive abilities (Paris & Winograd, 1990; Wenden, 1998). Influenced by time pressure (and the high-stakes nature) of tests, test takers constantly assess their test-taking and reading comprehension processes and judge the degree of accuracy to which they complete the test tasks (Cohen & Upton, 2006).

(c) **Monitoring strategies** refer to test takers' checking and regulating their own thoughts and performance while performing cognitive activities. Test takers engage in monitoring activities which rest upon their evaluations and modify their reading and test-taking plans as well as strategies (Cohen & Upton, 2006; Jacobs & Paris, 1987; Wenden, 1998).

In addition, drawing on Cohen's (2006) framework of test-taking strategies, each of the three types of metacognitive strategies can be further split into two subcategories: reading management strategies (RMS) and test management strategies (TMS). This is also in line with the focus of this study (i.e., language learner strategies and test management strategies).

(d) **Strategies for general progression** refer to the strategies used by readers in the general progression of the text from the beginning to the end which often comes after they overview the text (Pressley & Afflerbach, 1995). Automatic decoding of text occurs in this phase in which much of the comprehension is effortless (Johnson & Afflerbach, 1985).

(e) **Strategies for identifying important information** are those strategies employed by readers and test takers to refine their understanding of the text constantly when the new input is not consistent with their initial hypotheses (Pressley & Afflerbach, 1995).

(f) **Inference-making strategies** refer to readers' ability to "go beyond the information given in the text" (Pressley & Afflerbach, 1995, p. 46) through implication in order to "fill in meaning gaps in text" (p. 49).

(g) **Integrating strategies** are applied when readers manipulate the text to fit the information across the text based on their understanding of the text as well as their prior knowledge and experience of the world (see Kintsch & van Dijk, 1978).

(h) **Interpreting strategies** concern those strategies used in the interpretive processes in reading which involve making text more concrete (e.g., the instantiation of schemata and generalization of the visual images).

In conclusion, it is postulated that the eight types of strategies are used during reading. Following this, a strategy use questionnaire is developed based on the hypothesis. As such, the results of the statistical analysis will provide the testing of the hypothesis.

The hypothesized reading comprehension test model. It was postulated that there are two underlying factors in the reading comprehension test: LEX_GR and TxtCOM. In addition, Skimming and Scanning (SKSN) and Reading in Depth (RID) load on TxtCOM, while banked cloze (BCLZ) and multiple-choice cloze (MCLZ) load on LEX_GR.

Considerable research on reading comprehension has shown that comprehension cannot occur without successful operation of lower-level processes such as word recognition, syntactic parsing, and semantic proposition encoding (e.g., Gough & Tunmer, 1986; Grabe, 2009; LaBerge & Samuels, 1974). The lower-level processing knowledge was generally termed lexico-grammatical knowledge (Celce-Murcia & Larsen-Freeman, 1999; Purpura, 2004). Lexico-grammatical ability is directly related to L2 reading ability; i.e., test takers' knowledge of word recognition and syntactic parsing is expected to affect their reading ability greatly and directly (see Phakiti, 2008b; Zhang & Zhang, 2013). Therefore, it is hypothesized that reading test performance as measured by the CET-4 Reading subtest has two underlying factors, TxtCOM and LEX_GR, and that LEX_GR has a direct effect on TxtCOM.

According to the test syllabus of the CET-4 (National College English Testing Committee, 2006), specific skills assessed in the reading test include the following: (a) the ability to distinguish and understand main ideas and important details and (b) the ability to understand the passage by means of language skills. The former is represented by passage comprehension items in SKSN and RID sections, whereas the latter is operationalized by cloze items in BCLZ and MCLZ sections. Additionally, contrary to the earlier assertion that cloze tests measured higher-order processing abilities (Hinofotis, 1980; Oller, 1979), more recent studies have shown that cloze tests serve as a measure of lower-order proficiency such as grammar and vocabulary (Anderson 1979; Markham, 1985; Purpura, 1999, 2004; Saito, 2003; Shanahan, Kamil, & Tobin, 1982). Therefore, it is hypothesized that SKSN and RID load on TxtCOM, while BCLZ and MCLZ load on LEX_GR.

The hypothesized model of the relationships between strategy use and test performance. It was hypothesized that test takers' metacognitive and cognitive strategies have close relationships with their reading test performance. In other words, planning strategies, evaluating strategies, monitoring strategies, general progression strategies, strategies for identifying important information, inference-making strategies, integrating strategies, and interpreting strategies are supposed to enhance test takers' test performance positively.

Based on previous research on strategy use on reading comprehension, strategy use has close links with reading comprehension performance (see Brown, 1980; Carrell, 1989a; Paris & Jacobs, 1984; Phakiti, 2003; Pressley & Afflerbach, 1995; Sheorey & Mokhtari, 2001; Zhang, 2010). Empirical studies also show the causal relations between strategy use and readers' performance in reading comprehension (e.g., Cain, Oakhill, & Bryant, 2004; Phakiti, 2003; Roeschl-Heils, Schneider, & van Kraayenoord, 2003). In addition, studies on test-taking strategies (Cohen &

Upton, 2006; Phakiti, 2003, 2008b; Purpura, 1999) indicate that strategy use improves test performance.

The hypothesized models of the relationships between metacognitive and cognitive strategies in relation to language use. Researchers have come to the consensus that metacognition plays an important role in language use. However, the relationships between metacognitive and cognitive strategies in relation to language use are still not clear. Some researchers have pointed out that the distinction between metacognitive and cognitive strategies is "fuzzy" (Baker, 1991; Chapelle, Grabe, & Berns, 1997) and "difficult to demarcate" (Paris et al., 1991, p. 610); i.e., metacognition is unitary. Other researchers have argued that metacognitive and cognitive strategies are key components of language learners' metacognitive awareness; i.e., metacognition is componential and separable (e.g., O'Malley & Chamot, 1990; Oxford, 1990; Wenden, 1998). And yet other researchers have demonstrated that metacognitive strategy use and cognitive strategy use are related to each other closely (e.g., Phakiti, 2003, 2008b; Purpura, 1997, 1998). In addition, Purpura (1999) and Phakiti (2003) raised the query regarding the construct of test takers' metacognition. Phakiti (2003) argued that an important task for language testing researchers is to "measure the defined strategy construct" (p. 47). Therefore, on the basis of the existing literature, three models (i.e., unitary, higher-order, and correlated models) were hypothesized to examine the underlying structure of metacognition and its effect on test takers' reading test performance (see Figs. 3.1, 3.2, 3.3 for graphic demonstrations of the models). How these models are tested will be described in Chap. 4.

1. *Unitary model*. It was hypothesized in the unitary model that test takers' metacognitive and cognitive strategies play a unitary role in enhancing their reading test performance. In other words, metacognitive and cognitive strategies work in synergy in affecting test performance.
2. *Higher-order model*. According to the higher-order model, test takers' strategy use, which is mainly substantiated by two separate components (i.e., metacognitive and cognitive strategy use), was hypothesized to have direct effects on students' test performance.
3. *Correlated model*. In the correlated model, it was hypothesized that test takers' metacognitive strategy use is correlated with their cognitive strategy use. In addition, metacognitive strategy use and cognitive strategy use were hypothesized to have a direct effect on students' test performance, respectively.

In summary, on the basis of relevant empirical studies and theories, three models (i.e., unitary mode, high-order model, and correlated model) were hypothesized. As shown in Figs. 3.1, 3.2, and 3.3, the postulated models are latent models investigating the relationships between language users' strategy use and reading test performance. Literature showed that SEM appears to be the most appropriate method to test such latent models and investigate the relationships between test takers' strategy use and test performance (e.g., In'nami & Koizumi, 2011; Kunnan, 1998; Phakiti, 2008b; Purpura, 1997, 1999). The present study, therefore,

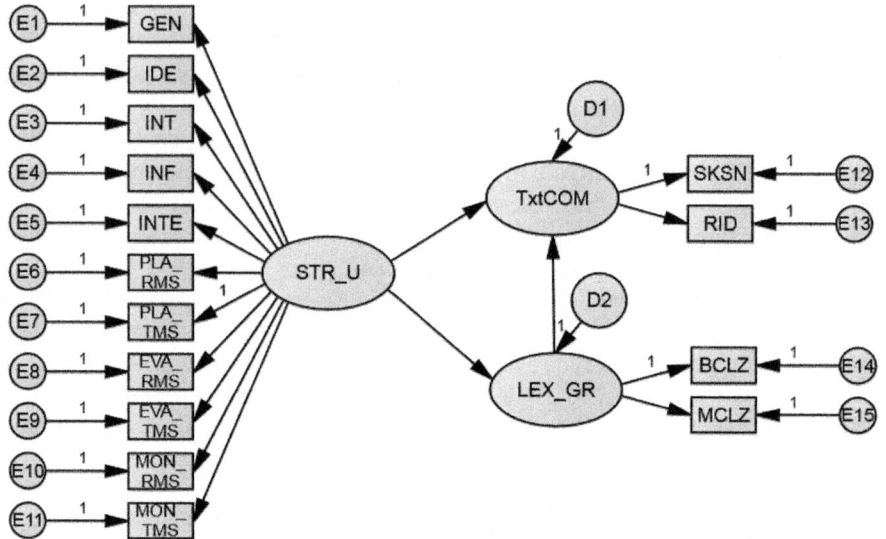

Fig. 3.1 The hypothesized unitary model. *GEN* general progression strategies, *IDE* identifying important information strategies, *INT* integrating strategies, *INF* inference-making strategies, *INTER* interpreting strategies, *PLA_RMS* planning reading management strategies, *PLA_TMS* planning test management strategies, *EVA_RMS* evaluating reading management strategies, *EVA_TMS* evaluating test management strategies, *MON_RMS* monitoring reading management strategies, *MON_TMS* monitoring test management strategies, *STR_U* strategy use, *TxtCOM* text comprehension reading ability, *LEX_GR* lexico-grammatical reading ability, *SKSN* Skimming and Scanning, *RID* Reading in Depth, *BCLZ* banked cloze, *MCLZ* multiple-choice cloze

investigates the relationships between Chinese college test takers' metacognitive and cognitive strategy use and reading test performance on the CET-4 Reading subtest by testing the hypothesized models using an SEM approach.

In summary, this chapter reviewed the literature pertinent to this study. It first defined reading comprehension based on extant voluminous literature. Relevant reading models were discussed, and response formats of assessing reading comprehension were introduced. Since this study is concerned with measuring test takers' strategy use in the reading comprehension test, relevant literature regarding reporting strategy use in reading comprehension was presented. Additionally, empirical studies on the relationship between strategy use and language performance, test-taking strategies, Chinese college students' strategy use and language performance, and gender differences in strategy use and language performance were reviewed. Based on relevant empirical studies and theories, hypothesized models were then postulated for further testing and investigation in the following part of the study. Finally, this chapter ended with a summary of the issues discussed in this section.

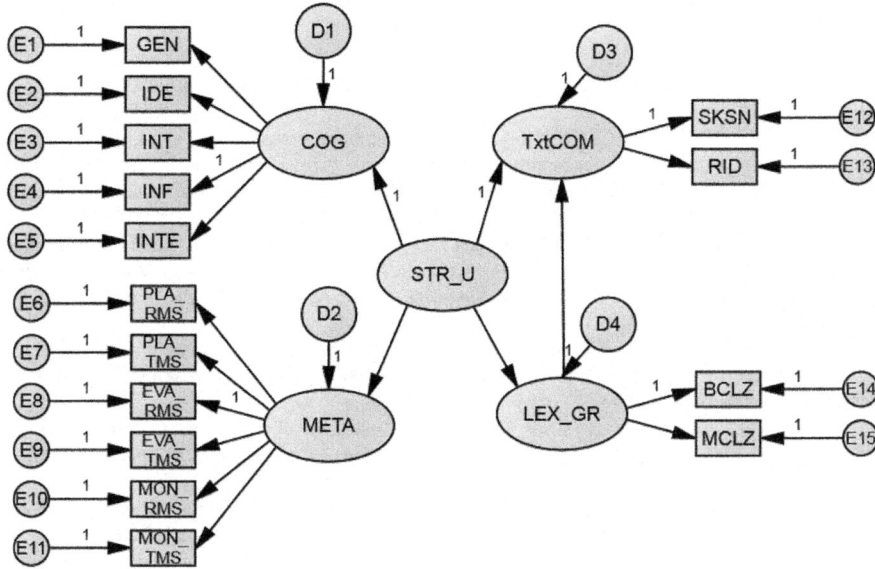

Fig. 3.2 The hypothesized higher-order model

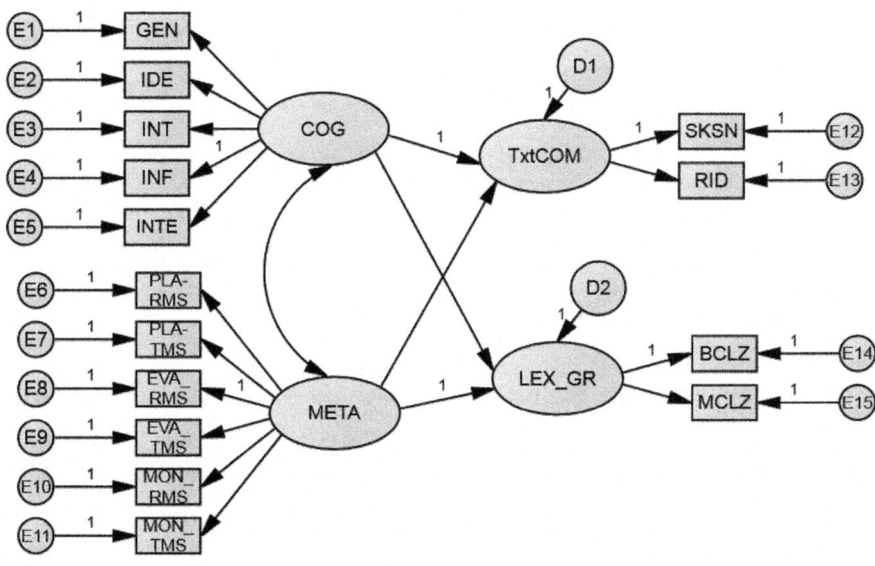

Fig. 3.3 The hypothesized correlated model

References

Adam, M. (1990). *Beginning to read: Thinking and learning about print*. Cambridge, MA: MIT Press.

Adam, B., Bell, L., & Perfetti, C. (1995). A trading relationship between reading skill and domain knowledge in children's text comprehension. *Discourse Processes, 20,* 307–323.

Adolf, S. M., Catts, H. W., & Little, T. (2006). Should the simple view of reading include a fluency component? *Reading and Writing: An Interdisciplinary Journal, 19,* 933–958.

Alderson, J. C. (1993). The relationship between grammar and reading in an English for Academic purposes test battery. In D. Douglas & C. Chapelle (Eds.), *A new decade of language testing research: Selected papers from the 1990 language testing research colloquium* (pp. 203–219). Alexandria, VA: TESOL.

Alderson, J. C. (2000). *Assessing reading*. Cambridge: Cambridge University Press.

Allan, A. (1992). Development and validation of a scale to measure test-wiseness in EFL/ESL reading test takers. *Language Testing, 9*(2), 101–122.

Anderson, T. H. (1979). Study skills and learning strategies. In H. E. O'Neil Jr. & C. D. Spielberger (Eds.), *Cognitive and affective learning strategies* (pp. 78–99). New York: Academic Press.

Anderson, N. J. (1989). *Reading comprehension tests versus academic reading: What are second language readers doing?* Unpublished PhD dissertation, University of Texas, Austin.

Anderson, N. J. (1991). Individual differences in strategy use in second language reading and testing. *Modern Language Journal, 75,* 460–472.

Anderson, N. J. (2005). L2 learning strategies. In E. Hinkel (Ed.), *Handbook of research in second language teaching and learning* (pp. 757–771). Mahwah, NJ: Lawrence Erlbaum.

Anderson, N. J., Bachman, L., Perkins, K., & Cohen, A. (1991). An exploratory study into the construct validity of a reading comprehension test: Triangulation of data sources. *Language Testing, 8*(1), 41–66.

Anderson, P. C., & Pearson, P. D. (1984). A schematic-theoretic view of basic processes in reading. In P. D. Pearson (Ed.), *Handbook of reading research* (pp. 255–292). White Plains, NY: Longman.

Aryadoust, V., Goh, C., & Lee, O. K. (2011). An investigation of differential item functioning in the MELAB listening test. *Language Assessment Quarterly, 8*(4), 361–385.

Bachman, L. F. (1990). *Fundamental consideration in language testing*. Oxford: Oxford University Press.

Bachman, L. F., Crushing, S. T., & Purpura, J. E. (1993). *Development of a questionnaire item bank to explore test-taker characteristics* (Interim Report submitted to University of Cambridge Local Examination Syndicate). Cambridge: UCLES.

Bachman, L. F., & Palmer, A. S. (1996). *Language testing in practice*. Oxford: Oxford University Press.

Bachman, L. F., & Palmer, A. S. (2010). *Language testing in practice*. Oxford: Oxford University Press.

Baker, L. (1991). Metacognition, reading and science education. In C. M. Santa & D. E. Alvermann (Eds.), *Science learning* (pp. 2–13). Newark, DE: International Reading Association.

Baker, L., & Brown, A. L. (1984). Metacognitive skills and reading. In P. D. Pearson, R. Barr, M. L. Kamil, & P. Mosenthal (Eds.), *Handbook of research in reading* (pp. 353–394). White Plains, NY: Longman.

Barnett, M. A. (1989). *More than meets the eye*. Englewood Cliffs, NJ: Prentice-Hall.

Bialystok, E. (2001). *Bilingualism in development: Language, literacy, and cognition*. New York: Cambridge University Press.

Block, E. (1986). The comprehension strategies of second language readers. *TESOL Quarterly, 20* (3), 463–493.

Block, E. (1992). See how they read: Comprehension monitoring of L1 and L2 readers. *TESOL Quarterly, 26*(2), 319–343.

Brown, A. L. (1980). Metacognitive development and reading. In R. J. Spiro, B. C. Bruce, & W. F. Brewer (Eds.), *Theoretical issues in reading comprehension: Perspectives from psychology, linguistics, artificial intelligence and education* (pp. 453–482). Hillsdale, NJ: Erlbaum.

Brown, A. L., Armbruster, B., & Baker, L. (1986). The role of metacognition in reading and studying. In J. Orasanu (Ed.), *Reading comprehension: From research to practice* (pp. 49–76). Hillsdale, NJ: Erlbaum.

Brown, A. L., Bransford, J. D., Ferrara, R., & Campione, J. C. (1983). Learning, remembering, and understanding. In L. H. Flavell & E. M. Markman (Eds.), *Handbook of child psychology* (pp. 77–106). New York: Wiley.

Buck, G., Tatsuoka, K. K., & Kostin, I. (1997). The subskills of reading: Rule-space analysis of a multiple-choice test of second language reading comprehension. *Language Learning, 47*, 423–466.

Bügel, K., & Buunk, B.P. (1996). Sex differences in foreign language text comprehension: The role of interests andprior knowledge. *Modern Language Journal, 80*(1), 15–31.

Cain, K., Oakhill, J., & Bryant, P. (2004). Children's reading comprehension ability: Concurrent prediction by working memory, verbal ability, and component skills. *Journal of Educational Psychology, 96*, 31–42.

Carrell, P. L. (1989a). SLA and classroom instruction: Reading. *Annual Review of Applied Linguistics, 9*, 223–242.

Carrell, P. L. (1989b). Metacognitive awareness and second language reading. *Modern Language Journal, 73*(2), 121–131.

Celce-Murcia, M., & Larsen-Freeman, D. (1999). *The grammar book: An ESL/EFL teacher's course.* Boston, MA: Heinle and Heinle.

Chapelle, C., Grabe, W., & Berns, M. (1997). Communicative language proficiency: Definitions and implications for TOEFL 2000. *TOEFL Monograph Series No. 10.* Princeton, NJ: Educational Testing Service.

Chen, R. S., & Vellutino, F. R. (1997). Prediction of reading ability: A cross-validation study of the simple view of reading. *Journal of Literacy Research, 29*, 1–24.

Chiu, M. M., & McBride-Chang, C. (2006). Gender, context, and reading: A comparison of students in 43 countries. *Scientific Studies of Reading, 10*(4), 331–362.

Coady, J. (1979). A psycholinguistic model for the ESL reader. In R. MacKay, B. Barkman, & R. R. Jordan (Eds.), *Reading in a second language: Hypothesis, organization and practice* (pp. 5–12). Rowley, MA: Newbury House.

Cohen, A. D. (1984). On taking language tests: What the students report. *Language Testing, 1*(1), 70–81.

Cohen, A. D. (1990). *Language learning: Insights for learners, teachers, and researchers.* New York: Newbury House.

Cohen, A. D. (1998). Strategies and process in test taking and SLA. In L. F. Bachman & A. D. Cohen (Eds.), *Interface between second language acquisition and language testing research* (pp. 90–111). Cambridge: Cambridge University Press.

Cohen, A. D. (2006). The coming age of research on test-taking strategies. *Language Assessment Quarterly, 3*(4), 307–331.

Cohen, A. D. (2013). Using test-wiseness strategy research in task development. In A. J. Kunnan (Ed.), *The companion to language assessment* (pp. 893–905). Hoboken, NJ: Wiley/ Blackwell.

Cohen, A. D., & Aphek, E. (1979). *Easifying second language learning.* Research report under the auspices of Brandeis University and submitted to the Jacob Hiatt Institute, Jerusalem. ERIC Document ED 163753.

Cohen, A. D., & Upton, T. A. (2006). *Strategies in responding to the new TOEFL reading tasks* (Monograph No. 33). Princeton, NJ: ETS. Retrieved from http://www.ets.org/Media/Research/pdf/RR-06-06.pdf.

Davis, A. (1968). *Language testing symposium: A psycholinguistic approach.* London: Oxford University Press.

Dörnyei, Z. (2007). *Research methods in applied linguistics*. Oxford: Oxford University Press.

Educational Testing Service. (2002). *LanguEdge Courseware: Handbook for scoring speaking and writing*. Princeton, NJ: Author.

Enright, M., Bridgemann, B., Cline, M., Eignor, D., Lee, Y.-W., & Powers, D. (2002). *Evaluating measures of communicative language abilities*. Paper presented at the annual TESOL Convention. Salt Lake City, UT.

Ericsson, K. A. (2002). Toward a procedure for eliciting verbal expression of nonverbal experience without reactivity: Interpreting the verbal overshadowing effect within the theoretical framework for protocol analysis. *Applied Cognitive Psychology, 16*, 981–987.

Farr, R., Pritchard, R., & Smitten, B. (1990). A description of what happens when an examinee takes a multiple-choice reading comprehension test. *Journal of Educational Measurement, 27*(3), 209–226.

Flavell, J. H. (1979). Metacognition and cognitive monitoring: A new area of cognitive-developmental inquiry. *American Psychologist, 34*(10), 906–911.

Flavell, J. H., Miller, P. H., & Miller, S. A. (2002). *Cognitive development* (4th ed.). Upper Saddle River, NJ: Prentice Hall.

Fransson, A. (1984). Cramming or understanding? Effects of intrinsic and extrinsic motivation on approach to learning and test performance. In J. C. Alderson & A. H. Urquhart (Eds.), *Reading in a foreign language* (pp. 86–121). London: Longman.

Frederiksen, C. H. (1977). Structure and process in discourse production and comprehension. In P. A. Carpenter & M. A. Just (Eds.), *Cognitive processes in comprehension* (pp. 313–322). Hillsdale, NJ: Lawrence Erlbaum.

Gagnè, E. D., Yekovich, C. W., & Yekovich, F. R. (1993). *The cognitive psychology of school learning*. New York: Harper Collins.

Gan, Z., Humphreys, G., & Hamp-Lyons, L. (2004). Understanding successful and unsuccessful EFL students in Chinese universities. *Modern Language Journal, 88*, 229–244.

Garner, R. (1987). *Metacognition and reading comprehension*. Norwood, NJ: Ablex.

Goh, C. (1998). How learners with different listening abilities use comprehension strategies and tactics. *Language Teaching Research, 2*, 124–147.

Goh, C. (2008). Metacognitive instruction for second language listening development: Theory, practice and research implications. *RELC Journal, 39*(2), 188–213.

Goh, C. M. C., & Zhang, L. M. (2013). Metacognitive theory and research in second language listening and reading: A comparative critical review. *Contemporary Foreign Language Studies, 396*(12), 94–110.

Goodman, K. S. (1967). Reading: A psycholinguistic guessing game. *Journal of the Reading Specialist, 6*, 126–135.

Goodman, K. S. (1986). *What's whole in whole language*. Portsmouth, NH: Heinemann Educational Books.

Goodman, K. S. (1994). Reading, writing, and written texts: A transactional sociolinguistic view. In R. B. Ruddell, M. R. Ruddell, & H. Singer (Eds.), *Theoretical models and processes of reading* (pp. 1093–1130). Newark: The International Reading Association.

Goodman, K. S. (1996). *On reading*. Portsmouth, NH: Heinemann.

Gordon, C. (1987). *The effect of testing method on achievement in reading comprehension tests in English as a foreign language*. Unpublished Master's thesis, School of Education, Tel Aviv University, Tel Aviv, Israel.

Gough, P. B. (1972). One second of reading. In J. F. Kavanagh & I. G. Mattingly (Eds.), *Language by ear and by eye*. Cambridge, MA: MIT Press.

Gough, P., Hoover, W., & Peterson, C. (1996). Some observations on a simple view of reading. In C. Cornoldi & J. Oakhill (Eds.), *Reading comprehension difficulties* (pp. 1–13). Mahwah, NJ: Lawrence Erlbaum.

Gough, P., Juel, C., & Griffith, P. (1992). Reading, spelling, and the orthographic cipher. In P. Gough, L. Ehri, & R. Treiman (Eds.), *Reading acquisition* (pp. 35–48). Hillsdale, NJ: Lawrence Erlbaum.

Gough, P. B., & Tunmer, W. (1986). Decoding, reading, and reading disability. *Remedial and Special Education, 7,* 6–10.

Gough, P., & Wren, S. (1999). Constructing meaning: The role of decoding. In J. Oakhill & R. Beard (Eds.), *Reading development and the teaching of reading* (pp. 59–78). Malden, MA: Blackwell.

Grabe, W. (1991). Current development in second language reading research. *TESOL Quarterly, 25*(3), 375–406.

Grabe, W. (2000). Reading research and its implications for reading assessment. In A. J. Kunnan (Ed.), *Fairness and validation in language assessment* (pp. 226–262). Cambridge: Cambridge University Press.

Grabe, W. (2009). *Reading in a second language: Moving from theory to practice.* Cambridge: Cambridge University Press.

Green, J. M., & Oxford, R. (1995). A closer look at learning strategies, L2 proficiency, and gender. *TESOL Quarterly, 29,* 261–297.

Griffin, R., MacKewn, A., Moster, E., & Van Vuren, K. (2012). Do learning and study skills affect academic performance? An empirical investigation. *Contemporary Issues in Education Research, 5*(2), 109–116.

Gu, Y., & Johnson, R. K. (1996). Vocabulary learning strategies and language learning outcomes. *Language Learning, 46*(4), 643–679.

Halliday, M. A. K., & Hasan, R. (1976). *Cohesion in English.* London: Longman.

Hinofotis, F. B. (1980). Cloze as an alternative method of ESL placement and proficiency testing. In J. W. Oller & K. Perkins (Eds.), *Research in language testing* (pp. 121–128). Rowley, MA: Newbury House.

Homberg, T. J., & Spaan, M. C. (1981). ESL Reading proficiency assessment: Testing strategies. In M. Hines & W. Rutherford (Eds.), *On TESOL'81* (pp. 25–33). Washington, DC: TESOL.

Hoover, W. A., & Gough, P. B. (1990). The simple view of reading. *Reading and Writing: An Interdisciplinary Journal, 2,* 127–160.

Hoover, W. A., & Tunmer, W. E. (1993). The components of reading. In G. G. Thompson, W. E. Tunmer, & T. Nicholson (Eds.), *Reading acquisition processes* (pp. 1–19). Clevedon: Multilingual Matters.

Hudson, T. (2007). *Teaching second language reading.* Oxford: Oxford University Press.

In'nami, Y., & Koizumi, R. (2011). Factor structure of the revised TOEIC® test: A multiple-sample analysis. *Language Testing, 29*(1), 131–152.

Jacobs, J. E., & Paris, S. G. (1987). Children's metacognition about reading: Issues in definition, measurement, and instruction. *Educational Psychologist, 22,* 255–278.

Johnson, P., & Afflerbach, P. (1985). The process of constructing main ideas from text. *Cognition and Instruction, 2,* 207–232.

Juel, C., Griffith, P. L., & Gough, P. B. (1986). Acquisition of literacy: A longitudinal study of children in first and second grade. *Journal of Educational Psychology, 78,* 243–255.

Kern, R. G. (1989). Second language reading strategy instruction: Its effects on comprehension and wordinference ability. *Modern Language Journal, 73*(2), 135–149.

Kintsch, W. (1988). The use of knowledge in discourse processing: A construction–integration model. *Psychological Review, 95,* 163–182.

Kintsch, W. (1998). *Comprehension: A paradigm for cognition.* New York: Cambridge University Press.

Kintsch, W., & van Dijk, T. A. (1978). Toward a model of text comprehension and production. *Psychological Review, 85,* 363–394.

Koda, K. (2005). *Insights into second language reading.* New York: Cambridge University Press.

Koda, K. (2007). Reading and language learning: Crosslinguistic constraints on second language reading development. In K. Koda (Ed.), *Reading and language learning* (pp. 1–44). Special issue of *Language Learning Supplement, 57,* 1–44.

Kunnan, A. J. (1990). DIF in native language and gender groups in an ESL placement test. *TESOL Quarterly, 24*(4), 741–746.

Kunnan, A. J. (1998). An introduction to structural equation modeling for language assessment research. *Language Testing, 15*(3), 295–332.

LaBerge, D., & Samuels, S. J. (1974). Toward a theory of automatic information processing. *Cognitive Psychology, 6*(2), 293–323.

Logan, S., & Johnson, R. S. (2009). Gender differences in reading: Examining where these differences lie. *Journal of Research in Reading, 32*(2), 199–214.

Logan, S., & Johnson, R. S. (2010). Investigating gender differences in reading. *Educational Review, 62*(2), 175–187.

Logan, S., & Medford, E. (2011). Gender differences in the strength of association between motivation, competency beliefs, and reading skill. *Educational Research, 53*(1), 85–94.

Long, D. L., Johns, C. L., & Morris, P. E. (2006). Comprehension ability in mature readers. In M. J. Traxler & M. A. Gernsbacher (Eds.), *Handbook of psycholinguistics* (2nd ed., pp. 801–834). Amsterdam: Elsevier.

Lunzer, E., Waite, M., & Dolan, T. (1979). Comprehension and comprehension test. In E. Lunzer & K. Gardner (Eds.), *The effective use of reading* (pp. 37–71). London: Heinemann Educational Books Ltd.

Lynch, B., & Hudson, T. (1991). EST reading. In M. Celce-Murcia (Ed.), *Teaching English as a second or foreign language* (2nd ed., pp. 216–232). Boston: Heinle and Heinle.

Macaro, E., & Erler, L. (2008). Raising the achievement of young-beginner readers of French through strategy instruction. *Applied Linguistics, 29*(1), 90–119.

MacLean, M., & d'Anglejan, A. (1986). Rational cloze and retrospection: Insights into first and second language reading comprehension. *Canadian Modern Language Review, 42*(4), 814–826.

Markham, P. L. (1985). The rational deletion cloze and global comprehension in German. *Language Learning, 35,* 423–430.

McGeown, S., Goodwin, H., Henderson, N., & Wright, P. (2012). Gender differences in reading motivation: Does sex or gender identity provide a better account? *Journal of Research in Reading, 35*(3), 328–336.

McNamara, D. S., Kintsch, E., Songer, N. B., & Kintsch, W. (1996). Are good texts always better? Text coherence, background knowledge, and levels of understanding in learning from text. *Cognition and Instruction, 14,* 1–43.

Messick, S. (1989). Validity. In R. L. Linn (Ed.), *Educational measurement* (pp. 13–103). New York: Macmillan.

Moe, A. J., & Irwin, J. W. (1986). Cohesion, coherence, and comprehension. In J. W. Irwin (Ed.), *Understanding and teaching cohesion comprehension.* International Reading Assoc: Delaware.

Mokhtari, K., & Reichard, C. A. (2002). Assessing students' metacognitive awareness of reading strategies. *Journal of Educational Psychology, 94*(2), 249–259.

Mokhtari, K., & Sheorey, R. (2002). Measuring ESL students' awareness of reading strategies. *Journal of Development Education, 25,* 2–10.

Mokhtari, K., Sheorey, R., & Reichard, C. A. (2008). Measuring the reading strategies of first and second language readers. In K. Mokhtari & R. Sheorey (Eds.), *Reading strategies of first- and second language learners.* Norwood, MA: Christopher-Gordon Publishers.

Munby, J. (1978). *Communicative syllabus design.* Cambridge: Cambridge University.

Myers, M., & Paris, S. (1978). Children's metacognitive knowledge about reading. *Journal of Educational Psychology, 70,* 680–690.

Nagy, W. (2007). Metalinguistic awareness and the vocabulary-comprehension connection. In R. Wagner, A. Muse, & K. Tannenbaum (Eds.), *Vocabulary acquisition: Implication for reading comprehension* (pp. 52–77). New York: Guilford.

National Assessment Governing Board. (2008). *Reading framework for the 2009 National Assessment of Educational Progress.* Washington, DC: NAGB.

National College English Testing Committee. (2006). *CET-4 test syllabus and sample test paper (2006 revised version).* Shanghai: Shanghai Foreign Language Education Press.

Nevo, N. (1989). Test-taking strategies on a multiple-choice test of reading comprehension. *Language Testing, 6,* 199–215.

O'Malley, J. M., & Chamot, A. U. (1990). *Learning strategies in second language acquisition.* Cambridge: Cambridge University Press.

Oller, J. (1979). *Language tests at school: A pragmatic approach.* London: Longman.

Oxford, R. L. (1990). *Language learning strategies: What every teacher should know.* New York: Newbury House.

Oxford, R., & Nyikos, M. (1989). Variables affecting choice of language learning strategies by university students. *Modern Language Journal, 73,* 292–300.

Oxford, R., Park-Oh, Y., Ito, I., & Sumrall, M. (1993). Learning a language by satellite: What influences achievement. *System, 21,* 31–48.

Paris, S. G., & Flukes, J. (2005). Assessing children's metacognition about strategic reading. In S. E. Israel, C. C. Block, K. L. Bauserman, & K. Kinnucan Welsh (Eds.), *Metacognition in literacy learning: Theory, assessment, instruction, and professional development* (pp. 121–139). Mahwah, NJ: Erlbaum.

Paris, S. G., & Hamilton, E. E. (2009). The development of children's reading comprehension. In S. E. Israel & G. G. Duffy (Eds.), *Handbook of research on reading comprehension* (pp. 32–53). New York: Routledge.

Paris, S. G., & Jacobs, J. (1984). The benefits of informed instruction for children's reading awareness and comprehension skills. *Child Development, 55,* 2083–2093.

Paris, S. G., Lipson, M. Y., & Wixson, K. K. (1983). Becoming a strategic reader. *Contemporary Educational Psychology, 8,* 239–316.

Paris, S. G., & Myers, M. (1981). Comprehension monitoring, memory and study strategies of good and poor readers. *Journal of Reading Behavior, 13,* 5–22.

Paris, S. G., Wasik, B., & Turner, J. (1991). The development of strategic readers. In R. Barr et al. (Eds.), *Handbook of reading research* (pp. 609–640). New York: Longman.

Paris, S. G., & Winograd, P. (1990). How metacognition can promote academic learning and instruction. In B. F. Jones & L. Idol (Eds.), *Dimensions of thinking and cognitive instruction* (pp. 15–51). Hillsdale, NJ: Erlbaum.

Pearson, P. D. (2009). The roots of reading comprehension instruction. In S. E. Israel & G. Duffy (Eds.), *Handbook of research on reading comprehension* (pp. 3–31). New York: Routledge.

Pearson, P. D., & Tierney, R. J. (1984). On becoming a thoughtful reader: Learning to read like a writer. In A. Purves & J. Niles (Eds.), *Becoming readers in a complex society.* Chicago, IL: National Society for the Study of Education.

Perfetti, C. (1985). *Reading ability.* New York: Oxford University Press.

Perfetti, C. (1992). The representation problem in reading acquisition. In P. Gough, L. Ehri, & R. Treiman (Eds.), *Reading acquisition.* Hillsdale, NJ: Lawrence Erlbaum.

Perfetti, C. (1994). Psycholinguistic and reading ability. In M. A. Gernsbacher (Ed.), *Handbook of psycholinguistics* (pp. 849–894). San Diego: Academic Press.

Perfetti, C. (1999). Comprehending written language: A blueprint for the teacher. In C. Brown & P. Hagoort (Eds.), *Neurocognition of language* (pp. 167–208). Oxford: Oxford University Press.

Perfetti, C. (2007). Reading ability: Lexical quality to comprehension. *Scientific Studies of Reading, 8,* 357–383.

Perfetti, C., & Hart, L. (2001). The lexical basis of comprehension skill. In D. Gorfien (Ed.), *On the consequences of meaning selection* (pp. 67–86). Washington, DC: American Psychological Association.

Perfetti, C., Marron, M., & Foltz, P. (1996). Sources of comprehension failure: Theoretical perspectives and case studies. In C. Cornoldi & J. Oakhill (Eds.), *Reading comprehension difficulties* (pp. 137–165). Mahwah, NJ: Lawrence Erlbaum.

Phakiti, A. (2003). A closer look at gender differences in strategy use in L2 reading. *Language Learning, 53*(4), 649–702.

Phakiti, A. (2006). Theoretical and pedagogical issues in ESL/EFL teaching of strategic reading. *University of Sidney Papers in TESOL, 1,* 19–50.

Phakiti, A. (2008a). Strategic competence as a fourth-order factor model: A structural equation modelling approach. *Language Assessment Quarterly, 5*(1), 20–42.

Phakiti, A. (2008b). Construct validation of Bachman and Palmer's (1996) strategic competence model over time in EFL reading tests. *Language Testing, 25*(2), 237–272.

Politzer, R., & McGroarty, M. (1985). An exploratory study of learning behaviors and their relationship to gains in linguistic and communicative competence. *TESOL Quarterly, 19*, 103–124.

Pressley, M. (2006). *Reading instruction that works: The case for balanced teaching* (3rd ed.). New York: Guilford.

Pressley, M., & Afflerbach, P. (1995). *Verbal protocols of reading: The nature of constructively responsive reading*. Hillsdale, NJ: Erlbaum.

Purpura, J. E. (1997). An analysis of the relationships between test takers' cognitive and metacognitive strategy use and second language test performance. *Language Learning, 47*, 289–325.

Purpura, J. E. (1998). Investigating the effects of strategy use and second language test performance with high- and low-ability test takers: A structural equation modeling approach. *Language Testing, 15*, 333–379.

Purpura, J. E. (1999). *Learner strategy use and performance on language tests: A structural equation modeling approach*. Cambridge: Cambridge University Press.

Purpura, J. E. (2004). *Assessing grammar*. Cambridge: Cambridge University Press.

Purpura, J. E. (2013). Cognition and language assessment. In A. J. Kunnan (Ed.), *The companion to language assessment* (pp. 100–124). Hoboken, NJ: Wiley/Blackwell.

RAND Reading Study Group. (2002). *Reading for understanding: Towards an R&D program in reading comprehension*. Report prepared for OERI.

Rayner, K., & Pollatsek, A. (1989). *The psychology of reading*. Englewood Cliffs, NJ: Prentice Hall.

Roeschl-Heils, A., Schneider, W., & van Kraayenoord, C. E. (2003). Reading, metacognition, and motivation: A follow-up study of German students 7 and 8. *European Journal of Psychology of Education, 18*, 75–86.

Rosenblatt, L. M. (1978). *The reader: The text: The poem*. Carbondale, IL: Southern Illinois University.

Rubin, J. (1975). What the "good" language learner can teach us? *TESOL Quarterly, 9*, 41–51.

Rumelhart, D. E. (1977). Understanding the summarizing stories. In D. LaBerge & S. J. Samuels (Eds.), *Basic processes in reading perception and comprehension* (pp. 265–303). Hillsdale, NJ: Lawrence Erlbaum.

Rumelhart, D. (1994). Toward an interactive model of reading. In R.B. Rudell & N.J. Unrau (Eds), *Theoreticalmodels and processes of reading* (5th ed., pp. 1149–1179). Newark: International Reading Association.

Rumelhart, D. (2004). Toward an interactive model of reading. In R. B. Rudell & N. J. Unrau (Eds.), *Theoretical models and processes of reading* (5th ed., pp. 1149–1179). Newark: International Reading Association.

Rupp, A. A., Ferne, T., & Choi, H. (2006). How assessing reading comprehension with multiple-choice questions shapes the construct: A cognitive processing perspective. *Language Testing, 23*, 441–474.

Saito, Y. (2003). Investigating the construct validity of the cloze section in the Examination for the Certificate of Proficiency in English. *Spaan Fellow Working Papers in Second or Foreign Language Assessment, 1*, 39–82.

Samuels, S. J. (1977). Introduction to theoretical models of reading. In W. Otto (Ed.), *Reading problems* (pp. 1–14). Boston: Addison-Wesley.

Samuels, S. J., & LaBerge, D. (1983). A critique of 'A theory of automaticity' in reading: Looking back: A retrospective analysis of the LaBerge-Samuels reading model. In L. Gentile, M. L. Kamil, & J. Blanchard (Eds.), *Reading research revisited* (pp. 34–56). Columbus, OH: C. E. Merrill.

Schmitt, M. C. (1990). A questionnaire to measure children's awareness of strategic reading processes. *The Reading Teacher, 43*(7), 454–464.

Shanahan, T., Kamil, M. L., & Tobin, A. W. (1982). Cloze as a measure of intersentential comprehension. *Reading Research Quarterly, 17,* 229–255.

Sheorey, R., & Mokhtari, K. (2001). Coping with academic materials: Differences in the reading strategies of native and non-native readers. *System: An International Journal of Educational Technology and Applied Linguistics, 29,* 431–449.

Sheorey, R., & Mokhtari, K. (2008). Differing perceptions of reading strategy use between native and non-native college students. In K. Mokhtari & R. Sheorey (Eds.), *Reading strategies of first and second language learners* (pp. 131–141). Norwood, MA: Christopher-Gordon Publishers.

Smith, F. (1971). *Understanding reading: A psycholinguistic analysis of reading and learning to read.* New York: Holt, Rinehart and Winston.

Smith, F. (1983). Reading like a writer. *Language Arts, 60*(5), 558–567.

Snow, C. E., Griffin, P., & Burns, M. S. (2005). *Knowledge to support the teaching of reading: Preparing teachers for a changing world.* San Francisco, CA: Jossey-Bass.

Song, X. (2005). Language learner strategy use and English proficiency on the Michigan English Language Assessment Battery. *Spaan Fellow Working Papers in Second or Foreign Language Assessment, 3,* 1–23.

Song, X., & Cheng, L. (2006). Language learner strategy use and test performance of Chinese learners of English. *Language Assessment Quarterly, 3*(3), 243–266.

Stanovich, K. E. (1980). Towards an interactive-compensatory model of individual differences in the development of reading fluency. *Reading Research Quarterly, 16,* 32–71.

Stanovich, K. E. (1986). Matthew effects in reading: Some consequences of individual differences in the acquisition of literacy. *Reading Research Quarterly, 21,* 360–407.

Stanovich, K. E. (2000). *Progress in understanding reading: Scientific foundations and new frontiers.* New York: Guilford Press.

Thorndike, R. L. (1917). Reading as reasoning. *Journal of Educational Psychology, 8*(6), 323–332.

Urquhart, S., & Weir, C. (1998). *Reading in a second language: Process, product and practice.* London: Longman.

van Dijk, T. A., & Kintsch, W. (1983). *Strategies of discourse comprehension.* New York: Academic Press.

Van Gelderen, A., Schoonen, R., de Glopper, K., Hulstjn, J., Simis, A., Snellings, P., et al. (2004). Linguistic knowledge, processing speed, and metacognitive knowledge in first- and second-language reading comprehension: A componential analysis. *Journal of Educational Psychology, 96,* 19–30.

Vandergrift, L. (1997). The comprehension strategies of second language (French) listeners: A descriptive study. *Foreign Language Annals, 30,* 387–406.

Vandergrift, L., & Goh, C. C. M. (2012). *Teaching and learning second language listening: Metacognition in action.* New York: Routledge.

Vandergrift, L., Goh, C. C. M., Mareschal, C. J., & Tafaghodtari, M. H. (2006). The Metacognitive Awareness Listening Questionnaire: Development and validation. *Language Learning, 56*(3), 431–462.

Vann, R. J., & Abraham, R. G. (1990). Strategies of unsuccessful language learners. *TESOL Quarterly, 24,* 177–198.

Wagner, D. A., Spratt, J. E., Gal, I., & Paris, S. G. (1989). Reading and believing: Beliefs, attributions, and reading achievement among Moroccan school children. *Journal of Educational Psychology, 81,* 283–293.

Walstad, W. B., & Robson, D. (1997). Differential item functioning and male-female differences on multiple choice tests in economics. *Journal of Economic Education, 28,* 155–171.

Wen, Q., & Johnson, R. (1997). L2 learner variables and English achievement: A study of tertiary-level English majors in China. *Applied Linguistics, 18,* 27–48.

Wenden, A. L. (1998). Metacognitive knowledge and language learning. *Applied Linguistics, 19*(4), 515–537.

Young, D.J., & Oxford, R. (1997). A gender-related analysis of strategies used to process written input in the nativelanguage and a foreign language. *Applied Language Learning, 8,* 43–73.

Yuill, N., & Oakhill, J. (1991). *Children's problems in text comprehension.* Cambridge: Cambridge University Press.

Zhang, L. J. (2002). Exploring EFL reading as a metacognitive experience: Reader awareness and reading performance. *Asian Journal of English Language Teaching, 12,* 65–90.

Zhang, L. J. (2010). A dynamic metacognitive systems account of Chinese university students' knowledge about EFL reading. *TESOL Quarterly, 44,* 320–353.

Zhang, L. M. (2014). A structural equation modeling approach to investigating test takers' strategy use and reading test performance. *Asian EFL Journal, 16*(1), 153–188.

Zhang, L. M., Aryadoust, V., & Zhang, L. J. (2013). Development and validation of the Test Takers' Metacognitive Awareness Reading Questionnaire. *The Asia-Pacific Education Researcher.* doi:10.1007/s40299-013-0083-z.

Zhang, L. M., Goh, C., & Kunnan, A. (2014). Analysis of test takers' metacognitive and cognitive strategy use and EFL reading test performance: A multi-sample SEM approach. *Language Assessment Quarterly, 11*(1), 76–120.

Zhang, L. M., & Zhang, L. J. (2013). Relationships between Chinese college test takers strategy use and EFL reading test performance: A structural equation modelling approach. *RELC Journal, 44*(1), 35–57.

Zimmerman, B. J., & Bandura, A. (1994). Impact of self regulatory influences on writing course attainment. *American Educational Research Journal, 31,* 845–862.

Zwaan, R., & Rapp, D. (2006). Discourse comprehension. In M. Traxler & M. A. Gernsbacher (Eds.), *Handbook of psycholinguistics* (2nd ed., pp. 725–764). Burlington, MA: Academic Press.

Chapter 4
Study Procedures and Data Collection

Abstract This chapter starts with an introduction of the research design. A description of the participants in the study is then provided. This is followed by an elaboration on the two research instruments used in this study—the Reading Test Strategy Use Questionnaire (ReTSUQ) and the CET-4 Reading subtest. The procedures for data collection and scoring are explained. Finally, the statistical analyses employed in the study are discussed.

4.1 Research Design

The research design adopted in this study is an ex post facto correlational research design. Ex post facto research is done when variables are studied in retrospect and ex post facto correlational research attempts to study the relationships among a set of variables occurring in a natural setting in which the researcher will not manipulate variables (Wiersma & Jurs, 2009). In other words, the study employed quantitative methods to investigate Chinese college test takers' strategy use and test performance on the CET-4 Reading subtest non-experimentally. Given the adaptation of the ex post facto research design in the present study, no firm causal claims are warranted by the findings of this study.

To measure test takers' strategy use on the reading comprehension test, the ReTSUQ was first developed on the basis of relevant empirical studies and theories. With the questionnaire, test takers' strategy use on the test was elicited, and the relationships between Chinese test takers' strategy use and reading test performance were investigated through a multi-sample SEM approach. Further, gender differences in strategy use and reading test performance were examined using a multi-group SEM approach. In other words, two minor studies are included in this book. Study 1 was designed to test the three hypothesized models and investigate the relationships between Chinese test takers' strategy use and reading test performance. Based on the findings from Study 1, Study 2 then examined the gender differences in strategy use and reading test performance.

© Springer Nature Singapore Pte Ltd. 2018
L. Zhang, *Metacognitive and Cognitive Strategy Use in Reading Comprehension*,
https://doi.org/10.1007/978-981-10-6325-1_4

4.2 Study Participants

The participants in this study were Chinese undergraduate students of non-English majors from five universities in three big cities in the northern part of mainland China. Due to resource limitations, the primary sampling method was convenient sampling. In addition, two general principles were followed in selecting the participating universities to aim for better representativeness of the population. First, the participants should be from the three major types of universities in China: the arts-oriented, science-oriented, and comprehensive universities. Second, the chosen universities should recruit their students from all over the country. Given the large population of the CET-4 test takers and the large number of participants required by the research method adopted in this study, the convenient sampling approach is useful in gaining access to a large number of participants in a relatively short period of time. However, it is obvious that this sampling method is limited in selecting a sample representative of the population in a rigorous manner. In other words, the generalization of the findings from this study to a larger population might be limited by this choice of sampling method.

The students from the arts-oriented university were majors in finance-related subjects such as accounting, banking, taxation, and international trade. Those from the science-oriented universities majored in engineering-related subjects including computer engineering, mechanical engineering, civil engineering, and automation, students from the comprehensive universities specialized in such disciplines as languages, mathematics, physics, and psychology.

Before entering colleges and universities, these participants had studied English as a required school subject for at least six years in their high schools. After being enrolled in colleges and universities, they learn English as a compulsory course in the first two years of their four-year undergraduate programs. In this program, English is normally instructed in the form of intensive reading, listening, and speaking. According to the national College English Curriculum Requirement (Ministry of Education, 2007), college students are expected to develop their ability to use English in myriad ways in order to communicate effectively in their future career and social interactions. The CET-4 was designed for college students who had completed the two-year compulsory College English courses as a measure of their general English proficiency.

4.2.1 Participants in Study 1

Study 1 concerns the investigation of Chinese test takers' strategy use and reading test performance. In this study, 593[1] Chinese first-year college students were invited

---

[1]Initially, 631 participants were involved in the study. However, 38 cases were dropped from the study in the data preparation process (see Sect. 2.1 for a detailed description).

to participate in this study. As freshmen newly admitted into the universities, they were still taking the compulsory English courses at the time of the data collection. In all the five universities, first-year non-English major students are not allowed to take part in the CET-4 until the end of the first academic year in the universities. These participants were invited to fill out the consent form and sit for the CET-4 Reading subtest[2] before they responded to the questionnaire. There were 274 (46.2%) male and 310 (52.3%) female participants, with nine (1.5%) students not providing their gender information. The age of these participants ranged from 18 to 25 ($M = 19.37$; SD $= 0.98$). The participants were required to report their scores of English and Chinese subjects on the National Tertiary Matriculation Examination (NTME). Participants' English score on the NTME ranged from 75.0 to 149.0 ($M = 125.11$; SD $= 0.50$). On average, they had received 9.19 (SD $= 2.41$) years of formal English instruction by the time of the study. Table 4.1 shows the distribution of the participants from the five universities. Table 4.2 displays the numbers and percentages of the participants according to their age, years of learning English, and English proficiency levels as measured by their NTME test scores. In addition, none of the participants had practiced the June 2010 version of the CET-4 Reading subtest prior to the study.

4.2.2 Participants in Study 2

Study 2 is on gender differences in strategy use and test performance on the reading comprehension test. Nine participants who did not provide their gender information in Study 1 were excluded from the study, leaving 584 participants in total. Among these participants, there were 274 (46.9%) male and 310 (53.1%) female students between the ages of 18–24 ($M = 19.38$; SD $= 0.98$). These participants' English score on the NTME ranged from 75.0 to 145.0 ($M = 125.03$; SD $= 0.50$) while their Chinese score ranged from 62.5 to 138.0 ($M = 113.20$; SD $= 0.40$). On average, they had received 9.18 (SD $= 2.40$) years of formal English instruction by the time of the study. Table 4.3 presents the distribution of the participants from the five universities. Table 4.4 shows the numbers and percentages of the participants according to their age, years of learning English, and English proficiency level as measured by the NTME test scores.

---

[2]The CET-4 Reading subtest used in this study is from the retired June 2010 version of the CET-4 test (Fang 2010).

Table 4.1 Distribution of participants from five universities for Study 1 (N = 593)

University	Type of university	Number of participants	Percentage of participants (%)
U1	Arts-oriented	123	20.74
U2	Science-oriented	74	12.48
U3	Science-oriented	171	28.84
U4	Comprehensive	167	28.16
U5	Comprehensive	58	9.78
	Total	593	100

Table 4.2 Descriptive information of participants for Study 1 (N = 593)

	Number and percentage of distribution of participants				
Age	<17	17–18	19–20	21–22	>22
	3 (0.54%)	175 (31.36%)	347 (62.19%)	24 (4.30%)	9 (1.61%)
Years of learning English	<6	6–8	9–11	12–14	>14
	12 (2.25%)	243 (45.59%)	201 (37.71%)	72 (13.51%)	5 (0.94%)
English proficiency level	<109	109–119	120–129	130–139	>139
	58 (10.64%)	82 (15.05%)	168 (30.83%)	220 (40.37%)	17 (3.12%)

Table 4.3 Distribution of participants from five universities for Study 2 (N = 584)

University	Type of university	Number of participants	Percentage of participants (%)
U1	Arts-oriented	120	20.55
U2	Science-oriented	74	12.67
U3	Science-oriented	166	28.42
U4	Comprehensive	166	28.42
U5	Comprehensive	58	9.93
	Total	584	100

Table 4.4 Descriptive information of participants for Study 2 (N = 584)

	Number and percentage of distribution of participants				
Age	<17	17–18	19–20	21–22	>22
	6 (1.09%)	170 (30.85%)	342 (62.07%)	23 (4.17%)	10 (1.81%)
Years of learning English	<6	6–8	9–11	12–14	>14
	11 (2.09%)	242 (46.01%)	198 (37.64%)	70 (13.31%)	5 (0.95%)
English proficiency level	<109	109–119	120–129	130–139	>139
	58 (10.80%)	81 (15.08%)	166 (30.91%)	216 (40.22%)	16 (2.98%)

4.3 Research Instruments

Two research instruments were used in this study: the ReTSUQ and the CET-4 Reading subtest. In this section, a description of the two instruments is provided first, followed by an explanation of how the instruments were developed and validated.

Reading Test Strategy Use Questionnaire (ReTSUQ). Based on the theory of metacognition (Paris & Winograd, 1990; Wenden, 1998), Cohen and Upton's (2006) framework, and Pressley and Afflerbach's (1995) constructively responsive reading model, the ReTSUQ was used to measure Chinese college test takers' strategy use on the reading comprehension test. There are 38 items in the final version of the questionnaire, which measure seven subscales: planning (PLA), evaluating (EVA), monitoring (MON), general progression (GEN), identifying important information (IDE), integrating (INT), and inference-making (INF) strategies (see Table 4.8). Strategy use items on the questionnaire were selected from the literature on learning strategies (e.g., O'Malley & Chamot, 1990; Oxford, 1990; Purpura, 1999), reading strategies (e.g., Carrell, 1989b; Mokhtari & Reichard, 2002; Phakiti, 2003, 2008; Pressley & Afflerbach, 1995; Sheorey & Mokhtari, 2001), and test-taking studies (e.g., Anderson, 1991; Anderson, Bachman, Perkins, & Cohen, 1991; Cohen & Upton, 2006). The questionnaire uses a six-point Likert scale: 0 (never), 1 (rarely), 2 (sometimes), 3 (often), 4 (usually), and 5 (always). Appendix B displays the 38-item questionnaire.

The CET-4 Reading subtest. A commercially published version of the CET-4 Reading subtest (Fang, 2010) was used in this study to measure test takers' reading test performance. It has four sections: Skimming and Scanning (10 items), banked cloze (10 items), Reading in Depth (10 items), and cloze (20 items). SKSN assesses students' ability to understand the main ideas and acquire particular information through fast reading (National College English Testing Committee, 2006). In this part, students are required to read one or two long passages with around 1000 words followed by ten questions in the form of MCQs, sentence completion, or true or false questions. BCLZ is designed to assess students' ability to use English words in actual contexts. In this part, students are required to read one passage with around 200 words and then choose one word for each of the ten MCQ cloze questions from a bank of fifteen words. RID is used to evaluate students' ability to understand main ideas, important facts and make inferences about the meanings of some specific words from the context. Students are asked to read two passages, each with around 300 words, and then answer ten MCQs. In the MCLZ section, students need to read one passage of around 250 words and answer 20 MCQ cloze questions. According to the test specifications, participants are required to complete the test within 55 min.

The following section describes the development and validation of the two research instruments employed in Study 1 and Study 2: the ReTSUQ and the CET-4 Reading subtest. First, descriptive statistics were calculated for the ReTSUQ, and then EFA and CFA were conducted. Based on the results of CFA, composite variables were formed for further use in the SEM analyses. Similarly, descriptive statistics of the CET-4 Reading subtest were calculated. To conduct EFA with the dichotomous test data, the matrix of tetrachoric correlation was generated with PRELIS 2 and imported to SPSS. On the basis of the EFA results, CFA was conducted and the measurement model of the test was hypothesized and tested.

4.3.1 Development and Validation of the ReTSUQ

Based on Pressley and Afflerbach's (1995) constructively responsive reading model, the theory of metacognition (Paris & Winograd, 1990; Wenden, 1998), Bachman and Palmer's (2010) language use model, Cohen and Upton's (2006) framework, and empirical studies on learning strategies (e.g., O'Malley & Chamot, 1990; Oxford, 1990; Purpura, 1999), reading strategies (e.g., Carrell, 1989a; Mokhtari & Reichard, 2002; Sheorey & Mokhtari, 2001; Phakiti, 2003, 2008), and test-taking strategies (e.g., Anderson, 1991; Anderson et al., 1991; Cohen& Upton, 2006), the ReTSUQ with 58 items was developed initially. These items were grouped conceptually into eight subscales of planning strategies, evaluating strategies, monitoring strategies, general progression strategies, strategies for identifying important information, inference-making strategies, integrating strategies, and interpreting strategies. Planning, evaluating, and monitoring strategies fall into the category of metacognitive strategy use, whereas general progression strategies, strategies for identifying important information, inference-making strategies, integrating strategies, and interpreting strategies belong to cognitive strategy use. Based on Cohen and Upton (2006), two categories in each of the three subscales of metacognitive strategies were included: reading management strategies (RMS) and test management strategies (TMS). The former are strategies managing the reading comprehension process while the latter refer to the strategies directing the test-taking process. Table 4.5 shows the categories and number of items in the strategy use questionnaire.

The next part illustrates each category of strategies with example items from the ReTSUQ.

(a) **Planning strategies (PLA)** help test takers achieve their pre-established goals. For example, before completing reading tasks, test takers identify and assess the characteristics of reading tasks and formulate their plans. They adapt their reading activities to their plans and test demands (Cohen & Upton, 2006; Jacobs & Paris, 1987; Wenden, 1998).
Example items:
RMS: I have a purpose as to what to read and in what order.
TMS: I know what to do if my plan does not work out while completing this reading test.

Table 4.5 Categories and numbers of items in the ReTSUQ

Strategy type	Strategy categories		Number of items
Metacognitive strategies (META)	Planning (PLA)	Reading management strategies (RMS)	3
		Test management strategies (TMS)	4
	Evaluating (EVA)	Reading management strategies (RMS)	3
		Test management strategies (TMS)	5
	Monitoring (MON)	Reading management strategies (RMS)	5
		Test management strategies (TMS)	5
Cognitive strategies (COG)	General progression (GEN)		4
	Identifying important information (IDE)		9
	Integrating (INT)		6
	Inference-making (INF)		8
	Interpreting (INTER)		6
	Total		58

(b) **Evaluating strategies (EVA)** refer to the cognitive processes that test takers apply to assess tasks and their own personal cognitive abilities (Paris & Winograd, 1990; Wenden, 1998). Influenced by time pressure (and the high-stakes nature) of tests, test takers constantly assess their test-taking and reading comprehension processes and judge the degree of accuracy to which they are completing the test tasks (Cohen & Upton, 2006).
Example items:
RMS: I know when I understand something and when I do not.
TMS: I check my own performance and progress as I complete the test.

(c) **Monitoring strategies (MON)** refer to test takers' checking and regulating their own thoughts and performance while performing cognitive activities. Test takers engage in monitoring activities which rest upon their evaluations and modify their reading and test-taking plans as well as strategies (Cohen & Upton, 2006; Jacobs & Paris, 1987; Wenden, 1998).
Example items:
RMS: When the text becomes difficult, I reread the problematic part to increase my understanding.
TMS: I budget my time wisely on the test.

(d) **Strategies for general progression (GEN)** refer to the strategies used by readers in the general progression of the text from the beginning to the end which often comes after "before-reading overviewing" (Pressley & Afflerbach, 1995, p. 37).

Example item:

I preview the text first by noting its characteristics like length and structure.

(e) **Strategies for identifying important information (IDE)** are those strategies employed by readers to refine their understanding of the text constantly when the new input is not consistent with their initial hypotheses (Afflerbach, 1990; Pressley & Afflerbach, 1995).

Example item:

I preview key sentences to understand the text better.

(f) **Inference-making strategies (INF)** refer to readers' ability to "go beyond the information given in the text" (Pressley & Afflerbach, 1995, p. 46) in order to "fill in meaning gaps in text" (p. 49).

Example item:

I try to make inference of the meanings of new words from context clues.

(g) **Integrating strategies (INT)** are applied when readers manipulate the text to fit the information across the text based on their understanding of the text as well as their prior knowledge and experience of the world (see Kintsch and van Dijk, 1978).

Example item:

I try to use my prior knowledge to help my understanding.

(h) **Interpreting strategies (INTER)** concern those strategies used in the interpretive processes in reading which involve making text more concrete (e.g., the instantiation of schemata and generalization of the visual images) (Wade, Trathen, & Schraw, 1990).

Example item:

I try to visualize information to help my understanding.

In conclusion, it was postulated that the eight types of strategies substantiate test takers' metacognitive awareness in reading comprehension tests. In the following part of the study, a strategy use questionnaire was developed based on the hypothesis. As such, the results of the statistical analysis will provide the testing of the hypothesis.

4.3.1.1 Piloting the ReTSUQ

Initially, the 58-item questionnaire was piloted with a group of 78 students to identify ambiguous or confusing items with regard to wording, format, and content. Among these participants, 66 (84.6%) were male and 12 (15.4%) were female students. They were between the ages of 18 and 24 ($M = 19.89$; SD = 1.00) and had received formal English instructions for an average of 8.98 years (SD = 2.04). Accordingly, two items were deleted and problematic items were reworded, leaving an inventory of 56 items tapping into eight postulated subscales. The questionnaire used a six-point Likert scale: 0 (never), 1 (rarely), 2 (sometimes), 3 (often), 4 (usually), and 5 (always) to avoid the "undecided" categories (Dörnyei, 2007, p. 28).

4.3.1.2   Administrating the ReTSUQ

The 56-item questionnaire was then administered to a sample of 650 college students to validate and analyze it further. As second-year college students, these participants, who were between the ages of 18 and 24 ($M = 20.58$; SD $= 1.21$), had taken the CET-4 at the end of their first academic year at universities. Their average English score on the NTME was 121.34 (SD $= 27.36$) and their average CET-4 score was 514.91 (SD $= 70.28$). In addition, they had received formal English instruction for an average of 9.86 years (SD $= 2.26$) by the time of the data collection. Of these respondents, 264 (40.6%) were male and 348 (53.5%) were female students with 38 (5.8%) students not providing their gender information.

Next, a series of statistical analyses was conducted for the purpose of investigating the clustering of the items and validating the instrument.

4.3.1.3   Descriptive Statistics of the ReTSUQ

Descriptive statistics for all the 56 items are presented in Table 4.6. The means varied from 2.36 to 3.96 while the standard deviation ranged from 1.00 to 1.49. The values of skewness and kurtosis were all within the accepted range of ±3, which indicated that the questionnaire items were normally distributed (Bachman, 2004).

4.3.1.4   EFA for the ReTSUQ

EFA was performed on the 56-item ReTSUQ to investigate the factor structure and the clustering of the items of the questionnaire through the computer software program, IBM SPSS Statistics Version 20. First, a principal component analysis (PCA) was conducted on the 56 items of the ReTSUQ to decide the appropriate number of factors that could be extracted. Table 4.7 presents the results of the unrotated PCA.

According to the commonly used criterion that the eigenvalue should be greater than one, 15 factors were extracted from the analysis as shown in Table 4.7. However, since the 15-factor solution was too excessive, the scree plot was examined further (Cattell, 1966). In addition, the differences between two succeeding factors were also considered in deciding the number of factors retained for following EFA analyses. Finally, the examination suggested that six, seven, or eight factors could be retained in the subsequent analysis due to reasons of parsimony and meaningful interpretation.

Next, principal factor analysis and promax rotation method were employed to conduct the following analysis because they appeared to have maximized

Table 4.6 Descriptive statistics for the ReTSUQ ($N = 650$)

	Mean	SD	Skewness	Kurtosis
PLA_RMS1	3.00	1.29	−0.29	−0.61
PLA_RMS2	3.14	1.08	−0.30	−0.21
PLA_TMS3	2.40	1.44	0.07	−0.87
PLA_TMS4	2.99	1.22	−0.12	−0.70
PLA_TMS5	3.20	1.30	−0.48	−0.40
EVA_RMS6	2.61	1.32	−0.12	−0.65
EVA_RMS7	3.50	1.08	−0.36	−0.48
EVA_RMS8	3.74	1.05	−0.55	−0.35
EVA_TMS9	2.36	1.30	0.07	−0.76
EVA_TMS10	2.98	1.24	−0.40	−0.32
EVA_TMS11	3.32	1.14	−0.34	−0.39
EVA_TMS12	3.68	1.24	−0.88	0.30
EVA_TMS13	3.13	1.21	−0.34	−0.45
MON_RMS14	3.77	1.12	−0.77	0.11
MON_RMS15	2.51	1.34	−0.09	−0.82
MON_RMS16	3.58	1.11	−0.61	−0.20
MON_RMS17	3.48	1.08	−0.55	0.07
MON_RMS18	3.88	1.00	−0.57	−0.47
MON_TMS19	3.46	1.17	−0.44	−0.36
MON_TMS20	3.21	1.17	−0.37	−0.45
MON_TMS21	3.58	1.07	−0.59	−0.02
MON_TMS22	2.94	1.12	−0.33	−0.21
MON_TMS23	3.70	1.12	−0.65	−0.04
GEN24	3.00	1.49	−0.33	−0.96
GEN25	2.67	1.39	−0.02	−0.91
GEN26	3.50	1.37	−0.70	−0.29
GEN27	2.91	1.26	−0.20	−0.59
IDE28	3.47	1.07	−0.47	−0.09
IDE29	3.08	1.22	−0.24	−0.60
IDE30	2.58	1.30	−0.04	−0.79
IDE31	3.14	1.21	−0.33	−0.50
IDE32	3.21	1.19	−0.40	−0.42
IDE33	3.54	1.14	−0.60	−0.08
IDE34	3.08	1.21	−0.26	−0.50
IDE35	3.40	1.16	−0.45	−0.49
IDE36	3.42	1.33	−0.55	−0.48
INF37	3.48	1.28	−0.60	−0.40
INF38	3.72	1.02	−0.62	0.07
INF39	3.70	1.05	−0.62	0.01
INF40	3.72	1.00	−0.58	0.06

(continued)

Table 4.6 (continued)

	Mean	SD	Skewness	Kurtosis
INF41	2.81	1.27	−0.30	−0.58
INF42	2.66	1.28	−0.12	−0.70
INT43	3.39	1.16	−0.38	−0.33
INT44	3.48	1.11	−0.44	−0.41
INT45	2.99	1.14	−0.23	−0.45
INT46	3.17	1.25	−0.40	−0.44
INT47	2.95	1.26	−0.32	−0.44
INT48	2.90	1.21	−0.21	−0.52
INT49	3.56	1.16	−0.72	0.30
INT50	3.60	1.10	−0.56	−0.20
INTER51	2.42	1.48	0.08	−0.99
INTER52	3.96	1.15	−1.05	0.63
INTER53	2.65	1.43	−0.13	−0.96
INTER54	3.08	1.19	−0.37	−0.35
INTER55	2.99	1.25	−0.39	−0.31
INTER56	2.99	1.32	−0.36	−0.52

PLA_RMS planning (reading management strategies), *PLA_TMS* planning (test management strategies), *EVA_RMS* evaluating (reading management strategies), *EVA_TMS* evaluating (test management strategies), *MON_RMS* monitoring (reading management strategies), *MON_TMS* monitoring (test management strategies), *GEN* strategies for general progression, *IDE* strategies for identifying important information, *INF* making inference strategies, *INT* integrating strategies, *INTER* interpreting strategies

interpretation of the data for this study. To compare the results and ensure a maximum interpretation of the data, six-, seven-, and eight-factor solutions were tested. A seven-factor promax rotation seemed apparent in the analysis. The factor extraction yielded seven factors with eigenvalues greater than 1.0, accounting for 45.26% of the total variance of test takers' strategy use. The seven-factor solution was then examined for unsatisfactory items. It was decided then that items with high loadings on more than one factor and those that did not load saliently on any of the factors were deleted out of consideration for simplicity in structure. The degree of each item's contribution to or detraction from the reliability of the factor was also examined. Factor loadings greater than 0.30 were reported.

After iterative processes, 18 items were deleted, which led to a remaining total of 38 items measuring seven subscales, i.e., planning strategies (PLA), evaluating strategies (EVA), monitoring strategies (MON), general progression strategies (GEN), strategies for identifying important information (IDE), integrating strategies (INT), and inference-making (INF) strategies. For the sake of clarity, the questionnaire items were reordered after EFA analyses. The pattern matrix of EFA analyses on the ReTSUQ is shown in Appendix D. The subscales and the reliability estimates of the questionnaire are presented in Table 4.8. The subscales provided

Table 4.7 Results of unrotated principal component analysis

Factors extracted	Eigenvalues	Differences in eigenvalues	% of variance	Cumulative % of variance
1	9.83	5.81	17.55	17.55
2	4.02	1.91	7.18	24.72
3	2.11	0.19	3.77	28.49
4	1.92	0.25	3.43	31.92
5	1.67	0.09	2.98	34.90
6	1.58	0.11	2.82	37.72
7	1.47	0.09	2.62	40.33
8	1.37	0.08	2.45	42.79
9	1.29	0.06	2.30	45.09
10	1.23	0.05	2.19	47.28
11	1.18	0.08	2.11	49.39
12	1.10	0.01	1.96	51.36
13	1.09	0.05	1.95	53.30
14	1.04	0.01	1.86	55.16
15	1.03	–	1.84	57.00

Extraction method: principal component analysis

the basis for the formation of the composite variables used in subsequent analyses of Study 1 and Study 2. As shown in Table 4.8, the reliability estimates of the subscales ranged from 0.49 to 0.84. The reliability estimates for GEN and IDE were low at 0.49 and 0.56, respectively. It is possible that the statistical results based on these two subscales might be affected in terms of its rigorousness and accuracy. As a limitation to the present study, it could be addressed in future relevant studies with different samples. In addition, the overall reliability estimate is 0.89, indicating the overall reliability of the ReTSUQ as a tool for the measure of strategy use.

4.3.1.5 CFA for the ReTSUQ

To confirm the factorial structure of the ReTSUQ, the item-level CFA was conducted on the 38-item questionnaire with the 593 participants. Based on the results of the previous EFA at the item level of the ReTSUQ, a seven-factor model of PLA, EVA, MON, GEN, IDE, INT, and INF was hypothesized. The seven factors were hypothesized to covary with each other.

Model fit indices. CFA/SEM model fit indices were used to investigate the fit of the proposed CFA/SEM model. According to Byrne (2006) and Kline (2011), these model fit indices can be classified into four general types: incremental or comparative fit indices, absolute fit indices, residual-based fit indices, and predictive fit indices.

Table 4.8 Subscales and reliability estimates of the ReTSUQ

	PLA	EVA	MON	GEN	IDE	INT	INF	Total
Number of items used	6	8	10	3	4	4	3	38
Items used	1, 2, 3, 4, 5, 6	7, 8, 9, 10, 11, 12, 13, 14	15, 16, 17, 18, 19, 20, 21, 22, 23, 24	25, 26, 27	28,29, 30, 31	32,33, 34, 35	36, 37, 38	
Reliability (Cronbach's α)	0.62	0.87	0.79	0.49	0.56	0.70	0.67	0.89

PLA planning, *EVA* evaluating, *MON* monitoring, *GEN* general progression, *IDE* identifying important information, *INT* integrating, *INF* inference-making

First, incremental or comparative fit indices measure the relative improvement in fit of the hypothesized model in comparison with the null model (Hu & Bentler, 1999). Examples include the Comparative Fit Index (CFI), the normed fit index (NFI), and the Tucker–Lewis index (TLI) or the non-normed fit index (NNFI). Second, the absolute fit indices assess the proportion of variance explained by the hypothesized model in the sample variance/covariance matrix (In'nami & Koizumi, 2011), such as the goodness-of-fit index (GFI). Third, residual-based fit indices evaluate the differences between observed and predicted variance and covariance of the hypothesized model. The standardized root-mean-square residual (SRMR) and the root-mean-square error of approximation (RMSEA) belong to this kind of indices. Fourth, the predictive fit indices measure the probability of the model "to fit in similar-sized samples from the same population" (In'nami & Koizumi, 2011, p. 252), which is used to select the best-fitting model among competing models. The Akaike Information Criterion (AIC), the Consistent Akaike Information Criterion (CAIC), and the Expected Cross-Validation Index (ECVI) are examples of this type of fit indices.

Multiple fit indices were calculated in this study to investigate the fit of the tested models in this study. The chi-square (χ^2) index should be non-significant ideally because it is the comparison between the implied covariance matrix and the produced one. A non-significant chi-square (χ^2) index indicates that the proposed model fits the sample data. Since the chi-square (χ^2) index is sensitive to sample size, researchers developed the normed chi-square (NC) index (χ^2/df) (Kline, 2011) and an NC value of less than three is considered to indicate a well-fitting model. The CFI should be equal to or greater than 0.90 for a reasonably good model fit (Hu & Bentler, 1999). In addition, absolute fit indices were calculated. The RMSEA shows how well a model fits the population and should be less than 0.08 to indicate reasonable error of approximation (Browne & Cudeck, 1993). A narrow RMSEA 90% confidence interval (CI) is indicative of better model fit. The SRMR evaluates the differences between observed and predicted variance and covariance. Values below 0.10 indicate good model fit (Kline, 2011). Lower values of AIC and CAIC indicate good model fit. IBM SPSS AMOS computer program Version 20.0 (Arbuckle, 2011) was employed to perform CFA. As the most widely used type of estimation method (Anderson & Gerbing, 1988; Bollen, 1989; Kelloway, 1998), maximum likelihood was used in the CFA analyses in this study.

Table 4.9 shows the fit indices for the tested CFA model. The values of the fit indices indicated that this model fits the data well. As shown in Table 4.9, the ratio of χ^2 to df is 1.70, which is less than 3.0; the incremental indices TLI and CFI are at least 0.90; the absolute indices RMSEA and SRMR are 0.034 and 0.047, which are both less than 0.05, indicating good model fit (Byrne, 2011). Although the value of χ^2 is significant, it is sensitive to a large sample size (Kline, 2011). Therefore, the results of CFA provided confirmative evidence for the previous EFA analyses about the clustering of the questionnaire items. This also answers the first research question in this study with regards to the trait structure of Chinese college test takers' strategy use on the CET-4 Reading subtest as measured by the ReTSUQ which will be discussed in more detail in the coming section.

4.3.2 Validation of the Reading Test

To investigate the factorial structure of the test and validate it as a measure of students' reading comprehension ability, a series of EFA and CFA were performed on the 50-item reading test. For the purpose of cross-validation, the data set ($N = 593$) was split randomly into two parts (i.e., $N = 296$ and $N = 297$) (Bollen, 1989). Item-level EFAs were conducted with the first sample (i.e., $N = 296$). Based on the results of EFA, the measurement model was configured and tested by CFA with the other half of the data set (i.e., $N = 297$). The results of these analyses were used in the subsequent SEM analyses.

4.3.2.1 Descriptive Statistics of the CET-4 Reading Subtest

In this part, item-level data of the CET-4 Reading subtest were analyzed. First, the descriptive statistics of the 50-item reading comprehension test were calculated. These results are shown in Table 4.10. The means ranged from 0.27 to 0.87 and the standard deviation ranged from 0.34 to 0.52. The values of skewness and kurtosis were all within the accepted range of ±3, which indicated that the test items were normally distributed (Bachman, 2004).

Table 4.9 Fit indices for CFA model to confirm the factor structure of the ReTSUQ

χ^2	df	χ^2/df	TLI	CFI	RMSEA	RMSEA 90% CI	SRMR
1000.64*	590	1.70	0.90	0.91	0.034	0.031–0.038	0.047

TLI Tucker–Lewis index, *CFI* Comparative Fit Index, *RMSEA* root-mean-square error of approximation, *RMSEA 90% CI* RMSEA 90% confidence interval, *SRMR* standardized root mean residual
*p < 0.05

4.3.2.2   Exploratory Factor Analysis for the CET-4 Reading Subtest

For the purpose of EFA, a matrix of tetrachoric correlation using all 50 items was generated in PRELIS 2 and exported into IBM SPSS Statistics Version 20 for further analysis. Then, a series of EFAs was performed on each section of the test. First, PCA was employed to extract the initial factors. According to Tabachnick and Fidell (2013), the number of factors to retain was based on the evaluation of the scree plot, the eigenvalues, and the interpretability. Based on the initial principal components extracted, different models were tested with appropriate extraction and rotation methods aiming for the maximum and most meaningful interpretation of the data. One-, two-, and three-factor models for each section were tested. The results showed that a two-factor model was most interpretable and meaningful for each section both statistically and substantively.

For the SKSN section, the PCA and oblimin procedures yielded two factors which accounted for 54.9% of the total variance. After examining the items in each section, some were termed "skimming items" (Items 1, 3, 4, 5, 6, 7), and others were termed "scanning items" (Items 2, 8, 9, 10). Table 4.11 presents the pattern matrix and factor correlation matrix of the section of SKSN on the reading test.

Similarly, with PCA and promax procedures, two factors emerged in BCLZ which accounted for 52.7% of the variance. Table 4.12 displays the pattern matrix and factor correlation matrix of the section of BCLZ on the CET-4 Reading subtest. As shown in Table 4.12, although Items 11 and 16 had loadings greater than 0.30 on Factor 2, they loaded more strongly onto Factor 1. After examining the two items further in terms of the reading skills they measure, they were assigned to the group of items clustered on Factor 1. Similarly, Items 18 and 19 were assigned to the group loading on Factor 2.

It is argued that cloze tests involve skills including grammar, vocabulary, and reading comprehension which are interrelated to some degree in all items (Hale et al., 1988). In other words, some items require test takers' sensitivity to "long-range textual constraints" (Hale et al., 1988, p. 10) while other items may only need their attention to "short-range constraints" of semantics and syntax (p. 11). Based on this and studying the items, Factor 1 was named "short-range constraints items" (items 11, 14, 15, 16 and 20) and Factor 2 was named "long-range constraints items" (items 12, 13, 17, 18 and 19).

With principal axis factoring and promax rotation procedures, EFA on the ten items in the RID section yielded two eigenvalues greater than 1.0, accounting for

Table 4.10 Descriptive statistics of the CET-4 Reading subtest ($N = 593$)

	Item	Mean	SD	Skewness	Kurtosis	Reliability (Cronbach's α)
	Item1	0.81	0.39	−1.59	0.54	
	Item2	0.55	0.50	−0.22	−1.96	
	Item3	0.58	0.49	−0.32	−1.91	
	Item4	0.83	0.38	−1.77	1.15	
SKSN	Item5	0.83	0.37	−1.79	1.21	0.69
	Item6	0.87	0.34	−2.23	2.99	
	Item7	0.80	0.40	−1.53	0.33	
	Item8	0.60	0.49	−0.40	−1.85	
	Item9	0.59	0.49	−0.35	−1.88	
	Item10	0.76	0.43	−1.20	−0.56	
	Item11	0.59	0.49	−0.38	−1.86	
	Item12	0.76	0.43	−1.21	−0.53	
	Item13	0.42	0.49	0.34	−1.89	
	Item14	0.37	0.48	0.52	−1.74	
	Item15	0.64	0.48	−0.60	−1.65	
BCLZ	Item16	0.48	0.50	0.07	−2.00	0.74
	Item17	0.50	0.50	0.01	−2.01	
	Item18	0.56	0.50	−0.25	−1.95	
	Item19	0.55	0.50	−0.21	−1.96	
	Item20	0.64	0.48	−0.59	−1.66	
	Item21	0.29	0.46	0.91	−1.18	
	Item22	0.77	0.42	−1.26	−0.42	
	Item23	0.75	0.44	−1.14	−.70	
	Item24	0.81	0.39	−1.61	0.59	
	Item25	0.67	0.47	−0.75	−1.45	
RID	Item26	0.72	0.45	−0.96	−1.07	0.54
	Item27	0.76	0.43	−1.24	−0.48	
	Item28	0.29	0.45	0.94	−1.13	
	Item29	0.73	0.45	−1.01	−0.98	
	Item30	0.66	0.47	−0.69	−1.53	
	Item31	0.69	0.46	−0.81	−1.36	
	Item32	0.47	0.50	0.13	−1.99	
	Item33	0.55	0.50	−0.20	−1.97	
	Item34	0.56	0.52	0.28	1.25	
	Item35	0.60	0.49	−0.41	−1.84	
	Item36	0.66	0.44	−0.68	−1.54	
	Item37	0.48	0.50	0.10	−2.00	

(continued)

Table 4.10 (continued)

	Item	Mean	SD	Skewness	Kurtosis	Reliability (Cronbach's α)
MCLZ	Item38	0.51	0.50	−0.05	−2.00	
	Item39	0.61	0.49	−0.45	−1.80	
	Item40	0.58	0.49	−0.31	−1.91	
	Item41	0.55	0.50	−0.22	−1.96	0.88
	Item42	0.27	0.45	1.02	−0.96	
	Item43	0.48	0.50	0.07	−2.00	
	Item44	0.59	0.49	−0.36	−1.88	
	Item45	0.72	0.45	−1.00	−1.00	
	Item46	0.50	0.50	0.02	−2.01	
	Item47	0.69	0.47	−0.80	−1.36	
	Item48	0.65	0.48	−0.64	−1.60	
	Item49	0.59	0.49	−0.35	−1.88	
	Item50	0.34	0.47	0.70	−1.50	
Total						0.90

Table 4.11 Pattern matrix and factor correlation matrix of section SKSN on the CET-4 Reading subtest

	Factor 1	Factor 2
Item_1	**0.69**	−0.08
Item_3	**0.51**	−0.09
Item_4	**0.74**	0.14
Item_5	**0.74**	0.11
Item_6	**0.81**	0.03
Item_7	**0.63**	0.10
Item_2	0.02	**0.52**
Item_8	−0.10	**0.87**
Item_9	0.13	**0.80**
Item_10	0.03	**0.83**
Factor 1	1.00	
Factor 2	0.40	1.00

29.5% of the variance. The two-factor solution produced two factors—"reading for explicit meaning" (Items 21, 23, 25, 26, 27, 29, 30) and "reading for implicit meaning" (Items 22, 24, 28) (Grabe, 1997; Kintsch, 1998). The small variance accounted for by the two factors emerging from the EFA on the ten items in the RID section suggests that the test design for this section might need to be improved. This could be further tested in a relevant study with different samples. Table 4.13 presents the pattern matrix and factor correlation matrix of this section.

Finally, with PCA and promax rotation procedures, EFA on the 20 items in the MCLZ section generated two eigenvalues greater than 1.0 which explained 51.7%

Table 4.12 Pattern matrix and factor correlation matrix of section BCLZ on the CET-4 Reading subtest

	Factor 1	Factor 2
Item_11	**0.46**	0.35
Item_14	**0.67**	0.13
Item_15	**0.70**	−0.14
Item_16	**0.36**	0.32
Item_20	**0.89**	−0.08
Item_12	0.28	**0.63**
Item_13	−0.45	**0.99**
Item_17	0.19	**0.59**
Item_18	0.31	**0.42**
Item_19	0.30	**0.48**
Factor 1	1.00	
Factor 2	0.51	1.00

Table 4.13 Pattern matrix and factor correlation matrix of section RID on the CET-4 Reading subtest

	Factor 1	Factor 2
Item_21	**0.34**	−0.22
Item_23	**0.38**	−0.13
Item_25	**0.52**	0.04
Item_26	**0.46**	0.01
Item_27	**0.58**	0.10
Item_29	**0.56**	0.14
Item_30	**0.71**	−0.12
Item_22	−0.02	**0.87**
Item_24	0.05	**0.40**
Item_28	0.18	**−0.32**
Factor 1	1.00	
Factor 2	0.55	1.00

of the total variance. As what was discussed previously for the BCLZ section, cloze tests involve skills including grammar, vocabulary, and reading comprehension which are interrelated to some degree in all items (Hale et al., 1988). Some items require test takers' sensitivity to "long-range textual constraints" (p. 10), while other items may only need their attention to "short-range constraints" of semantics and syntax (p. 11). Based on this and studying the items, one factor was named "short-range constraints" (Items 31, 32, 35, 36, 37, 38, 39, 40, 41, 42, 43, 44, 45, 46, 47, 48, 49) and the other factor was named "long-range constraints" (Items 33, 34, and 50). The pattern matrix and factor correlation matrix of this section are shown in Table 4.14.

In the following section, CFA was conducted on the CET-4 Reading subtest to confirm the underlying factors of the test on the basis of the results of EFA.

Table 4.14 Pattern matrix and factor correlation matrix of section MCLZ on the CET-4 Reading subtest

	Factor 1	Factor 2
Item_31	**0.37**	0.27
Item_32	**0.38**	0.34
Item_35	**0.57**	0.10
Item_36	**0.87**	0.01
Item_37	**0.66**	−0.13
Item_38	**0.72**	−0.15
Item_39	**0.69**	0.20
Item_40	**0.50**	0.24
Item_41	**0.59**	0.12
Item_42	**0.62**	−0.60
Item_43	**0.48**	0.32
Item_44	**0.81**	−0.15
Item_45	**0.80**	0.11
Item_46	**0.64**	−0.06
Item_47	**0.84**	0.03
Item_48	**0.54**	0.40
Item_49	**0.62**	0.20
Item_33	0.28	**0.49**
Item_34	0.32	**0.48**
Item_50	−0.31	**0.96**
Factor 1	1.00	
Factor 2	0.56	1.00

4.3.2.3 CFA for the CET-4 Reading Subtest

Based on the results of the EFA, CFA was performed on the CET-4 Reading subtest with 297 participants (i.e., the other half of the 593 participants). As discussed earlier, it was hypothesized that there are two underlying factors as measured by the reading comprehension test: LEX_GR and TxtCOM. It was, therefore, further hypothesized that "skimming items" (SK), "scanning items" (SN), "reading for explicit meaning" (EM), and "reading for implicit meaning" (i.e., the extracted factors from SKSN and RID sections) load on TxtCOM, while "short-range constraints items" (SR1 and SR2) and "long-range constraints items" (LR1 and LR2) (i.e., the extracted factors from BCLZ and MCLZ sections). This hypothesized model (i.e., Model 1) was tested with 297 participants. The fit indices of the tested model are shown in Table 4.15.

However, as shown in Table 4.15, the fit indices for Model 1 are not satisfactory in that CFI is 0.89, TLI is 0.84, RMSEA is 0.10, and SRMR is 0.065, indicating that Model 1 may not be the most appropriate model which reflects the factor structure of the CET-4 Reading subtest.

To identify the model which interprets the data best, Model 2 was hypothesized on the basis of the test design. According to the National College English Testing

Table 4.15 Fit indices for Model 1 to confirm the factor structure of the CET-4 Reading subtest

	χ^2	df	χ^2/df	TLI	CFI	RMSEA	RMSEA 90% CI	SRMR
Model 1	79.440*	19	4.181	0.84	0.89	0.11	0.081–0.128	0.065

TLI Tucker–Lewis index, *CFI* Comparative Fit Index, *RMSEA* root-mean-square error of approximation, *RMSEA 90% CI* RMSEA 90% confidence interval, *SRMR* standardized root mean residual

* $p < 0.05$

Committee (2006), students' reading ability is measured in four sections in the CET-4 Reading subtest: RID, BCLZ, SKSN, and MCLZ. It was hypothesized that SKSN and RID load on TxtCOM while BCLZ and MCLZ load on LEX_GR. The hypothesized model was tested with 297 participants. The fit indices of the test model are shown in Table 4.16. Although χ^2/df is slightly more than 3, other indices indicate good model fit. The values of incremental fit indices TLI and CFI are above 0.95. The value of absolute fit index RMSEA is 0.084, which is less than 0.10 (Kline, 2011), while the value of SRMR is 0.020, smaller than 0.050 (Byrne, 2011). Given the good model fit indices, the model of the CET-4 Reading subtest is used in the following Study 1 and Study 2 as the measurement model of the test.

Table 4.17 presents the four composite variables used in the following analyses and the reliability estimates of the test. As shown in Table 4.17, the reliability estimates of the subsections of the test range from 0.57 to 0.88 The low-reliability estimate of the RID section (i.e., Cronbach's $\alpha = 0.57$) might affect the results of the study to some degree, which is a limitation of this study. However, the general reliability estimate is 0.90 indicating that overall, the test is reliable as a measure of students' reading ability.

4.4 Data Collection and Scoring

This section describes the procedures for data collection and scoring.

4.4.1 Administration of Research Instruments

Before the administration of the questionnaire and the CET-4 Reading subtest, the purpose of the study was explained to the participants either by the researcher or the research assistants who had been trained before the study. To ensure that the participants understood the questionnaire and purpose of the study appropriately, the questionnaire, the letter of information, and the consent form were not only provided in English, but were also translated into Chinese. Both the English and

Table 4.16 Fit indices for Model 2 to confirm the factor structure of the CET-4 Reading subtest

χ^2	df	χ^2/df	TLI	CFI	RMSEA	RMSEA 90% CI	SRMR
6.159*	2	3.079	0.96	0.99	0.084	0.010–0.163	0.020

* $p < 0.05$

Table 4.17 Subsections of the CET-4 Reading subtest with reliability estimates

	SKSN	BCLZ	RID	MCLZ	Total
No. of items	10	10	9	19	48
Items used	1, 2, 3, 4, 5, 6, 7, 8, 9, 10	11, 12, 13, 14, 15, 16, 17, 18, 19, 20	21 22, 23, 24, 25, 26, 27, 29, 30	31, 32, 33, 34, 35, 36, 37, 38, 39, 40, 41, 43, 44, 45, 46, 47, 48, 49, 50	
Reliability (Cronbach's α)	0.69	0.74	0.57	0.88	0.90

SKSN Skimming and Scanning, *RID* Reading in Depth, *BCLZ* banked cloze, *MCLZ* multiple-choice cloze

Chinese versions of the questionnaire, the letter of information, and the consent form are provided in Appendix A.

After the letters of information and consent forms were filled out by participants, the test and the questionnaire were administered to the participants. Participants were given 50 min to complete the 38-item strategy use questionnaire, and 55 min to write the CET-4 Reading subtest. However, since the version of the CET-4 Reading subtest administered was a retired test, it is possible that the participants may not have behaved exactly as they would have in the real CET-4 test conditions.

4.4.2   Data Scoring and Preparation

All test items were scored dichotomously with only one key to each question. All test papers were marked and double-checked to ensure all the items were scored accurately. In accordance with the Syllabus for College English Test (National College English Testing Committee, 2006), each correctly answered item in the sections of SKSN, BCLZ, RID, and MCLZ was assigned a score of 1, 0.5, 2, and 0.5 points, respectively. Thus, the total score of the CET-4 Reading subtest was 45 points and the full score for each section of SKSN, BCLZ, RID, and MCLZ was 10, 5, 20, and 10 points each.

Since this study is concerned with the relationships between test takers' strategy use and reading test performance which involves both the questionnaire and the test, an identification number was assigned to both the questionnaire and test for each participant. If the participant did not complete either of the instruments, the case was excluded from the study. Regarding the issue of treatment of the missing data, it was decided that if three or more questions were left unanswered in a particular section, the data were treated as missing (Purpura, 1999). Then, a listwise-deletion was used for cases that had missing values on any variables. Following these procedures, 38 cases were dropped from the sample of 631, which left a total of 593 cases to be used in the further analysis in Study 1. In Study 2, data from the nine students who failed to provide gender information were deleted, which left 584 cases in total for analyses.

All the data were keyed into the IBM SPSS Statistics Version 20 computer program for further analysis.

4.5   Statistical Analyses

After descriptive statistics were estimated, reliability analyses and EFA were conducted, and SEM and multi-group SEM analysis were carried out to investigate and provide answers to the proposed research questions.

4.5.1   Structural Equation Modeling (SEM)

Before SEM analysis was conducted, CFA was carried out first. Based on the results of previous EFA and extant literature, three models of strategy use and reading test performance (unitary, higher-order, and correlated) were hypothesized and tested. Before commencing the investigation of the relationships between the observed and latent variables in the structural models, CFA was conducted to examine the trait structure of the measurement models, i.e., the strategy use and the reading test models. After the measurement models were established, analyses were conducted further to examine the relationships in the structural models.

In SEM analyses, the relationships between latent and observed variables of the three strategy use and reading test performance models (see Figs. 3.1, 3.2, 3.3) were examined. The model which produced the best-fit indices would be chosen as the baseline model used in the subsequent multi-group SEM analyses.

4.5.2   Multi-group Structural Equation Modeling

Similarly, two steps were involved in the multi-group SEM analysis. First, on the basis of the results of the single-group SEM analysis and previous relevant litera- ture, multi-group SEM analysis was conducted on groups of participants of similar characteristics. For purposes of carrying out this analysis, the 593 participants were randomly split into two groups. Factor invariance across the two groups was tested to examine the generalizability of the factor structure and to cross-validate the findings in the previous single-group analyses.

Further, multi-group SEM analyses based on gender groups were conducted by dividing the participants into male and female groups. The baseline model derived from the single-group SEM analyses and previous literature on gender differences in strategy use and reading test performance provided a basis for this analysis. In this analysis, first, separate baseline models were established for each gender group and then estimated simultaneously with cross-group equality constraints released. The invariance of the factorial structure of the strategy use questionnaire, the reading comprehension test, and the relationships between them were examined.

4.5.3 Computer Software Programs Used

IBM SPSS Statistics Version 20 computer program was used for descriptive statistics, internal consistency reliability, and EFA. PRELIS 2 was used to generate the matrix of tetrachoric correlation of the 50 test items before EFAs were conducted. Further, the computer program, IBM SPSS AMOS Version 20.0 (Arbuckle, 2011) was employed to perform CFA and SEM. As the most widely used type of estimation method (Anderson & Gerbing, 1988; Bollen, 1989; Kelloway, 1998), maximum likelihood was used in the SEM analyses in this study.

In summary, this chapter gave an account of the research methodology used in this study. First, the participants in Study 1 and Study 2 were described in detail. The two major instruments (i.e., the ReTSUQ and the CET-4 Reading subtest) were then presented and introduced. The development and validation of the research instruments were also described. First, the process of developing the ReTSUQ was introduced in detail. Then, the EFA was performed to investigate the clustering of the questionnaire items. As a validating process, CFA was conducted to confirm and cross-validate the results of the EFA. Similarly, a series of EFAs was performed on each section of the CET-4 Reading subtest, which was followed by CFA to test the hypothesized model of the trait structure of the reading comprehension test. The results and findings of item-level analyses of the ReTSUQ and the CET-4 Reading subtest provided bases for further analyses in this study. In addition, a detailed introduction of data collection and scoring procedures was provided. The statistical analyses employed in the study were then discussed and presented.

References

Afflerbach, P. P. (1990). The influence of prior knowledge on expert readers' main idea construction strategies. *Reading Research Quarterly, 25*(1), 31–46.

Anderson, J. C., & Gerbing, D. W. (1988). Structural equation modeling in practice: A review and recommended two-step approach. *Psychological Bulletin, 103*(3), 411–423.

Anderson, N. J. (1991). Individual differences in strategy use in second language reading and testing. *Modern Language Journal, 75,* 460–472.

Anderson, N. J., Bachman, L., Perkins, K., & Cohen, A. (1991). An exploratory study into the construct validity of a reading comprehension test: Triangulation of data sources. *Language Testing, 8*(1), 41–66.

Arbuckle, J. L. (2011). *IBM SPSS Amos 20.0 [Computer Program].* New York: IBM.

Bachman, L. F. (2004). *Statistical analyses for language assessment.* Cambridge: Cambridge University Press.

Bachman, L. F., & Palmer, A. S. (2010). *Language testing in practice.* Oxford: Oxford University Press.

Bollen, K. A. (1989). *Structural equations with latent variables.* New York: Wiley.

Browne, M. W., & Cudeck, R. (1993). Alternative ways of assessing model fit. In K. A. Bollen & J. S. Long (Eds.), *Testing structural equation models* (pp. 136–162). Newbury Park, CA: Sage.

Byrne, B. M. (2006). *Structural equation modeling with EQS: Basic concepts, applications, and programming* (2nd ed.). Mahwah, NJ: Lawrence Erlbaum Associates.

Byrne, B. M. (2011). *Structural equation modeling with Mplus: Basic concepts, applications, and programming.* New York: Routledge.

Carrell, P. L. (1989a). SLA and classroom instruction: Reading. *Annual Review of Applied Linguistics, 9,* 223–242.

Carrell, P. L. (1989b). Metacognitive awareness and second language reading. *Modern Language Journal, 73*(2), 121–131.

Cattell, R. B. (1966). The scree test for the number of factors. *Multivariate Behavioral Research, 1* (2), 245–276.

Cohen, A. D., & Upton, T. A. (2006). *Strategies in responding to the new TOEFL reading tasks* (Monograph No. 33). Princeton, NJ: ETS. Retrieved from http://www.ets.org/Media/Research/ pdf/RR-06-06.pdf.

Dörnyei, Z. (2007). *Research methods in applied linguistics.* Oxford: Oxford University Press.

Fang, Z. (2010). *Complete guide to the College English Test* (Vol. 4). Beijing: Foreign Language Teaching and Research Press.

Grabe, W. (1997). *Developments in reading research and their implications for computer-adaptive reading assessment.* Paper presented at 19th Annual Language Testing Research Colloquium, Orlando, FL.

Hale, G. A., Stansfield, C. W., Rock, D. A., Hicks, M. M., Butler, F. A., & Oller, J. W. (1988). *Multiple-choice cloze items and the test of English as a foreign language (Research Reports No. 26).* Princeton, NJ: Educational Testing Service.

Hu, L., & Bentler, P. M. (1999). Cutoff criteria for fit indexes in covariance structure analysis: Conventional criteria versus new alternative. *Structural Equation Modeling, 6,* 1–55.

In'nami, Y., & Koizumi, R. (2011). Factor structure of the revised TOEIC® test: A multiple-sample analysis.*Language Testing, 29*(1), 131–152.

Jacobs, J. E., & Paris, S. G. (1987). Children's metacognition about reading: Issues in definition, measurement, and instruction. *Educational Psychologist, 22,* 255–278.

Kelloway, E. K. (1998). *Using LISREL for structural equation modeling: A researcher's guide.* Thousand Oaks, CA: Sage.

Kintsch, W. (1998). *Comprehension: A paradigm for cognition.* New York: Cambridge University Press.

Kintsch, W., & van Dijk, T. A. (1978). Toward a model of text comprehension and production. *Psychological Review, 85,* 363–394.

Kline, R. B. (2011). *Principles and practices of structural equation modeling* (2nd ed.). New York: Guilford.

Ministry of Education. (2007). *College English curriculum requirements.* Shanghai: Shanghai Foreign Language Education Press.

Mokhtari, K., & Reichard, C. A. (2002). Assessing students' metacognitive awareness of reading strategies. *Journal of Educational Psychology, 94*(2), 249–259.

National College English Testing Committee. (2006). *CET-4 test syllabus and sample test paper (2006 Revised Version)*. Shanghai: Shanghai Foreign Language Education Press.

O'Malley, J. M., & Chamot, A. U. (1990). *Learning strategies in second language acquisition*. Cambridge: Cambridge University Press.

Oxford, R. L. (1990). *Language learning strategies: What every teacher should know*. New York: Newbury House.

Paris, S. G., & Winograd, P. (1990). How metacognition can promote academic learning and instruction. In B. F. Jones & L. Idol (Eds.), *Dimensions of thinking and cognitive instruction* (pp. 15–51). Hillsdale, NJ: Erlbaum.

Phakiti, A. (2003). A closer look at gender differences in strategy use in L2 reading. *Language Learning, 53*(4), 649–702.

Phakiti, A. (2008). Construct validation of Bachman and Palmer's (1996) strategic competence model over time in EFL reading tests. *Language Testing, 25*(2), 237–272.

Pressley, M., & Afflerbach, P. (1995). *Verbal protocols of reading: The nature of constructively responsive reading*. Hillsdale, NJ: Erlbaum.

Purpura, J. E. (1999). *Learner strategy use and performance on language tests: A structural equation modeling approach*. Cambridge: Cambridge University Press.

Sheoery, R., & Mokhtari, K. (2001). Coping with academic materials: Differences in the reading strategies of native and non-native readers. *System: An International Journal of Educational Technology and Applied Linguistics, 29*, 431–449.

Tabachnick, B. G., & Fidell, L. S. (2013). *Using multivariate statistics* (6th ed.). London: Pearson Education.

Wade, S. E., Trathen, W., & Schraw, G. (1990). An analysis of spontaneous study strategies. *Reading Research Quarterly, 25,* 147–166.

Wiersma, W., & Jurs, S. (2009). *Research methods in education: An introduction*. MA: Pearson.

Wenden, A. L. (1998). Metacognitive Knowledge and Language Learning1. *Applied Linguistics, 19*(4), 515–537.

Chapter 5
Effects of Metacognitive and Cognitive Strategy Use on Reading Test Performance

Abstract This chapter presents the results of the study regarding the effect of metacognitive and cognitive strategy use on reading test performance. Descriptive statistics are introduced first, followed by the analysis of structural equation modeling (SEM) performed for two samples of similar characteristics. After the baseline model is established based on single-group SEM analysis, the results of SEM analyses conducted for cross-validation are displayed. The last section in the chapter discusses the findings from Study 1.

This chapter presents the results from the quantitative analyses in Study 1. Findings from Study 1 are shown in terms of descriptive statistics, SEM analysis for two samples, and SEM analysis for cross-validation. The results support the invariance of factor loadings, measurement error variances, structural regression coefficients, and factor variances for the unitary model in Study 1.

Study 1 investigates the relationships between test takers' metacognitive and cognitive strategy use. In addition, it also examines if the factor structure of the relationships between Chinese college test takers' reading strategy use and reading test performance is invariant across samples of similar characteristics.

To achieve the research goals, three hypothesized models of metacognition and reading test performance were tested: (a) the unitary model (see Fig. 3.1); (b) the higher-order model (see Fig. 3.2); and (c) the correlated model (see Fig. 3.3). In addition, the data were randomly split into two halves ($N = 296$ for Sample 1 and $N = 297$ for Sample 2) (MacCallum, Roznowski, Mar, & Reith, 1994) to conduct multi-sample SEM analyses.

First, descriptive statistics and reliability at the item and subscale levels of the questionnaire, and subsection level of the reading test were calculated for each sample. Assumptions regarding univariate normality and multivariate normality were also inspected. Values of skewness within ±3 and kurtosis within ±10 indicate univariate normality (Kline, 2011). Multivariate normality was evaluated using Mardia's coefficient, with a value of 5.00 or below representing multivariate normality (Byrne, 2006).

© Springer Nature Singapore Pte Ltd. 2018
L. Zhang, *Metacognitive and Cognitive Strategy Use in Reading Comprehension*,
https://doi.org/10.1007/978-981-10-6325-1_5

Second, a baseline model was identified prior to conducting multi-sample analyses by testing the three hypothesized models separately (In'nami & Koizumi, 2011). After the baseline model was selected, cross-group invariance was tested by imposing constraints on sets of parameters in a logically ordered and increasingly restrictive manner (Byrne, 2011).

Finally, after the best fitting model among the three hypothesized models was selected for both samples, a multi-sample SEM analysis was performed to cross-validate the selected model to test the invariance of factor loadings, measurement error variances, structural regression coefficients, and factor variances of the baseline model. The following section presents the results of the analyses.

5.1 Descriptive Statistics

Descriptive statistics at the item level and subscale level of the questionnaire, and subsection level of the reading test were calculated (see Tables 5.1, 5.2, and 5.3). All values of skewness and kurtosis were found to be within the accepted range for univariate normality. Multivariate normality was indicated by a Mardia's coefficient of 3.136 for Sample 1 and 3.605 for Sample 2. Reliability estimates are shown in Tables 5.1 and 5.2. It is possible that the low reliability estimates of the subscale of general progression (0.49) and subsection of Reading in Depth (0.54) may affect the results of this study to some degree. However, both the questionnaire and the test overall appeared to be reliable measuring instruments as indicated by the high overall reliability estimates (Cronbach's α = 0.89 and 0.90, respectively).

5.2 SEM Analysis for Two Samples

First, to establish the baseline model, the three hypothesized models were tested with both samples. As shown in Table 5.4, the unitary model fit the data well. On top of the fact that the chi-square statistics were significant (χ^2 = 109.74, df = 43, $p < 0.05$ for Sample 1; χ^2 = 67.53, df = 43, $p < 0.05$ for Sample 2), the other fit indices showed a good model fit with the data: CFI = 0.92, RMSEA = 0.073 [90% CI 0.056–0.089], and SRMR = 0.057 for Sample 1; CFI = 0.97, RMSEA = 0.044 [90% CI 0.022–0.063], and SRMR = 0.044 for Sample 2. In addition, although the higher-order model also seemed to fit the data well, it had the problem of negative error variance associated with COG and META for Sample 1 (as shown in Fig. 5.3) and with META and MCLZ for Sample 2 (as shown in Fig. 5.4). If the problematic variance is fixed to zero to solve the problem, the model becomes meaningless and not interpretable. The correlated model, on the other hand, had the problem that the covariance matrix of COG and META is not positive definite. Additionally, it

Table 5.1 Descriptive statistics for the ReTSUQ ($N = 593$)

	Strategy	Mean	SD	Skewness	Kurtosis	Reliability (Cronbach's α)
PLA	PLA1	2.69	1.42	0.02	−0.91	
	PLA2	3.06	1.16	−0.08	−0.65	
	PLA3	2.92	1.27	−0.19	−0.81	
	PLA4	3.37	1.27	−0.41	−0.67	0.62
	PLA5	2.47	1.45	0.28	−0.95	
	PLA6	4.05	1.15	−1.16	0.69	
EVA	EVA7	2.56	1.32	0.08	−0.80	
	EVA8	2.37	1.22	0.29	−0.62	
	EVA9	2.48	1.29	0.17	−0.64	
	EVA10	2.94	1.33	−0.12	−0.90	0.84
	EVA11	2.71	1.15	0.11	−0.59	
	EVA12	2.91	1.22	−0.16	−0.64	
	EVA13	2.65	1.34	0.17	−0.97	
	EVA14	3.16	1.18	−0.20	−0.59	
MON	MON15	3.63	1.09	−0.47	−0.50	
	MON16	3.32	1.11	−0.25	−0.63	
	MON17	3.68	1.07	−0.76	0.33	
	MON18	3.53	1.07	−0.53	0.01	
	MON19	3.52	1.17	−0.46	−0.58	
	MON20	3.23	1.13	−0.31	−0.38	0.79
	MON21	3.65	1.03	−0.65	0.18	
	MON22	3.87	1.09	−0.81	0.10	
	MON23	3.17	1.28	−0.33	−0.70	
	MON24	3.85	1.00	−0.74	0.19	
GEN	GEN25	3.09	1.35	−0.21	−0.85	
	GEN26	2.90	1.30	−0.05	−0.79	0.49
	GEN27	3.72	1.37	−0.79	−0.48	
IDE	IDE28	3.18	1.19	−0.29	−0.51	
	IDE29	3.71	1.20	−0.76	−0.19	0.56
	IDE30	3.36	1.24	−0.38	−0.68	
	IDE31	3.44	1.34	−0.53	−0.69	
INT	INT32	3.91	1.06	−0.10	0.78	
	INT33	3.95	0.95	−0.89	0.84	0.70
	INT34	3.63	1.13	−0.72	0.20	
	INT35	3.63	1.11	−0.56	−0.22	
INF	INF36	3.71	1.08	−0.64	−0.09	
	INF37	3.65	1.07	−0.58	−0.16	0.67
	INF38	3.13	1.16	−0.22	−0.47	
Total	38					0.89

Table 5.2 Descriptive statistics of the CET-4 Reading subtest at the subscale level ($N = 593$)

	Item no.	Mean	SD	Skewness	Kurtosis	Reliability (Cronbach's α)
SKSN	10	0.72	0.43	−1.14	0.19	0.69
BCLZ	10	0.55	0.49	−0.23	1.73	0.74
RID	10	0.65	0.44	−0.68	−0.84	0.54
CLZ	20	0.55	0.48	−0.20	−1.57	0.88
Total	50					0.90

showed poor model fit across both samples. Based on these findings, the unitary model was selected as the baseline model as it fits the data well both statistically and substantively. Thus, the unitary model was later used in the cross-validation analysis. Table 5.4 presents the fit indices for the three models with the two samples. The tested models with standardized regression coefficients are shown in Figs. 5.1, 5.2, 5.3, 5.4, 5.5 and 5.6.

5.3   SEM Analysis for Cross-validation

In the multi-sample cross-validation analysis, the unitary model was tested across samples (1) with no constraints; (2) with factor loading constrained; (3) with factor loadings and error variance constrained; (4) with factor loadings, error variance, and structural regression coefficients constrained; and (5) with factor loadings, error variance, structural regression coefficients, and factor variance constrained (see Bae & Bachman, 1998; Byrne, 2011; In'nami & Koizumi, 2011; Purpura, 1998). The test was conducted in an increasingly restrictive manner with the most stringent constraints imposed in the last model (Model 5).

First, the baseline model (i.e., the unitary model) was tested across two samples with no equality constraints. As shown in Table 5.5, the fit indices showed that this model fits the data well with both samples: CFI = 0.951, RMESA = 0.042 [90% CI 0.033–0.051] and SRMR = 0.0568.

Second, the invariance of factor loadings was tested by placing constraints on factor loadings with both samples, meaning constraining all factor loadings across samples as equal. This was more stringent compared with the first step with no constraints. As indicated in Table 5.5, Model 2 yielded good fit indices: CFI = 0.950, RMSEA = 0.041 [90% CI 0.032–0.049], and SRMR = 0.0555.

Third, constraints were placed on factor loadings and error variances across the samples to test the invariance of these parameters. As a result, Model 3 produced good model fit to the data: CFI = 0.948, RMSEA = 0.039 [90% CI 0.031–0.047], and SRMR = 0.0563 (see Table 5.5).

Fourth, a more stringent step was taken to test the invariance of the factor loadings, error variances, and structural regression coefficients by constraining all

Table 5.3 Descriptive statistics for Sample 1 and Sample 2 of the ReTSUQ and the CET-4 Reading subtest

		ReTSUQ							CET-4 Reading subtest			
		GEN	IDE	INT	INF	PLA	EVA	MON	SKSN	BCLZ	RID	MCLZ
Mean	Sample* 1	3.09	3.41	3.75	3.52	3.23	2.71	3.56	3.09	3.41	3.75	3.52
	Sample* 2	3.12	3.41	3.82	3.47	3.25	2.73	3.56	3.12	3.41	3.82	3.47
SD	Sample 1	0.67	0.68	0.72	0.85	0.84	0.69	0.59	0.67	0.68	0.72	0.85
	Sample 2	0.78	0.74	0.75	0.86	0.91	0.73	0.66	0.78	0.74	0.75	0.86
Skewness	Sample 1	0.01	−0.13	−0.28	−0.35	−0.26	−0.17	−0.03	0.01	−0.13	−0.28	−0.35
	Sample 2	−0.01	−0.23	−0.36	−0.28	−0.32	0.11	−0.27	−0.01	−0.23	−0.36	−0.28
Kurtosis	Sample 1	0.39	0.020	−0.40	−0.29	−0.13	−0.01	−0.25	0.39	0.02	−0.40	−0.29
	Sample 2	−0.23	−0.40	−0.30	−0.26	−0.01	−0.19	−0.20	−0.23	−0.40	−0.30	−0.26

* Sample 1: N = 296; Sample 2: N = 297

Table 5.4 Fit indices for the three models with the two samples

	Sample 1			Sample 2		
	Unitary model	Higher-order model	Correlated model	Unitary model	Higher-order model	Correlated model
χ^2	109.74*	111.31*	202.58*	67.53*	81.55*	165.64*
df	43	40	41	43	40	41
χ^2/df	2.55	2.78	4.94	1.57	2.04	4.04
CFI	0.92	0.91	0.80	0.97	0.96	0.87
RMSEA	0.073	0.078	0.116	0.044	0.059	0.101
RMSEA 90% CI	0.056–0.089	0.061–0.095	0.100–0.132	0.022–0.063	0.041–0.078	0.086–0.118
AIC	177.74	185.31	274.58	135.53	155.55	237.64
CAIC	278.06	300.85	368.66	228.45	259.25	337.43
SRMR	0.057	0.071	NA	0.044	0.059	0.101

df degree of freedom, *CFI* Comparative Fit Index, *RMSEA* root mean square error of approximation, *RMSEA 90% CI* RMSEA 90% confidence interval, *AIC* Akaike information criteria, *CAIC* consistent Akaike information criteria, *SRMR* standardized root mean square residual, *NA* not available
*$p < 0.05$

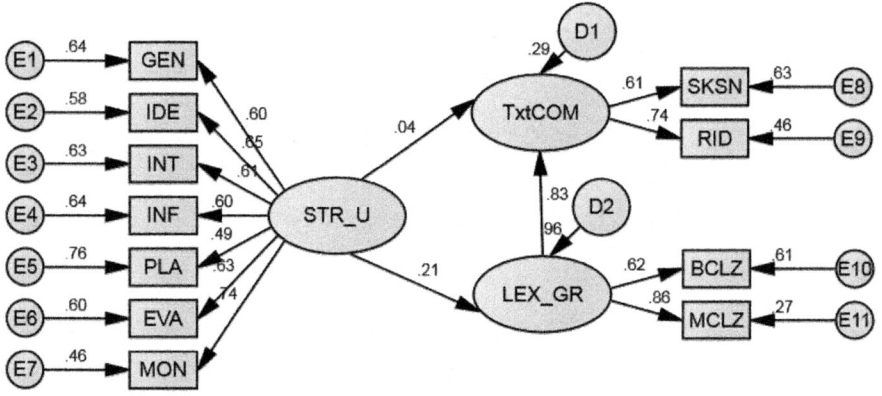

Fig. 5.1 Tested unitary model with Sample 1 with standardized estimates ($N = 296$)

these parameters across the two samples. As shown in Table 5.5, the fit indices of Model 4 showed that this model fits the data well: CFI = 0.949, RMSEA = 0.038 [90% CI 0.030–0.047], and SRMR = 0.0610.

Finally, invariance of the factor loadings, error variances, structural regression coefficients, and factor variances was tested. Constraints were placed on all these parameters, which is the most stringent level of the invariance test. As shown in Table 5.5, Model 5 fit the data well: CFI = 0.948, RMSEA = 0.038 [90% CI 0.030–0.046], and SRMR = 0.0616, indicating that all the factor loadings, error

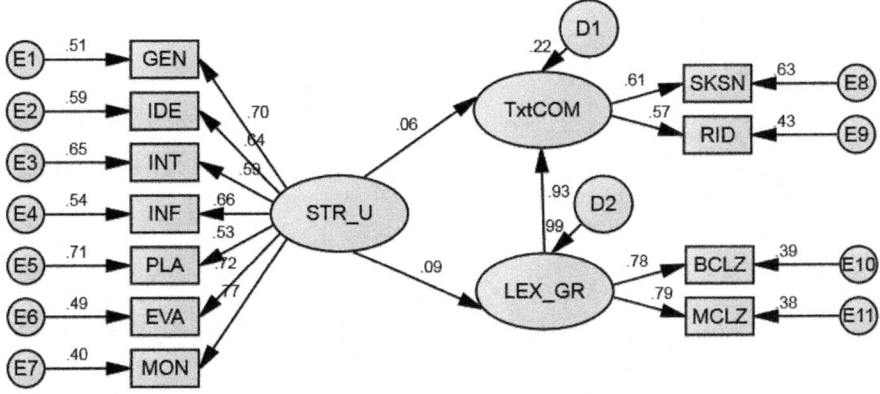

Fig. 5.2 Tested unitary model with Sample 2 with standardized estimates ($N = 297$)

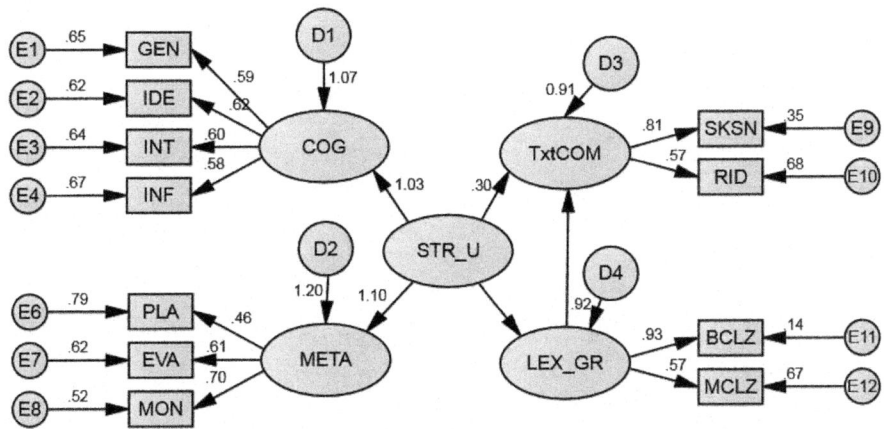

Fig. 5.3 Tested higher-order model with Sample 1 with standardized estimates ($N = 296$)

variance, structural regression coefficients, and factor variance were equal across the sample.

As discussed above and shown in Table 5.5, all the five tested models fit the data well. Since Model 2, Model 3, Model 4, and Model 5 are all nested within Model 1, chi-square difference tests were then conducted to examine if the four models were significantly different from Model 1. As shown in Table 5.6, the chi-square difference tests showed that all the four models were not significantly different from Model 1, suggesting that the invariance of factor loadings, error variance, structural regression coefficients, and factor variance was supported across Sample 1 and Sample 2. Figure 5.7 shows the final model tested with all factor loadings, error variance, structural regression coefficients, and factor variance constrained, which will be discussed further in the following section.

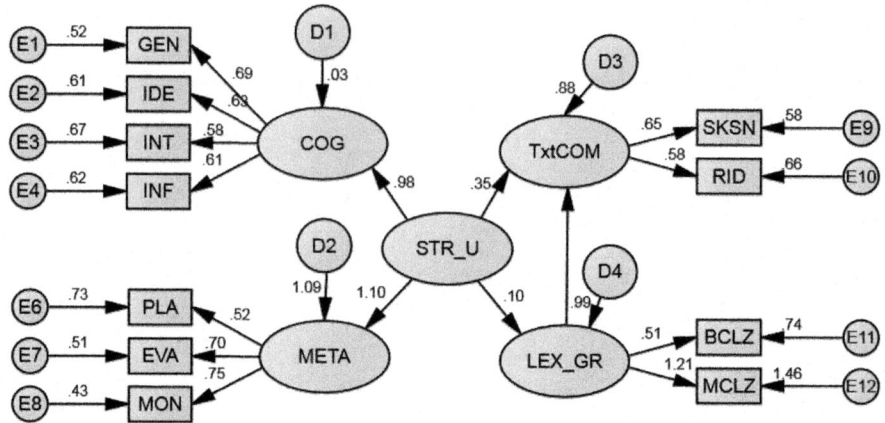

Fig. 5.4 Tested higher-order model with Sample 2 with standardized estimates ($N = 297$)

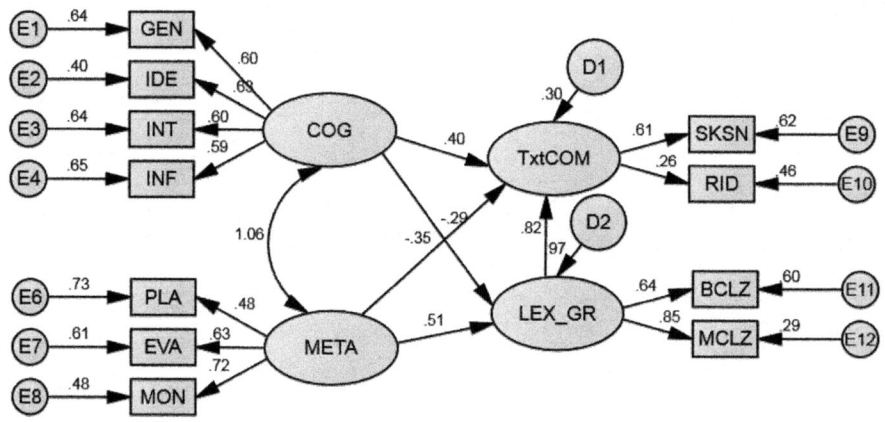

Fig. 5.5 Tested correlated model with Sample 1 with standardized estimates ($N = 296$)

5.4 Discussion

Four research questions were raised regarding Study 1 which investigates the relationships between Chinese college test takers' strategy use and reading test performance. This section discusses the results of the statistical analyses.

Research Question 1: What is the trait structure of Chinese college test takers' strategy use on the retired CET-4 Reading subtest as measured by the ReTSUQ?

Results of the analyses in the present study showed that seven categories emerged from the group of strategies used by these Chinese college test takers on

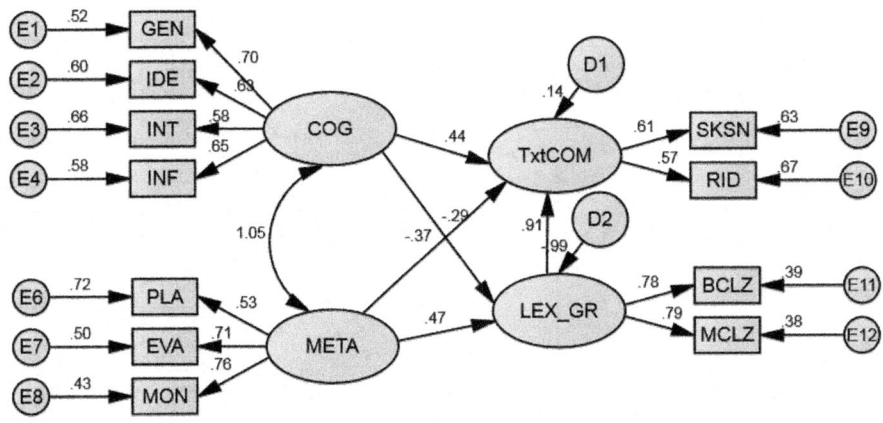

Fig. 5.6 Tested correlated model with Sample 2 with standardized estimates ($N = 297$)

Table 5.5 Fit indices for the unitary model for cross-validation

	Model 1	Model 2	Model 3	Model 4	Model 5
χ^2	169.018	178.041	192.25	194.691	199.732
df	82	90	101	104	107
CFI	0.951	0.950	0.948	0.949	0.948
RMSEA	0.042	0.041	0.039	0.038	0.038
RMSEA 90% CI	0.033–0.051	0.032–0.049	0.031–0.047	0.030–0.047	0.030–0.046
AIC	331.018	306.041	298.25	294.691	293.732
SRMR	0.0568	0.0555	0.0563	0.0610	0.0616

df degree of freedom; CFI Comparative Fit Index; RMSEA root mean square error of approximation, RMSEA 90% CI RMSEA 90% confidence interval, AIC Akaike information criteria, SRMR standardized root mean square residual, NA not available
*$p < 0.05$

Table 5.6 Chi-square difference test results

	Model 1 versus Model 2	Model 1 versus Model 2	Model 1 versus Model 2	Model 1 versus Model 2
$\Delta\chi^2$	9.023	14.209	1.841	5.641
Δdf	8	11	3	3
p value	0.340	0.222	0.606	0.130
Significance	ns	ns	ns	ns

ns not significant

the CET-4 Reading subtest, which are planning strategies (PLA), evaluating strategies (EVA), monitoring strategies (MON), general progression strategies (GEN), strategies for identifying important information (IDE), integrating strategies

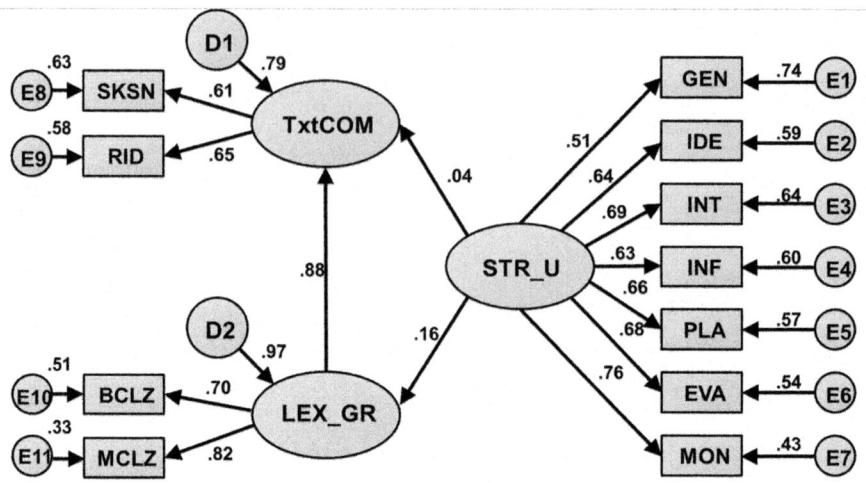

Fig. 5.7 Final SEM model

(INT), and inference-making (INF) strategies. PLAs refer to the strategies test takers use to achieve their pre-established goals in the process of their reading comprehension and test completion (e.g., Cohen & Upton, 2006; Wenden, 1998); EVAs are strategies that test takers employ to evaluate their cognitive abilities and performance on the reading comprehension test (e.g., Paris & Winograd, 1990; Wenden, 1998); MONs include test takers' strategies in checking and regulating their own performance in completing reading test tasks (e.g., Cohen & Upton, 2006; Jacobs & Paris, 1987; Wenden, 1998); GENs are the strategies readers and test takers use in the process of general reading after their overview of the text (e.g., Pressley & Afflerbach, 1995); IDEs refer to the strategies used by readers to confirm their initial hypotheses about the text and to refine their understanding (e.g., Afflerbach, 1990; Pressley & Afflerbach, 1995); GENs are those used by readers when they manipulate the text to fit the information across the text on the basis of their comprehension and prior knowledge and experience (e.g., Kintsch & van Dijk, 1978; Pressley & Afflerbach, 1995); and INFs refer to the strategies readers use to make inference about the information beyond the text to fill the gaps in meaning (e.g., Pressley & Afflerbach, 1995).

Based on the categorizations above, we can see that the Chinese college test takers use both metacognitive and cognitive strategies on the CET-4 Reading subtest. Metacognitive strategies include planning, evaluating, and monitoring strategies, whereas cognitive strategies comprise general progression strategies, strategies for identifying important information, integrating strategies, and inference-making strategies. Although reading management strategies (RMS) and test management strategies (TMS) were included in each of the three subscales of metacognitive strategies, neither of them emerged as individual categories in the process of EFA. Instead, the emerging factors in metacognitive strategies were the conventionally categorized planning, evaluating, and monitoring strategies. This shows that although test management strategies were found to play an important role in test takers' performance (e.g., Cohen, 2006; Phakiti, 2003, 2008), they failed to emerge as a separate factor in affecting test takers' reading comprehension and test completion, at least for this group of Chinese college test takers. This finding is congruent with other studies of test management strategies (e.g., Phakiti, 2008; Yoshizawa, 2002) in which test management strategies are found to be embedded in the category of metacognitive strategies although they "assist in producing a correct answer responsibly" (Cohen, 2013, p, 3).

In Cohen's (2006) framework, test-taking strategies comprise language learner strategies, test management strategies, and test-wiseness strategies. In the current study, as test takers were required to respond to the reading comprehension tasks, language learner strategies are equivalent to test takers' reading strategies which comprise metacognitive and cognitive strategies. The results from RQ1 showed that the classification of test takers' strategy use into distinct groups might have been convenient for research and further examination. For example, researchers might find it easier to investigate how learners use strategies after categorizing them into subscales. But in actual use situations, they are hardly distinguishable in that no separate factors of test management strategies emerged. Instead, test takers' management of reading comprehension and test-taking processes are better represented by the three frequently termed factors of metacognitive strategies (i.e., planning, evaluating, and monitoring). This shows that test management strategies are metacognitive in nature (Cohen & Upton, 2006). That is to say, while engaging in reading comprehension tests, students have to manage their reading comprehension as well as test-taking processes, which make strategy use in test contexts a very complicated issue (Purpura, 1999). Paradoxically, this points to the necessity of categorizing strategies into subscales for better understanding and instruction.

In addition, metacognitive strategies appear to define the latent strategy use better than cognitive strategies. For example, as shown in Fig. 5.7, STR_U regressed on the three types of metacognitive strategies (i.e., PLA, EVA, and MON) with greater coefficients than on the other four types of cognitive strategies (i.e., GEN, IDE, INT, and INF), indicating that these metacognitive strategies explain the latent variable of STR_U better than cognitive strategies. This finding seems to provide empirical support for Bachman and Palmer's (2010) framework of strategic competence to some degree in that metacognitive strategies are the core of strategic competence and test takers' focal attributes, whereas cognitive strategies are one of test takers' peripheral attributes.

With regard to cognitive strategies, it was found that these Chinese college readers and test takers appeared to follow the pattern of reading explicated by Pressley and Afflerbach (1995). For example, on the basis of Pressley and Afflerbach's reading model, five categories of cognitive reading strategies used by these test takers on the CET-4 Reading subtest were postulated which comprise general progression strategies, strategies for identifying important information, integrating strategies, inference-making strategies, and interpreting strategies. Although interpreting strategies did not emerge as a separate factor in EFA, all of the other four types of reading strategies were included in their strategy use on the reading comprehension test. This finding shows that CET-4 readers appeared to engage in many of the expected processes of comprehension on the reading comprehension test, which provides affirmative evidence in support of the validity of the reading comprehension test. However, interpretive strategies, although postulated as one of the types of cognitive strategies employed in students' reading comprehension process, were not found to be an important set of strategies for the Chinese college test takers. This suggests that Pressley and Afflerbach's (1995) model might be sensitive to differences in subjects' cultural and educational backgrounds, suggesting that it might need to be reviewed further. However, the plausibility of this tentative conclusion still needs empirical studies to further test and conclusively prove.

In summary, the analyses about the strategies used by the Chinese college test takers showed that both metacognitive and cognitive strategies were employed in the process of their reading comprehension and test completion. In addition, metacognitive strategies appeared to affect test takers' reading test performance more importantly.

Research Question 2: What is the trait structure of the EFL reading test performance as measured by the retired CET-4 Reading subtest?

In the tested model of the retired CET-4 Reading subtest, two underlying factors explained the EFL reading test performance: LEX_GR and TxtCOM. Based on the regression coefficient shown in Fig. 5.7 (i.e., $\beta = 0.88$), LEX_GR appeared to have a direct and significant effect on TxtCOM. This finding is consistent with an array of similar studies such as Phakiti (2008), Purpura (1997), and Saito (2003). In Phakiti's longitudinal study about the EFL reading test, the values were 0.99 and 0.82 in the Time 1 and Time 2 situations, respectively. In Purpura's and Saito's studies on second language test performance, LEX_GR directly and significantly affected reading ability with high values of 0.99 and 0.95, respectively.

As shown in Fig. 5.1, SKSN and RID loaded significantly and heavily on TxtCOM with coefficients of 0.61 and 0.65, respectively. LEX_GR was well measured by test takers' performance on BCLZ and MCLZ sections with relatively high and significant loadings of 0.70 and 0.82, respectively, meaning these two sections explained the variance of LEX_GR well. Contrary to the assertion that cloze tests measured higher-order processing abilities (Hinofotis, 1980; Oller, 1979), more studies have shown that cloze tests served as good measures of lower-order proficiency such as grammar and vocabulary (e.g., Anderson, 1979; Markham, 1985; Purpura, 1999, 2004; Saito 2003; Shanahan, Kamil, & Tobin, 1982). This has been further backed up by the results of this study in that BCLZ and MCLZ appeared to measure LEX_GR well. This is because cloze test scores are not only affected by test takers' general language proficiency, but also by other contextual factors such as text topic, deletion ratio (Abraham & Chapelle, 1992).

In addition, it can be regarded as supportive evidence for the validity claims of the test. According to the test syllabus of the CET-4 (National College English

Testing Committee, 2006), specific skills assessed in the reading test include: (a) the ability to distinguish and understand the main idea and important details; (b) the ability to understand the passage by means of language skills. The finding indicated that BCLZ and MCLZ provided good measures for the latter. Furthermore, after a major revision to the CET-4 in 2007, the Vocabulary and Structure section was replaced by the BCLZ section because more attention was given to contextualized language use compared with context-free knowledge of language (Jin, 2008; National College English Testing Committee, 2006). This is related to the CET-4 reform which is supposed to reflect the revision of the College English Curriculum Requirements (Ministry of Education, 2007). In addition, the high loading of the BCLZ section on LEX_GR ($\beta = 0.70$) seemed to show that the new test format played an expected role in tapping into test takers' lexico-grammatical reading ability. Similarly, the new test format of Skimming and Scanning ($\beta = 0.61$) also appeared to be a section which assessed college test takers' text comprehension ability effectively, as shown in the analysis.

Additionally, it was found that LEX_GR) predicted TxtCOM well in that the former had a high path coefficient of 0.88 on the latter. This indicates that the former affected the latter greatly, but also showed that they were distinct constructs. This result is congruent with other relevant reading theories and empirical studies (e.g., Aryadoust & Zhang, 2016; Gough & Tunmer, 1986; Grabe, 2009; LaBerge & Samuels, 1974; Phakiti, 2008; Purpura, 2004; Zhang & Zhang, 2013). For example, according to LaBerge and Samuels (1974) and Gough and Tunmer (1986), readers' comprehension of the text is based primarily on their word decoding abilities, i.e., their LEX_GR, a conclusion backed up by numerous empirical studies on reading (e.g., Phakiti, 2008; Purpura, 2004; Zhang & Zhang, 2013). In other words, fundamental skills of reading are important in building up reading comprehension ability. This indicates that more efforts should be put into this area when designing classroom reading instructions. For example, teachers can provide more explicit instruction on vocabulary and help students achieve automaticity in word processing, which may enhance their comprehension effectively. In addition, the underlying structure of the tested model of the CET-4 Reading subtest showed that students' LEX_GR and TxtCOM were evaluated in the test. This has provided support for the claim that both students' decoding and comprehension ability are assessed and evaluated (National College English Testing Committee, 2006).

Research Question 3: What is the relationship between test takers' metacognitive and cognitive strategy use? In other words, of the three models—the unitary, higher-order, and correlated—which model of strategy use and reading test performance fits the data best?

On the basis of relevant literature, the unitary, higher-order, and correlated models were hypothesized, tested, and compared to identify a baseline model. The analyses showed that the unitary model proved to be the best fitting model as the baseline model for the cross-validation study. Although the higher-order model also yielded good model fit, a decision was made not to select it due to the impossibility of solving the problem of negative error variance. Therefore, the unitary model was selected as the baseline model for the cross-validation study.

Regarding the functions of metacognitive and cognitive strategies, and how they are interrelated in language use, scholars have provided taxonomies related to the nature of these strategies, suggesting that it is possible, at least in theory, to distinguish different types of strategies within the overarching construct of strategy use. For example, O'Malley and Chamot (1990) classified learner strategies into three types: metacognitive, cognitive, and socio-affective strategies, whereas Oxford (1990) divided learning strategies into six kinds: memory, cognitive, compensation, metacognitive, affective, and social strategies in her Strategy Inventory for Language Learners. The analyses from this study suggest that metacognitive and cognitive strategies may not be so clearly distinguishable in actual use situations.

Purpura (1997, 1998, 1999) and Phakiti (2003, 2008) concluded that metacognitive and cognitive strategies appeared to be correlated with each other although they both raised queries about the relationship between metacognitive and cognitive strategy use in the test context. For example, Purpura (1999) pointed out explicitly that "cognitive strategy use seems to function in concert with metacognitive strategy use" (p. 127), indicating that test takers need to use both metacognitive and cognitive strategies simultaneously to optimize their test performance. Phakiti (2003) also found that "most cognitive strategies occurred in association with metacognitive strategies" (p. 43). Therefore, he argued that metacognitive and cognitive strategy use seemed to "form a continuum" (p. 44).

On the basis of the analysis, the good fit of the unitary model with the data lends support to researchers' earlier views (Baker, 1991; Chapelle, Grabe, & Berns, 1997; Paris, Wasik, & Turner, 1991) that the distinction between metacognitive and cognitive strategies hinges on the variation of topics, tasks, and individuals involved. This appears to show that when language users are faced with a series of complex behaviors or decisions, the strategies they employ to deal with the required tasks are not clearly distinguishable. In the test context, a wide range of sources of information and task demands are presented to test takers under time constraints. Therefore, they tend to use multiple strategies simultaneously to deal with language and test tasks demands in order to maximize their test performance. This is substantiated by the unitary model in which metacognitive and cognitive strategies function in synergy and collectively explain a significant portion of variance in reading test performance in a unitary manner. The synergy of metacognitive and cognitive strategies has also been observed in listening, the other receptive language skill (Goh, 2008). In other words, when language users are faced with a wide range of complicated task demands, they are likely to employ multiple strategies concurrently to tackle language and test task demands in order to maximize their test performance. In high-stakes test contexts, such as the CET-4 in China, students have to deal with both reading and test tasks' demands, indicating that they are required to arrive at appropriate understanding of the text and select the correct answer under time constraints. In other words, the dividing line between metacognitive and cognitive strategies is "fuzzy" and difficult to mark out in actual use situations, although for research purposes they are termed differently and treated as conceptually distinct strategies (e.g., O'Malley & Chamot, 1990; Oxford, 1990). To sum up, test takers' metacognitive awareness is substantiated by both metacognitive and cognitive strategies. In other words, test takers use the two types of strategies collectively and simultaneously.

Our findings about the relationships between metacognitive and cognitive strategies in test contexts appear to provide empirical evidence for Bachman and Palmer's (2010) revised language use model. In their updated model, Bachman and Palmer include cognitive strategies as part of language users/test takers' peripheral attributes, whereas metacognitive strategies are still perceived as the core of strategic competence, which is one of the two components of test takers' language ability (the other being test takers' focal attributes). As argued by Bachman and Palmer (1996), strategic competence provides a link among other characteristics of the individual. However, it is still not clear how metacognitive strategies are related to cognitive strategies in actual language use situations. This study serves as one of the first empirical studies to explore the relationships between metacognitive and cognitive strategies in actual reading test contexts. As shown in the analysis, in their reading and test-taking process, test takers employed both metacognitive and cognitive strategies which functioned in synergy to maximize their test performance. This finding provides validating evidence for Bachman and Palmer's (2010) language use model.

Research Question 4: What are the relationships between Chinese college test takers' metacognitive and cognitive strategy use and reading test performance? Specifically, is the factor structure of the relationships between Chinese college test takers' reading strategy use and reading test performance invariant across samples?

The cross-validation study showed invariance of the factor loadings, error variances, structural regression coefficients, and factor variances across the two samples, indicating that the unitary model of test takers' strategy use and reading test performance was generalizable across samples. This showed that metacognitive and cognitive strategies appeared to play a unitary role in enhancing their reading test performance.

Based on the final model identified (see Fig. 5.7), it was found that the seven measured variables of metacognitive and cognitive strategy use loaded on STR_U with values ranging from 0.51 to 0.76, suggesting that the latent variable STR_U was well defined by the measured variables. Among the seven subscales of strategy use, the three subscales of metacognitive strategy use had the highest loadings (i.e., $\beta = 0.76$ for MON, $\beta = 0.68$ for EVA, and $\beta = 0.66$ for PLA) which indicate that the questionnaire captures the metacognitive strategy use variables better than cognitive ones.

Regarding the factorial structure of the test, the findings are similar to Phakiti (2008) in that the CET-4 Reading subtest has two underlying factors: LEX_GR and TxtCOM. BCLZ ($\beta = 0.70$) and MCLZ ($\beta = 0.82$) loaded on LEX_GR significantly ($p < 0.05$), whereas SKSN and RID fell on TxtCOM at $\beta = 0.61$ and $\beta = 0.65$, suggesting the four measured variables defined the two latent variables well. Additionally, LEX_GR had a direct and significant effect on TxtCOM ($\beta = 0.88$), which indicated that the former affected the latter greatly but also showed that they were distinct constructs. This finding was consistent with relevant theories and empirical studies in that LEX_GR is found to affect TxtCOM to a great extent (see Gough & Tunmer, 1986; Grabe, 2009; LaBerge & Samuels, 1974; Phakiti, 2008; Zhang, 2014). It also indicates that the model of the CET-4 Reading subtest identified in this study appeared to be consistent with the test syllabus of the CET-4 (National College English Testing Committee, 2006).

With regard to the relationship between test takers' strategy use and reading test performance, it was found that test takers' strategy use affected their LEX_GR significantly ($\beta = 0.16$, $p < 0.05$), whereas it had an indirect effect on TxtCOM through LEX_GR. Several plausible reasons may explain this finding. First, Bachman and Palmer (2010) argued that strategy use is one part of test takers' characteristics among the many factors that affect performance on language tests. The dominating factor is their language knowledge. Similarly, Phakiti (2008) also found that cognitive strategy use explained 16–30% of test takers' lexico-grammatical performance, suggesting that the limited variance is accounted for by strategy use.

In addition, according to Rumelhart's (2004) and Stanovich's (1980) information processing model, readers construct meaning from the text using multiple tools such as their prior knowledge, past experience, and reading strategies. That is to say, they will compensate for their weak skills with their strong skills. As EFL learners who may typically have a limited set of vocabulary, the Chinese college test takers involved in this study tended to employ strategies to make up for their lack of proficiency in the target language. As shown in the analysis, strategy use played an important role in enhancing students' performance in the BCLZ and MCLZ items which tap into their LEX_GR. However, since the RID and SKSN items tap into students' TxtCOM which requires higher level skills, the compensatory role of strategies seems to be less obvious, indicating that strategy use may play a minor role in that strategies were not employed effectively in improving students' performance on these sections of the reading comprehension test.

Furthermore, empirical studies (e.g., Cohen & Aphek, 1979; Paris, 2002; Song, 2005) also showed that strategies may have positive, negative, or no effects on language performance. Also, Anderson (2005) pointed out that successful use of strategies hinges on several conditions: (1) the strategy is related well to language tasks encountered by language users; (2) the strategy is linked closely with other strategies relevant to the tasks at hand; and (3) the strategy is consistent with the language user's learning style. Furthermore, strategy use in test situations may be related to test takers' self-assessment and evaluation (Phakiti, 2008). In other words, if test takers fail to assess or evaluate themselves, it may lead to their poor strategy use. Thus, the limited role played by strategy use in Chinese college test takers' reading performance in this study may be due to their failure to link suitable strategies to the tasks at hand or their learning style or their inappropriate self-assessment in responding to the test tasks (Anderson, 2005).

In addition, this finding also concurs with Bachman's (1990) argument that strategy use is only one part of test takers' characteristics among the factors that affect performance on language tests (p. 187). According to Bachman and Palmer (2010), language ability comprises two components: language knowledge and strategic competence. The core of strategic competence is metacognitive strategies. Thus, strategy use is one part of their language ability and the dominating contributor to the variance of test scores is test takers' language knowledge (Saito, 2003; Song, 2004).

In summary, this chapter presented the results of Study 1, the investigation on Chinese test takers' strategy use and reading test performance. The results of preliminary analyses were first introduced, followed by the presentation of SEM analyses for two samples of similar characteristics. After the baseline model was established based on the single-group SEM analysis, SEM analyses for cross-validation were conducted and the results were displayed. In addition, this chapter also discussed the results in relation to the four research questions raised in Study 1. The results from the SEM analysis showed that the unitary model fits the data best in both samples. Further, it was found that Chinese college test takers' strategy use affected their LEX_GR significantly.

References

Abraham, R. G., & Chapelle, C. A. (1992). The meaning of cloze test scores: An item difficulty perspective. *Modern Language Journal, 76,* 79–468.

Afflerbach, P. P. (1990). The influence of prior knowledge on expert readers' main idea construction strategies. *Reading Research Quarterly, 25*(1), 31–46.

Anderson, N. J. (2005). L2 learning strategies. In E. Hinkel (Ed.), *Handbook of research in second language teaching and learning* (pp. 757–771). Mahwah, NJ: Lawrence Erlbaum.

Anderson, T. H. (1979). Study skills and learning strategies. In H. E. O'Neil Jr. & C. D. Spielberger (Eds.), *Cognitive and affective learning strategies* (pp. 78–99). New York: Academic Press.

Aryadoust, V., & Zhang, L. M. (2016). Fitting the mixed Rasch model to a reading comprehension test: Exploring individual difference profile in L2 reading. *Language Testing, 33*(4), 529–553.

Bachman, L. F. (1990). *Fundamental consideration in language testing*. Oxford, England: Oxford University Press.

Bachman, L. F., & Palmer, A. S. (1996). *Language testing in practice*. Oxford: Oxford University Press.

Bachman, L. F., & Palmer, A. S. (2010). *Language testing in practice*. Oxford: Oxford University Press.

Bae, J., & Bachman, L. F. (1998). A latent variable approach to listening and reading: Testing factorial invariance across two groups of children in the Korean/English two-way Immersion program. *Language Testing, 15,* 380–414.

Baker, L. (1991). Metacognition, reading and science education. In C. M. Santa & D. E. Alvermann (Eds.), *Science learning* (pp. 2–13). Newark, DE: International Reading Association.

Byrne, B. M. (2006). *Structural equation modeling with EQS: Basic concepts, applications, and programming* (2nd ed.). Mahwah, NJ: Lawrence Erlbaum Associates.

Byrne, B. M. (2011). *Structural equation modeling with Mplus: Basic concepts, applications, and programming*. New York: Routledge.

Chapelle, C., Grabe, W., & Berns, M. (1997). *Communicative language proficiency: Definitions and implications for TOEFL 2000. TOEFL monograph series No. 10.* Princeton, NJ: Educational Testing Service.

Cohen, A. D. (2006). The coming age of research on test-taking strategies. *Language Assessment Quarterly, 3*(4), 307–331.

Cohen, A. D. (2013). Using test-wiseness strategy research in task development. In A. J. Kunnan (Ed.), *The companion to language assessment* (pp. 893–905). Hoboken, NJ: Wiley/Blackwell.

Cohen, A. D., & Aphek, E. (1979). *Easifying second language learning.* Research report under the auspices of Brandeis University and submitted to the Jacob Hiatt Institute, Jerusalem. ERIC Document ED 163753.

Cohen, A. D., & Upton, T. A. (2006). *Strategies in responding to the new TOEFL reading tasks* (Monograph No. 33). Princeton, NJ: ETS. Retrieved from http://www.ets.org/Media/.

Goh, C. (2008). Metacognitive instruction for second language listening development: Theory, practice and research implications. *RELC Journal, 39*(2), 188–213.

Gough, P. B., & Tunmer, W. (1986). Decoding, reading, and reading disability. *Remedial and Special Education, 7,* 6–10.

Grabe, W. (2009). *Reading in a second language: Moving from theory to practice.* Cambridge: Cambridge University Press.

Hinofotis, F. B. (1980). Cloze as an alternative method of ESL placement and proficiency testing. In J. W. Oller & K. Perkins (Eds.), *Research in language testing* (pp. 121–128). Rowley, MA: Newbury House.

In'nami, Y., & Koizumi, R. (2011). Factor structure of the revised TOEIC® test: A multiple-sample analysis. *Language Testing, 29*(1), 131–152.

Jacobs, J.E., & Paris, S.G. (1987). Children's metacognition about reading: Issues in definition, measurement, and instruction. *Educational Psychologist, 22,* 255–278.

Jin, Y. (2008). Powerful tests, powerfulness test designers? Changes facing the college english test. *CELEA Journal, 31,* 3–11.

Kintsch, W., & van Dijk, T. A. (1978). Toward a model of text comprehension and production. *Psychological Review, 85,* 363–394.

Kline, R. B. (2011). *Principles and practices of structural equation modeling* (2nd ed.). New York: Guilford.

LaBerge, D., & Samuels, S. J. (1974). Toward a theory of automatic information processing. *Cognitive Psychology, 6*(2), 293–323.

MacCallum, R. C., Roznowski, M., Mar, C. M., & Reith, J. V. (1994). Alternative strategies for cross-validation of covariance structure models. *Multivariate Behavioural Research, 29,* 1–32.

Markham, P. L. (1985). The rational deletion cloze and global comprehension in German. *Language Learning, 35,* 423–430.

Ministry of Education. (2007). *College English curriculum requirements.* Shanghai: Shanghai Foreign Language Education Press.

National College English Testing Committee. (2006). *CET-4 test syllabus and sample test paper (2006 revised version).* Shanghai: Shanghai Foreign Language Education Press.

Oller, J. (1979). *Language tests at school: A pragmatic approach.* London: Longman.

O'Malley, J. M., & Chamot, A. U. (1990). *Learning strategies in second language acquisition.* Cambridge: Cambridge University Press.

Oxford, R. L. (1990). *Language learning strategies: What every teacher should know.* New York: Newbury House.

Paris, S. G., & Winograd, P. (1990). How metacognition can promote academic learning and instruction. In B.F. Jones & L. Idol (Eds.), *Dimensions of thinking and cognitive instruction* (pp.15–51). Hillsdale, NJ: Erlbaum.

Paris, S. G. (2002). When is metacognition helpful, debilitating, or benign? In P. Chambres, M. Izaute, & P. Marescaux (Eds.), *Metacognition: Process, function, and use* (pp. 105–120). Norwell, MA: Kluwer.

Paris, S. G., Wasik, B., & Turner, J. (1991). The development of strategic readers. In R. Barr et al. (Eds.), *Handbook of reading research* (pp. 609–640). New York: Longman.

Phakiti, A. (2003). A closer look at gender differences in strategy use in L2 reading. *Language Learning, 53*(4), 649–702.

Phakiti, A. (2008). Construct validation of Bachman and Palmer's (1996) strategic competence model over time in EFL reading tests. *Language Testing, 25*(2), 237–272.

Pressley, M., & Afflerbach, P. (1995). *Verbal protocols of reading: The nature of constructively responsive reading*. Hillsdale, NJ: Erlbaum.

Purpura, J. E. (1997). An analysis of the relationships between test takers' cognitive and metacognitive strategy use and second language test performance. *Language Learning, 47*, 289–325.

Purpura, J. E. (1998). Investigating the effects of strategy use and second language test performance with high- and low-ability test takers: A structural equation modeling approach. *Language Testing, 15*, 333–379.

Purpura, J. E. (1999). *Learner strategy use and performance on language tests: A structural equation modeling approach*. Cambridge: Cambridge University Press.

Purpura, J. E. (2004). *Assessing grammar*. Cambridge: Cambridge University Press.

Rumelhart, D. (2004). Toward an interactive model of reading. In R. B. Rudell & N. J. Unrau (Eds.), *Theoretical models and processes of reading* (5th ed., pp. 1149–1179). Newark: International Reading Association.

Saito, Y. (2003). Investigating the construct validity of the cloze section in the Examination for the Certificate of Proficiency in English. *Spaan Fellow Working Papers in Second or Foreign Language Assessment, 1*, 39–82.

Shanahan, T., Kamil, M. L., & Tobin, A. W. (1982). Cloze as a measure of intersentential comprehension. *Reading Research Quarterly, 17*, 229–255.

Song, W. (2004). Language learner strategy use and English proficiency on the Michigan English Language Assessment Battery. *Spaan Fellow Working Papers in Second or Foreign Language Assessment, 3*, 1–26.

Song, X. (2005). Language learner strategy use and English proficiency on the Michigan English Language Assessment Battery. *Spaan Fellow Working Papers in Second or Foreign Language Assessment, 3*, 1–23.

Stanovich, K. E. (1980). Towards an interactive-compensatory model of individual differences in the development of reading fluency. *Reading Research Quarterly, 16*, 32–71.

Wenden, A. L. (1998). Metacognitive knowledge and language learning. *Applied Linguistics, 19*(4), 515–537.

Yoshizawa, K. (2002). *Relationships among strategy use, foreign language aptitude, and second language proficiency: A structural equation modeling approach*. Unpublished doctoral dissertation. Philadelphia, PA: Temple University.

Zhang, L. M. (2014). A structural equation modeling approach to investigating test takers' strategy use and their EFL reading test performance. *Asian EFL Journal, 16*(1), 153–188.

Zhang, L. M., & Zhang, L. J. (2013). Relationships between Chinese college test takers strategy use and EFL reading test performance: A structural equation modelling approach. *RELC Journal, 44*(1), 35–57.

Chapter 6
Gender Differences in Metacognitive and Cognitive Strategy Use and Reading Test Performance

Abstract This chapter presents the results of the study on gender differences in metacognitive and cognitive strategy use and reading test performance. Similar to Chap. 5, the results of descriptive analyses are presented. Next, the results of single-group structural equation modeling (SEM) analyses conducted to establish the baseline model for each gender group are presented. Based on these displayed results, SEM analyses for cross-validation were conducted and the results are shown. Finally, the findings from Study 2 are discussed and introduced.

This chapter presents the results of the quantitative analyses in Study 2, which was designed to investigate gender differences in test takers' strategy use and reading test performance across male and female groups. Findings from Study 2 are shown in terms of descriptive statistics, SEM analysis for two samples, and SEM analysis for cross-validation. The results from Study 2 show that the invariance of the strategy use between gender groups is partially supported. In addition, this chapter discusses the results and findings from Study 2 and answers to research questions regarding this study. The following analytical procedures were adopted to answer the research questions from Study 2.

First, descriptive statistics and reliability at the item and subscale levels of the questionnaire, and subsection level of the reading test were calculated. The validity of assumptions regarding univariate normality and multivariate normality was also inspected. Values of skewness within ± 3 and kurtosis within ± 10 indicate univariate normality (Kline, 2011). Multivariate normality was evaluated using Mardia's coefficient, with a value of 5.00 or below indicating multivariate normality (Byrne, 2006).

Second, similar to Study 1, preliminary single-group analyses were conducted to identify a baseline model for each group prior to conducting multi-group analyses. If the baseline models were found to be identical, cross-group invariance was tested by placing constraints on sets of parameters in an increasingly restrictive manner (Byrne, 2011).

Finally, after the baseline model was established for male and female student groups respectively, multi-group SEM analyses were performed to cross-validate

Table 6.1 Descriptive statistics for the ReTSUQ ($N = 584$)

	Item	Mean	SD	Skewness	Kurtosis	Reliability (Cronbach's α)
PLA	PLA1	2.69	1.43	0.01	−0.92	
	PLA2	3.06	1.16	−0.08	−0.65	
	PLA3	2.91	1.27	−0.18	−0.82	0.62
	PLA4	3.36	1.28	−0.40	−0.68	
	PLA5	2.46	1.45	0.27	−0.95	
	PLA6	4.05	1.15	−1.17	0.70	
	EVA7	2.55	1.31	0.08	−0.78	
EVA	EVA8	2.37	1.22	0.29	−0.59	
	EVA9	2.49	1.29	0.16	−0.64	
	EVA10	2.93	1.33	−0.11	−0.90	
	EVA11	2.70	1.15	0.10	−0.59	0.84
	EVA12	2.90	1.21	−0.16	−0.63	
	EVA13	2.65	1.35	0.16	−0.97	
	EVA14	3.15	1.18	−0.20	−0.59	
MON	MON15	3.63	1.09	−0.47	−0.50	
	MON16	3.32	1.11	−0.24	−0.64	
	MON17	3.68	1.06	−0.76	0.34	
	MON18	3.53	1.06	−0.54	0.04	
	MON19	3.52	1.16	−0.46	−0.58	0.79
	MON20	3.21	1.13	−0.30	−0.36	
	MON21	3.64	1.03	−0.65	0.17	
	MON22	3.87	1.09	−0.81	0.11	
	MON23	3.18	1.28	−0.34	−0.70	
	MON24	3.85	1.00	−0.74	0.19	
GEN	GEN25	3.09	1.36	−0.21	−0.86	
	GEN26	2.90	1.30	−0.05	−0.80	0.49
	GEN27	3.71	1.37	−0.79	−0.48	
IDE	IDE28	3.17	1.19	−0.29	−0.51	
	IDE29	3.71	1.20	−0.76	−0.19	0.56
	IDE30	3.36	1.24	−0.37	−0.70	
	IDE31	3.44	1.34	−0.53	−0.70	
INT	INT32	3.90	1.07	−0.10	0.79	
	INT33	3.95	.95	−0.91	0.88	0.70
	INT34	3.63	1.13	−0.72	0.20	
	INT35	3.62	1.11	−0.56	−0.24	
INF	INF36	3.71	1.08	−0.65	−0.08	
	INF37	3.65	1.08	−0.59	−0.16	
	INF38	3.13	1.16	−0.22	−0.47	0.67
Total	38			0.89		

the two models to test the invariance of factor loadings, structural regression coefficients, and factor variances of the baseline model (Byrne, 2011). The following section presents the results of the analyses.

6.1 Descriptive Statistics

Descriptive statistics at the item and subscale levels of the questionnaire, and subsection level of the reading test were calculated (see Tables 6.1, 6.2, and 6.3). All values of skewness and kurtosis were within the accepted range for univariate normality. Multivariate normality was indicated by Mardia's coefficient being smaller than 5.00, with 2.04 for the male group and 4.81 for the female group. Reliability estimates as measured by Cronbach's α are shown in Tables 6.1 and 6.2. The values of reliability were 0.89 for the ReTSUQ and 0.90 for the CET-4 Reading subtest, indicating that both are reliable measurement instruments.

6.2 SEM Analysis for Two Groups

To establish the baseline models for each gender group, a series of models was tested based on the reviewed literature. The baseline models of strategy use and reading test performance for male and female groups are presented in Figs. 6.1 and 6.2. These two models seem to fit the data well (see the model fit indexes in Table 6.4), both statistically and substantively. The normed chi-square indexes (χ^2/df) for both models are below 3.0. CFI and TLI are all above 0.90, RMSEAs are less than 0.06, and RMSEA 90% CIs are narrow.

6.3 SEM Analysis for Cross-validation

In the multi-group cross-validation analysis, the invariance of factor loadings, factor covariance, and structural regression coefficients across the male and female groups were tested (see Bae & Bachman, 1998; Byrne, 2011; In'nami & Koizumi, 2011; Purpura, 1998). The test was conducted in an increasingly restrictive manner with the most stringent constraints added in the last model. In other words, the two baseline models were tested (1) with no constraints; (2) with factor loadings constrained; (3) factor loadings and structural regression coefficients constrained; (4) factor loadings, structural regression coefficients, and factor covariance constrained.

First, the two baseline models were tested for each male and female group with no equality constraints. As shown in Table 6.4, the fit indices showed that this

Table 6.2 Descriptive statistics of the CET-4 Reading subtest ($N = 584$)

	Item	Mean	SD	Skewness	Kurtosis	Reliability (Cronbach's α)
SKSN	Item1	0.81	0.39	−1.58	0.51	
	Item2	0.56	0.50	−0.23	−1.96	
	Item3	0.58	0.49	−0.32	−1.90	
	Item4	0.83	0.38	−1.77	1.12	
	Item5	0.83	0.37	−1.80	1.24	0.69
	Item6	0.87	0.34	−2.23	2.97	
	Item7	0.80	0.40	−1.54	0.38	
	Item8	0.60	0.49	−0.42	−1.83	
	Item9	0.59	0.49	−0.36	−1.88	
	Item10	0.76	0.43	−1.21	−0.53	
BCLZ	Item11	0.59	0.49	−0.39	−1.86	
	Item12	0.76	0.43	−1.2	−0.53	
	Item13	0.42	0.49	0.32	−1.90	
	Item14	0.37	0.48	0.53	−1.73	
	Item15	0.64	0.48	−0.59	−1.66	
	Item16	0.48	0.50	0.07	−2.00	0.74
	Item17	0.49	0.50	0.02	−2.01	
	Item18	0.56	0.50	−0.24	−1.96	
	Item19	0.55	0.50	−0.21	−1.96	
	Item20	0.64	0.48	−0.58	−1.67	
RID	Item21	0.29	0.46	0.90	−1.19	
	Item22	0.77	0.42	−1.27	−0.40	
	Item23	0.75	0.44	−1.14	−0.71	
	Item24	0.82	0.39	−1.64	0.70	
	Item25	0.68	0.47	−0.76	−1.43	
	Item26	0.72	0.45	−0.98	−1.05	0.54
	Item27	0.76	0.43	−1.23	−0.48	
	Item28	0.29	0.46	0.92	−1.15	
	Item29	0.73	0.45	−1.02	−0.97	
	Item30	0.66	0.47	−0.68	−1.54	
CLZ	Item31	0.68	0.47	−0.80	−1.37	
	Item32	0.47	0.50	0.11	−2.00	
	Item33	0.55	0.50	−0.21	−1.96	
	Item34	0.56	0.52	0.28	1.29	
	Item35	0.60	0.49	−0.41	1.84	
	Item36	0.66	0.47	−0.68	−1.54	
	Item37	0.47	0.50	0.10	−2.00	
	Item38	0.51	0.50	−0.06	−2.00	
	Item39	0.61	0.49	−0.46	−1.80	
	Item40	0.58	0.50	−0.31	−1.91	

(continued)

Table 6.2 (continued)

Item	Mean	SD	Skewness	Kurtosis	Reliability (Cronbach's α)
	0.56	0.50	−0.23	−1.96	0.88
Item42	0.27	0.45	1.02	−0.97	
Item43	0.48	0.50	0.07	−2.00	
Item44	0.59	0.49	−0.35	−1.89	
Item45	0.72	0.45	−0.10	−1.01	
Item46	0.50	0.50	0.01	−2.01	
Item47	0.69	0.46	−0.80	−1.36	
Item48	0.65	0.48	−0.63	−1.60	
Item49	0.59	0.49	−0.35	−1.89	
Item50	0.34	0.47	0.70	−1.52	
Total	50				0.90

Table 6.3 Descriptive statistics of the ReTSUQ and the CET-4 Reading subtest for male and females students ($N = 584$)

	Mean		SD		Skewness		Kurtosis	
	Males*	Females*	Males	Females	Males	Females	Males	Females
ReTSUQ								
Planning (PLA)	3.27	3.22	0.84	0.91	−0.18	−0.35	−0.40	0.12
Evaluating (EVA)	2.75	2.69	0.72	0.70	0.03	−0.06	0.05	−0.25
Monitoring (MON)	3.57	3.55	0.63	0.62	−0.16	−0.17	−0.32	−0.06
General progression (GEN)	3.08	3.14	0.75	0.72	0.12	−0.11	−0.24	0.36
Identifying important information (IDE)	3.43	3.39	0.71	0.72	−0.31	−0.10	−0.30	−0.11
Integrating (INT)	3.71	3.86	0.74	0.73	−0.23	−0.41	−0.56	−0.13
Inference-making (INF)	3.55	3.44	0.84	0.87	−0.28	−0.33	−0.45	−0.20
CET-4 Reading subtest								
Skimming and Scanning (SKSN)	6.20	7.05	2.23	1.83	−0.58	−1.15	−0.34	1.38
Banked cloze (BCLZ)	2.50	2.98	1.37	1.25	0.02	−0.36	−0.93	−0.52
Reading in Depth (RID)	11.80	12.72	3.80	3.64	−0.47	−0.86	−0.36	0.89
Multiple-choice cloze (MCLZ)	5.13	5.85	2.57	2.62	−0.41	−0.84	−0.78	−0.19

* Male: N = 274; Female: N = 310

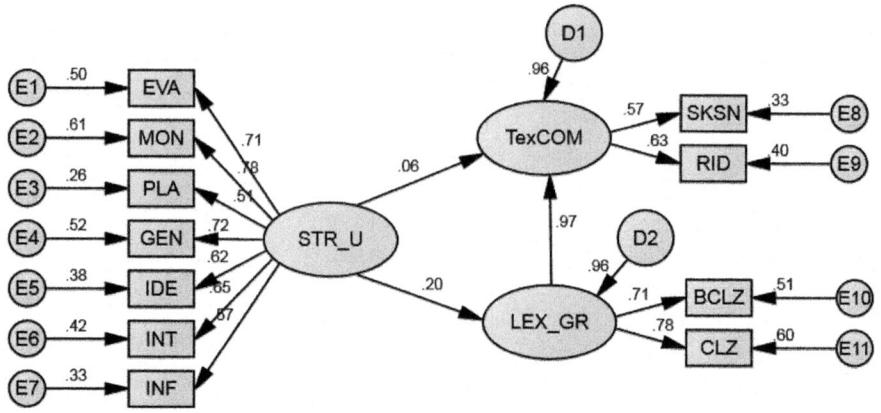

Fig. 6.1 The baseline model for the male group with standardized estimates

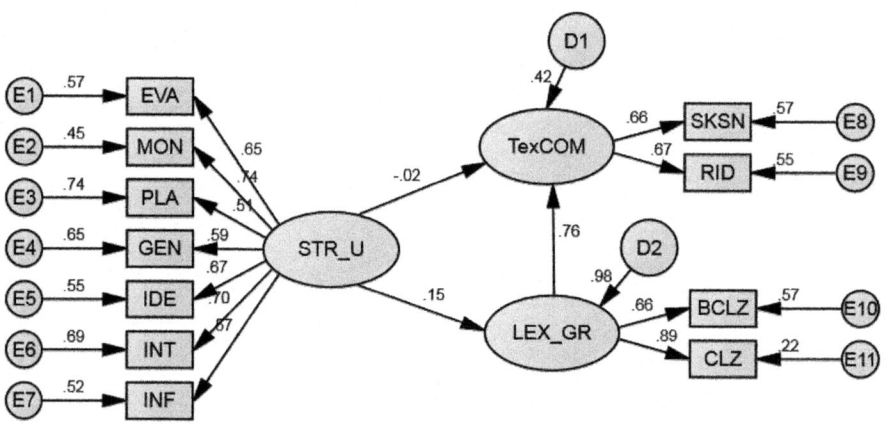

Fig. 6.2 The baseline model for the female group with standardized estimates

Table 6.4 Fit indices for the baseline models for male and female students

	χ^2	df	χ^2/df	CFI	TLI	RMSEA	RMSEA 90% CI	SRMR
Baseline model for the male group	68.394	41	1.668	0.969	0.958	0.049	0.028–0.070	0.390
Baseline model for the female group	79.590	41	1.941	0.958	0.944	0.055	0.037–0.073	0.439

df degree of freedom, *CFI* comparative fit index, *RMSEA* root mean square error of approximation, *RMSEA 90% CI* RMSEA 90% confidence interval, *SRMR* standardized root mean square residual
*$p < 0.05$

model fit the data well with both samples: CFI = 0.963, TLI = 0.951, RMSEA = 0.037 (90% CI 0.027–0.047), and SRMR = 0.039.

Second, the invariance of factor loadings was tested by placing constraints on factor loadings with both samples, meaning constraining all factor loadings across samples as equal. This was more stringent compared with the first step which imposed no constraints. As indicated in Table 6.5, Model 2 yielded good fit indices: CFI = 0.958, TLI = 0.949, RMSEA = 0.038 [90% CI 0.029–0.047], and SRMR = 0.044. However, the chi-square difference test showed that Model 2 was significantly different from Model 1 (see Table 6.6). As such, the subsequent invariance test was to pinpoint the location of the non-invariance (Byrne, 2001).

Third, constraints were placed on the factor loadings of the test model. If the invariance was found to hold across gender groups in this test, the measurement model of strategy use could be tested. The resultant Model 2(a) produced good model fit to the data: CFI = 0.962, TLI = 0.950, RMSEA = 0.037 [90% CI 0.028–0.047], and SRMR = 0.040 (see Table 6.5). The chi-square difference test results showed that Model 2(a) was not significantly different from Model 1. Next, the factor loadings were constrained from indicators to the strategy use one after another. One important principle in the process of the invariance test is that if a certain factor loading is found invariant across the groups, it should be retained cumulatively in the later test of invariance (Byrne, 2001).

Fourth, in the test of invariance of the strategy use model, first constraints were placed on EVA and the invariance test was then conducted. The results of the chi-square difference test indicated that Model 2(b) was significantly different from Model 1. Hence, the loading was set free and the test on invariance of MON was conducted. Similarly, it was found Model 2(c) was also significantly different from Model 1. Following the similar steps, all six loadings were tested in the strategy use model with the exception of INF, which had been restricted to 1.0 in the analysis. The results showed that EVA, MON, and GEN are invariant across gender groups, whereas PLA, IDE, INT, and INF are not equivalent between male and female students (see Tables 6.5 and 6.6).

Fifth, the invariance of structural models was tested by putting constraints on structural regression coefficients. The results of the chi-square difference test supported the notion of invariance of the structural model across gender groups (see Table 6.5). As shown in this table, Model 3 produced good fit indices: CFI = 0.960, TLI = 0.951, RMSEA = 0.037 [90% CI 0.028–0.046], and SRMR = 0.037.

Finally, invariance of the factor loadings with PLA, IDE, INT, and INF, structural regression coefficients, and factor variances was tested. Constraints were placed on all these parameters. As shown in Table 6.5, Model 4 fit the data well: CFI = 0.960, TLI = 0.953, RMSEA = 0.036 [90% CI 0.027–0.045], and SRMR = 0.048. The chi-square difference test showed that Model 4 is not significantly different from Model 1, indicating that the factor loadings with PLA, IDE, INT, and INF, structural regression coefficients, and factor variance were equal across the sample (see Figs. 6.3 and 6.4).

Table 6.5 Fit indices for models in cross-validation

	χ^2	df	χ^2/df	CFI	RMSEA	RMSEA 90% CI	AIC	SRMR
Model 1: Baseline: no equality constraints	147.984	82	1.805	0.963	0.037	0.027–0.047	291.984	0.039
Model 2: Factor loadings equal	165.383	90	1.838	0.958	0.038	0.029–0.047	293.383	0.044
Model 2(a): Factor loadings of the test model equal	152.034	84	1.810	0.962	0.037	0.028–0.047	292.034	0.040
Model 2(b): Factor loadings with EVA equal	155.925	85	1.834	0.960	0.038	0.028–0.047	293.925	0.042
Model 2(c): Factor loadings with MON equal	156.726	85	1.844	0.960	0.038	0.029–0.047	294.726	0.042
Model 2(d): Factor loadings with PLA equal	152.271	85	1.791	0.962	0.037	0.027–0.046	290.271	0.041
Model 2(e): Factor loadings with PLA, GEN equal	161.939	86	1.883	0.958	0.039	0.030–0.048	297.939	0.043
Model 2(f): Factor loadings with PLA, IDE equal	152.541	86	1.774	0.963	0.036	0.027–0.046	288.541	0.043
Model 2(g): Factor loadings with PLA, IDE, INT	157.068	87	1.805	0.961	0.037	0.028–0.046	291.068	0.042
Model 3: Factor loadings with PLA, IDE, INT, and structural regression coefficients equal	162.220	90	1.802	0.960	0.037	0.028–0.046	290.220	0.047
Model 4: Factor loadings with PLA, IDE, INT, structural regression coefficients, and factor variance equal	164.245	93	1.766	0.960	0.036	0.027–0.045	286.245	0.048

df degree of freedom, *CFI* comparative fit index, *TLI* Tucker–Lewis index (TLIs are consistently smaller than CFIs, which are not shown in Table 6.5 due to limited space), *RMSEA* root mean square error of approximation, *RMSEA 90% CI* RMSEA 90% confidence interval, *AIC* Akaike information criteria, *SRMR* standardized root mean square residual, *NA* not available

Table 6.6 Chi-square difference test results

	$\Delta\chi^2$	Δdf	p value	Significance
Model 1 versus Model 2	17.399	8	0.026	Significant
Model 1 versus Model 2(a)	4.050	2	0.132	ns
Model 1 versus Model 2(b)	7.941	3	0.047	Significant
Model 1 versus Model 2(c)	8.742	3	0.033	Significant
Model 1 versus Model 2(d)	4.287	3	0.232	ns
Model 1 versus Model 2(e)	13.955	4	0.007	Significant
Model 1 versus Model 2(f)	4.557	4	0.336	ns
Model 1 versus Model 2(g)	9.084	5	0.106	ns
Model 1 versus Model 3	14.236	8	0.076	ns
Model 1 versus Model 4	16.261	11	0.132	ns

ns not significant

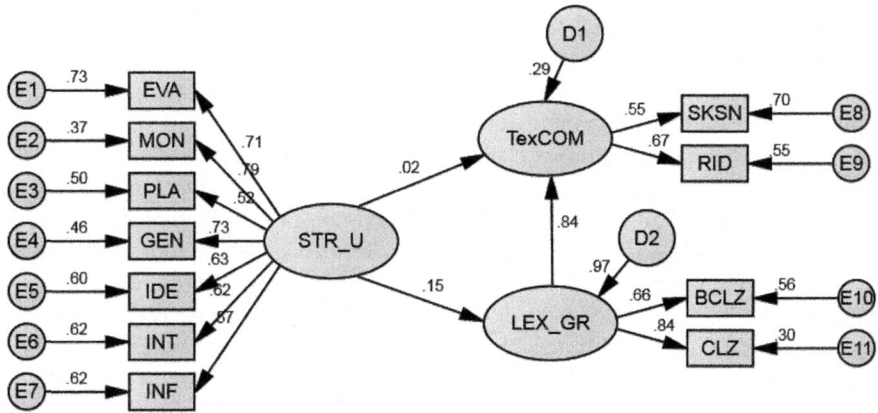

Fig. 6.3 The final model for the male group

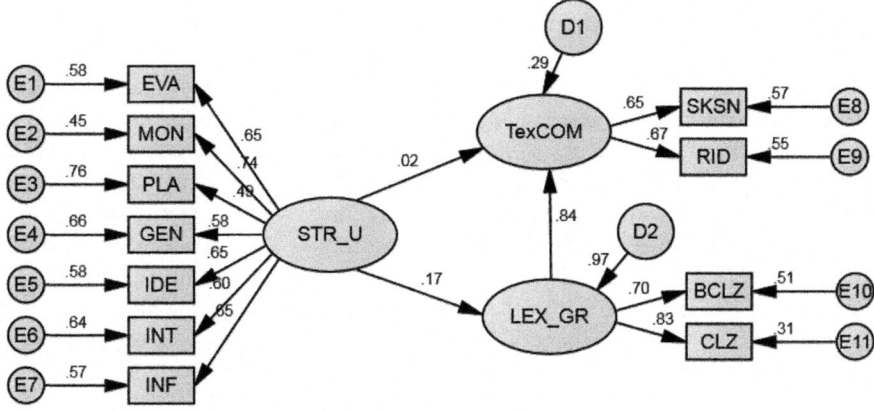

Fig. 6.4 The final model for the female group

6.4 Discussion

Three questions were put forward in Study 2 regarding gender differences in strategy use and reading test performance. This section discusses the results of statistical analyses in relation to these questions.

Research Question 5: Is the factorial structure of the reading comprehension test performance as measured by the retired CET-4 Reading subtest invariant across male and female students?

As shown in Figs. 6.3 and 6.4, the CET-4 Reading subtest had two underlying factors: LEX_GR and TxtCOM. Based on the invariance test of the factorial structure of the test model (Model 3 in Tables 6.5 and 6.6) which boils down to the chi-square difference test, it was found that the constraints on the factor loadings with SKSN, RID, BCLZ, and MCLZ did not produce a significantly different model from the baseline model. This indicates that the factorial structure of the reading comprehension test performance as measured by the CET-4 Reading subtest is generalizable across male and female groups in this study. In other words, it shows that the way male students respond to the reading comprehension test is not significantly different from that of the female students. This finding provides positive support for the validity argument for the reading comprehension test, suggesting that the test was not biased toward male or female groups.

As indicated by Muthén (cited in Bae & Bachman, 1998), measurement invariance is equivalent to differential item functioning (DIF) in essence, although one of the most frequently used methods of DIF analysis is through Rasch-based DIF analysis (Aryadoust, Goh, & Lee, 2011). Furthermore, the finding resonates with Hyde's (2005) the conclusion of gender similarities hypothesis, which found little evidence of gender differences on most psychological measures based on a review of 46 meta-analyses. In addition, Phakiti (2003) and McGeown, Goodwin, Henderson, and Wright (2012) also found that males and females did not differ in their reading comprehension performance.

Although male and female students are not significantly different based on the analysis, in the separate group analysis, TxtCOM is regressed on LEX_GR at a high value of 0.97 for the male group, whereas for the female group the loading was 21% lower ($\beta = 0.76$), as shown in Figs. 6.1 and 6.2. This indicates that compared with female students, male students' LEX_GR explained a greater variance of their TxtCOM, indicating that male students relied more on their fundamental skills of word processing in the process of reading comprehension than female readers. In other words, these male readers appear to be at a more fundamental stage than the female readers in this study, suggesting that they have overall lower reading ability compared with the female students. This is supported by their lower mean scores in all four sections of the reading comprehension test as shown in Table 6.3. The finding seems to be in line with the studies which showed that females performed better than males in comprehending written texts (e.g., Farhady, 1982; Logan & Johnson, 2009; Wen & Johnson, 1997). The interpretation for this finding might be that females are commonly perceived as better language learners in L2 learning (Chavez, 2001).

To sum up, based on the analysis, it was found that in spite of the differences between male and female students, their responses to the reading comprehension test across were not significantly different. In other words, the results from this study showed that male and female students are not significantly different from each other in their test performance.

Research Question 6: Is the factorial structure of the strategy use as measured by the strategy use questionnaire invariant across males and females?

In the SEM analysis, it was found that the seven types of strategies (i.e., PLA, EVA, MON, GEN, IDE, INT, and INF) accounted for the variance of the strategy use data well (see Figs. 5.10 and 5.11). Further multi-group SEM analyses showed that four types of strategies (i.e., PLA, IDE, INT, and INF) are generalizable across gender groups, but three types (i.e., EVA, MON, and GEN) are employed in significantly different manners between male and female groups (see Tables 6.5 and 6.6). As shown in the separate and simultaneous group analysis (see Figs. 6.3 and 6.4), EVA ($\beta = 0.71$ for the male group, and $\beta = 0.65$ for the female group) and MON ($\beta = 0.79$ for the male group, and $\beta = 0.74$ for the female group) are loaded on STR_U at a higher value in the male group than in the female group. This seems to indicate that metacognitive strategies (i.e., EVA and MON) are perceived as more important to male than female students. In addition, general progression strategies (i.e., GEN) ($\beta = 0.72$ and $\beta = 0.73$ for the male group, and $\beta = 0.59$ and $\beta = 0.58$ for the female group as shown in Figs. 6.1, 6.2, 6.3, and 6.4) appear to be more important to male than female students.

The finding that metacognitive strategies (i.e., EVA and MON) appeared to be more frequently needed by males than females is consistent with findings by Phakiti (2003) who concluded that males reported significantly higher use of metacognitive strategies than females. It is also congruent with Young and Oxford's (1997) finding that male students use more monitoring strategies in their processing of written texts. The similar finding that males employ more metacognitive strategies than females in test situations might be related to the gender differences in test anxiety. Compared with males, females have higher test anxiety (Zeidner, 1998), which may cause them to be worried and lack self-confidence. As a result, this may affect their overall employment of quality strategies. This has several implications for practice in language instruction and assessment. On the one hand, instructors could attempt to provide gender-related strategy instructions in test and non-test contexts; on the other hand, test designers may consider incorporating these gender differences in strategy use in designing tests.

Additionally, although the test of invariance holds regarding other types of strategies (i.e., PLA, IDE, INT, and INF) across the gender groups, there are still some differences arising from the comparison between them. For example, in the simultaneous group analysis (see Figs. 6.3 and 6.4), PLA had a higher loading on STR_U for the male group ($\beta = 0.52$ for male group, and $\beta = 0.49$ for the female group), whereas INF had a higher loading on STR_U higher for the female group than the male group ($\beta = 0.57$ for the male group, and $\beta = 0.65$ for the female group). On the other hand, in the separate and simultaneous analysis, IDE ($\beta = 0.62$ and 0.63 for the male group, and $\beta = 0.67$ and $\beta = 0.65$ for the female group), and INT ($\beta = 0.65$ and $\beta = 0.62$ for the male group, and $\beta = 0.70$ and $\beta = 0.60$ for the female group), all had higher loadings for the female group than the male group.

Taken together, it was concluded that metacognitive strategies (i.e., EVA, MON, and PLA) appeared to be more important to male than female students. While except for the general progression strategies (GEN) which are fundamental strategies in reading comprehension, the other cognitive strategies (IDE, INT, and INF) seemed to be more important to female than male students. The finding lends support to our answer to Research Question 5 which suggested that although both gender groups responded to the reading test similarly, male students relied more on fundamental skills of word recognition and syntactic parsing, etc., in the process of reading comprehension than female students. An information processing model of reading showed that readers construct meaning from the text using multiple tools such as their past experience, prior knowledge, or strategies. In the process of reading comprehension, these tools may help enhance readers' performance in a compensatory or interactive manner. In other words, it is likely that students may use their strong skills to compensate for their weak skills. As such, the male readers, who appear to be less proficient readers, tend to resort to the use of strategies to compensate for their inadequacy in language processing skills. Additionally, since this study concerns strategy use in the test context in which test takers have to manage their reading comprehension and test-taking processes (Cohen & Upton, 2006), it is understandable why less advanced male readers reported more use of metacognitive strategies. On the other hand, as more advanced readers, female students appeared to employ a more balanced combination of cognitive and metacognitive strategies as shown in the separate and simultaneous group analysis. This is supported by Pearson (2009) who argued that a "healthy repertoire of strategies" helps to repair comprehension failure and maximize comprehension of the text (p. 14).

In addition, as shown in Figs. 6.1, 6.2, 6.3, and 6.4, it is worth mentioning that MON ($\beta = 0.78$ and $\beta = 0.79$ for the male group, and $\beta = 0.74$ for the female group) and EVA ($\beta = 0.71$ for the male group, and $\beta = 0.65$ for the female group) were loaded on STR_U at high values for both groups in the separate and simultaneous group analysis, indicating that these metacognitive strategies are pivotal in taking the CET-4 Reading subtest. This finding resonates with Song (2005) who argued that monitoring strategies were especially important to MELAB test takers. In addition, it supports Bachman and Palmer's (2010) language use framework in that metacognitive strategies determine how test takers actualize their language knowledge.

In summary, the analysis of the strategy use model showed that males and females differ in some aspects of their strategy use (i.e., EVA, MON, and GEN) but are identical in others (i.e., PLA, IDE, INT, and INF) on the reading comprehension test. That is to say, they are similar in using planning, identifying, integrating, and inference-making strategies, but different in employing evaluating, monitoring, and general progression strategies in their reading comprehension test.

Research Question 7: Is the structure of the relationships between test takers' strategy use and reading test performance invariant across males and females?

The SEM analysis of the relationships between the test takers' strategy use and reading test performance showed that the test takers' strategy use affected their LEX_GR significantly ($\beta = 0.20$ for the male group, and $\beta = 0.15$ for the female group as shown in Figs. 6.1 and 6.2), whereas the effect of strategy use on TxtCOM was relatively weak for both gender groups ($\beta = 0.06$ for males and $\beta = -0.02$ for females). The multi-group SEM analysis (see Figs. 6.3 and 6.4) showed similar patterns but some divergence in the coefficients in that TxtCOM loaded on STR_U at 0.02, while LEX_GR on STR_U at 0.17 for both male and female groups. This indicated that the factorial structure of the structure model was invariant across the male and female group, meaning that structural model of strategy use was generalizable across two groups.

There are two possible interpretations for the relationships between test takers' strategy use and reading test performance across gender groups. On the one hand, as shown in Figs. 6.3 and 6.4, STR_U affected males' LEX_GR to a greater degree than females'. According to previous findings, males were shown to be less advanced readers; as such, strategy use seems to be more important to them in compensating for their lack of language ability (Rumelhart, 2004; Stanovich, 1980). On the other hand, strategies seemed to play an important role for the items tapping into test takers' lower level processing skills (i.e., LEX_GR). In contrast, for the items included in RID and SKSN which are designed to tap into test takers' higher level ability (i.e., TxtCOM), the function of strategy use in compensating for the lack of proficiency became less prominent. This is because higher-order skills, often linked to high language proficiency levels, are required to make correct responses to such items. If students' proficiency levels are limited, the quality or quantities of their strategy use may suffer. In other words, they may not be able to employ multiple strategies effectively in answering the more demanding items. This result is congruent with Phakiti's (2008) finding that cognitive strategy use explained 16–30% of test takers' lexico-grammatical performance. Additionally, this also concurs with Bachman's (1990) argument that strategy use is only one part of test takers' characteristics among the factors that affect performance on language tests.

To summarize, it was found that the relationships between test takers' strategy use and their reading test performance are generalizable across gender groups, indicating the congruence of the current finding with Hyde's (2005) gender similarities hypothesis which argued that males and females are "similar on most psychological variables" (p. 581).

In summary, this chapter presented the results of Study 2, gender differences in test takers' strategy use and reading test performance. First, preliminary analyses were performed and the results were presented. Next, single-group SEM analyses were conducted to establish the baseline model for each gender group. Based on the displayed results, SEM analyses for cross-validation were conducted and the results were shown. Additionally, this chapter discussed the results in relation to the three research questions raised in Study 2. Results indicated that the invariance of the factorial structure of the reading test and relationships between test takers' strategy use and reading test performance was supported. However, male and female students were found to be different in their use of some strategies. In conclusion, the results showed that although gender differences can be perceived in their reading ability level and strategy use pattern, there seems to be a degree of overlap between male and females in terms of the way they respond to reading comprehension tasks and employ strategies to tackle the tasks.

References

Aryadoust, V., Goh, C., & Lee, O. K. (2011). An investigation of differential item functioning in the MELAB listening test. *Language Assessment Quarterly, 8*(4), 361–385.

Bachman, L. F. (1990). *Fundamental consideration in language testing*. Oxford, England: Oxford University Press.

Bachman, L. F., & Palmer, A. S. (2010). *Language testing in practice*. Oxford, England: Oxford University Press.

Bae, J., & Bachman, L. F. (1998). A latent variable approach to listening and reading: Testing factorial invariance across two groups of children in the Korean/English Two-way Immersion program. *Language Testing, 15*, 380–414.

Byrne, B. M. (2001). *Structural equation modeling with AMOS: Basic concepts, applications, and programming*. Mahwah, NJ: Erlbaum.

Byrne, B. M. (2006). *Structural equation modeling with EQS: Basic concepts, applications, and programming* (2nd ed.). Mahwah, NJ: Lawrence Erlbaum Associates.

Byrne, B. M. (2011). *Structural equation modeling with Mplus: Basic concepts, applications*

Chavez, M. (2001). *Gender in the language classroom*. Boston: McGraw Hill.

Cohen, A. D., & Upton, T. A. (2006). *Strategies in responding to the new TOEFL reading tasks* (Monograph No. 33). Princeton, NJ: ETS. Retrieved from http:// www.ets.org/Media/Research/pdf/RR-06-06.pdf

Farhady, H. (1982). Measures of language proficiency from the learners' perspective. *TESOL Quarterly, 16*(1), 43–59.

Hyde, J. S. (2005). The gender similarities hypothesis. *American Psychologist, 60*(6), 581–592.

In'nami, Y., & Koizumi, R. (2011). Factor structure of the revised TOEIC® test: A multiple-sample analysis. *Language Testing, 29*(1), 131–152.

Kline, R. B. (2011). *Principles and practices of structural equation modeling* (2nd ed.). New York: Guilford.

Logan, S., & Johnson, R. S. (2009). Gender differences in reading: Examining where these differences lie. *Journal of Research in Reading, 32*(2), 199–214.

McGeown, S., Goodwin, H., Henderson, N., & Wright, P. (2012). Gender differences in reading motivation: Does sex or gender identity provide a better account? *Journal of Research in Reading, 35*(3), 328–336.

Pearson, P. D. (2009). The roots of reading comprehension instruction. In S. E. Israel & G. Duffy (Eds.), *Handbook of research on reading comprehension* (pp. 3–31). New York: Routledge.

Phakiti, A. (2003). A closer look at gender differences in strategy use in L2 reading. *Language Learning, 53*(4), 649–702.

Phakiti, A. (2008). Construct validation of Bachman and Palmer's (1996) strategic competence model over time in EFL reading tests. *Language Testing, 25*(2), 237–272.

Purpura, J. E. (1998). Investigating the effects of strategy use and second language test performance with high- and low-ability test takers: A structural equation modeling approach. *Language Testing, 15*, 333–379.

Rumelhart, D. (2004). Toward an interactive model of reading. In R. B. Rudell & N. J. Unrau (Eds.), *Theoretical models and processes of reading* (5th ed., pp. 1149–1179). Newark: International Reading Association.

Song, X. (2005). Language learner strategy use and English proficiency on the Michigan English Language Assessment Battery. *Spaan Fellow Working Papers in Second or Foreign Language Assessment, 3*, 1–23.

Stanovich, K. E. (1980). Towards an interactive-compensatory model of individual differences in the development of reading fluency. *Reading Research Quarterly, 16*, 32–71.

Wen, Q., & Johnson, R. (1997). L2 learner variables and English achievement: A study of tertiary-level English majors in China. *Applied Linguistics, 18*, 27–48.

Young, D. J., & Oxford, R. (1997). A gender-related analysis of strategies used to process written input in the native language and a foreign language. *Applied Language Learning, 8*, 43–73.

Zeidner, M. (1998). *Test anxiety: The state of the art.* New York, London: Plenum Press.

Chapter 7
Implications and Recommendations

Abstract This chapter discusses the implications of the current study, based on its findings pertaining to the effect of metacognitive and cognitive strategy use on reading test performance, as well as the gender differences in strategy use and reading test performance. Implications of the findings for classroom teachers and language assessment are provided, followed by recommendations for classroom instruction and future research in this field. Conclusions of the overall study are presented at the end of this chapter.

This chapter makes final conclusions on the basis of the empirical results described and introduced in previous chapters. Pedagogical, theoretical, and methodological implications derived from this study are discussed in relation to L2 reading assessment, instruction, and acquisition. Suggestions for classroom instruction and further research on the issue of strategy use on reading comprehension tests are introduced and presented.

This study was designed to investigate the relationships between Chinese college test takers' metacognitive and cognitive strategy use on a tertiary level EFL reading comprehension test widely used in mainland China, the CET-4 Reading subtest. Seven research questions were addressed in this study.

Results showed that (a) the strategies used by Chinese college test takers on the CET-4 Reading subtest fall under seven categories: planning strategies, evaluating strategies, monitoring strategies, general progression strategies, strategies for identifying important information, integrating strategies, and inference-making strategies; (b) factorial analysis showed that the CET-4 Reading subtest had two underlying factors: LEX_GR and TxtCOM; (c) test takers' strategy use affected test takers' LEX_GR significantly but its effect on TxtCOM was weak and insignificant; (d) metacognitive and cognitive strategies function in synergy in the test context to collectively enhance test takers' test performance, suggesting that metacognitive and cognitive strategies are difficult to separate in actual language use situations; (e) it was found that there was no significant difference in test takers' response to the reading comprehension test across gender groups; (f) although there were no significant differences in strategy use across gender groups in their response to the

© Springer Nature Singapore Pte Ltd. 2018   147
L. Zhang, *Metacognitive and Cognitive Strategy Use in Reading Comprehension*,
https://doi.org/10.1007/978-981-10-6325-1_7

reading comprehension test, male and female test takers differ in some aspects of their use of strategies but are identical in others; and (g) it was found that the relationships between test takers' strategy use and their reading test performance are generalizable across gender groups.

7.1   Implications for Classroom Teachers

This study has important pedagogical implications for classroom teachers who teach English as a second or foreign language.

7.1.1   Pedagogical Implications of Study 1

In Study 1, multi-sample analyses were used to cross-validate the unitary model of test takers' strategy use and reading test performance across two groups of similar characteristics. Results showed that the unitary model was generalized across samples among Chinese college test takers of the CET-4 Reading subtest.

The findings have pedagogical implications for school instructors. For example, this study found that test takers' strategy use can improve test takers' reading test performance (Cohen, 2006), but this is mainly limited to the items which measure lexico-grammatical knowledge that supports reading comprehension fundamentally. For the items which assess higher level reading ability, strategy use appears to play a less important role as the compensatory function of strategies may have a limited effect on the challenging items tapping into test takers' higher level reading skills (Rumelhart, 2004; Stanovich, 1980). This suggests that instruction on reading strategies or even test management strategies may only partially influence test takers' reading performance. Thus, classroom instructors would need to focus on the improvement of students' language knowledge in order to support their reading ability. At the same time, however, they would still need to help learners use relevant strategies which enable them to use not only contextual clues for word-level inference-making, but also more general discourse cues for higher order comprehension.

For students, this study showed that reading and test management strategies function well with easier items but not with more challenging ones. To improve reading test scores substantively, they not only need to practice using strategies during the test, but also have to make efforts to enhance their comprehensive language ability greatly. For example, students can improve their reading skills by building up their vocabulary knowledge, content knowledge, inference-making ability, etc. That way, their performance on reading comprehension tests is likely to improve in a significant manner.

7.1.2 Pedagogical Implications of Study 2

In Study 2, gender differences in strategy use and reading test performance were examined through the use of multi-group SEM. The results showed that the factorial structure of the reading comprehension test, some parts of the factorial structure of the strategy use (i.e., PLA, IDE, INT, and INF), and the relationships between test takers' strategy use and reading test performance are generalizable across male and female students. However, EVA, MON, and GEN in the strategy use model are not invariant across gender groups. These results were similar to Hyde's (2005) gender similarities hypothesis which showed that males and females are similar on most but not all psychological variables.

In other words, the finding is that while gender differences can be perceived through reading ability level and strategy use patterns, males and females are similar in the way of responding to reading comprehension tasks and employing strategies to tackle the tasks. This conclusion carries pedagogical implications for classroom teachers in that it is necessary that they should be aware of the existing differences across gender groups in implementing the curricula and carrying out academic activities. For example, teachers should be focusing on those strategies that a gender group does not seem to use in classroom instruction. Similarly, this finding offers some guidance to test developers in developing and designing tests in that there should be a fine balance between what is fair to a gender and what is deemed necessary to learn for students. A good example of gender balance in test development is that while selecting passages for reading comprehension tests, test developers should try to ensure the content of the passage is not biased toward any gender group. If every effort is made to avoid gender bias, chances are that the gender balance can be achieved.

7.2 Implications for the Field of Language Testing

This study provides the following implications in terms of theory, methodology, and practice for the field of language assessment and testing.

7.2.1 Theoretical Implications

This study has not only provided supporting evidence for the underlying structure of ESL/EFL reading test performance but also given implications for the relationships between metacognitive and cognitive strategies in test contexts, which extended the study about language users' metacognitive awareness to test contexts. In addition, it provided validating information for Bachman and Palmer's (2010) language use framework, especially regarding the role of strategic competence in this model.

Researchers have long been interested in defining the construct of L2 reading ability and investigating the factorial structure of reading test performance as measured by L2 reading comprehension tests (e.g., Child, 1988; Koda, 2007; Phakiti, 2008). The findings derived from Study 1 showed that there are two underlying factors on the EFL reading comprehension test as measured by the CET-4 Reading subtest: LEX_GR and TxtCOM. In addition, LEX_GR was found to have a direct effect on TxtCOM. This finding is very consistent with the Simple View of Reading in which comprehension is understood as a combination of word decoding abilities and text comprehension abilities (Gough & Tunmer, 1986). In addition, it also resonates with Phakiti (2008) study on Thai college students regarding the factorial structure of an L2 reading comprehension test. Additionally, it also extended the finding about the underlying structure of a L2 reading test in that Chinese college test takers were involved in this study. Thus, it provides further empirical evidence for the theoretical construct of second language reading ability.

Additionally, in Study 1, the relationships between metacognitive and cognitive strategy use on the reading comprehension test were investigated. Researchers have argued that students' metacognitive strategy use and cognitive strategy use are either two parallel components of a hierarchical model (e.g., O'Malley & Chamot, 1990; Oxford, 1990), or correlated with each other (Phakiti, 2008; Purpura, 1997). This study demonstrated empirically that they were unitary in actual use contexts, which concurs with some researchers' views (e.g., Baker, 1991; Chapelle, Grabe, & Berns, 1997; Goh, 2008; Paris, Wasik, & Turner, 1991). In other words, metacognitive and cognitive strategies function collectively in test contexts to enhance test takers' test performance. This suggests that metacognitive and cognitive strategies are hardly distinguishable in language use, especially in test contexts.

In addition, how students use these two types of strategies depends on the variation of topics, tasks, and individuals (e.g., Baker, 1991; Chapelle et al., 1997; Paris et al., 1991; Vandergrift, Goh, Mareschal, & Tafaghodtari, 2006). For example, in the test context, students have to deal with both reading and test task demands, which means that they are required to arrive at an appropriate level of understanding of the text and select the correct answer under time constraints. Therefore, the metacognitive and cognitive strategies they use form a continuum (Phakiti, 2008; Purpura, 1999), and it is difficult to draw a clear-cut dividing line between them, which suggests that there are some strategies that are not clearly cognitive or metacognitive. This is something that might be inherent in the construct. This finding about language users' metacognitive awareness, especially their use of metacognitive and cognitive strategy use in the test context, has therefore extended the investigation about language learners' metacognitive awareness in general and for reading in particular.

Furthermore, the above-mentioned findings about metacognitive and cognitive strategy use provide supporting evidence for Bachman and Palmer's (1996) model of language use. According to this model, language ability is composed of language knowledge and strategic competence. Strategic competence is perceived as a set of metacognitive strategies which provide management function in language use. Bachman and Palmer (2010) updated this model and included cognitive strategies. According to the new model, metacognitive strategies are perceived to be equivalent to strategic competence, whereas cognitive strategies are regarded as "what language users employ when they execute plans" (p. 43). The findings from this study demonstrated that both metacognitive and cognitive strategies play a part in improving test takers' reading test performance. Furthermore, it showed that metacognitive and cognitive strategies function in synergy and collectively in actual language use situations. This, therefore, provides empirical information for the validation of Bachman and Palmer's (2010) framework.

7.2.2   Methodological Implications

This study not only demonstrated CFA as a useful statistical procedure for investigating the factorial structure of the CET-4 Reading subtest, but also showed the usefulness of multi-group SEM for examining the relationships between test takers' strategy use and test performance.

This study was one of the first studies to use CFA to investigate the factorial structure of reading test performance as measured by the CET-4 Reading subtest, although it has been used in listening assessment research (e.g., Aryadoust, 2012, 2013). It demonstrated how the CFA approach could be employed to investigate the underlying structure of the EFL reading test. First, a set of item-level EFAs was conducted to examine the structure of item clustering. On the basis of the results of EFAs, composite variables were formed. Based on the previous empirical studies and relevant literature, the model of the CET-4 Reading test was then hypothesized and tested. This study provides exploratory information about the factorial structure of the test and how to examine the underlying factors of the CET-4 by means of the CFA approach.

In addition, the present study also illustrated how to use the multi-group SEM approach to investigate the relationships between strategy use and reading test performance. Although some researchers have employed the SEM approach to investigate similar issues (Phakiti, 2008; Purpura, 1999), no previous studies have tested the invariance of the factor structure of the relationships between reading strategy use and reading test performance across samples of similar characteristics. First, the data set used in this study was randomly split into two halves. Before doing the multi-group SEM analyses, single-group analyses were conducted to identify a baseline model for each group among the three postulated models of strategy use and test performance (i.e., the unitary model, hierarchical trait model, and correlated model). After the best fitting model among the three hypothesized models was selected for both samples, multi-sample SEM analyses were performed to cross-validate the selected model to test the invariance of factor loadings, measurement error variances, structural regression coefficients, and factor variances of the baseline model. This study, therefore, demonstrated how to examine strategy use on reading test performance through multi-group SEM across samples of similar characteristics. In other words, this study explored the possibility of using this method to examine the test-taking process, which has attracted increasing attention from language testing researchers.

Moreover, this study demonstrated how to investigate strategy use and reading test performance with multi-group SEM across gender groups. Although previous studies have examined gender differences in strategy use and reading test performance (Phakiti, 2003), this study was the first to utilize the multi-group SEM to examine the invariance of models with regard to gender effect on strategy use and reading test performance between gender groups. First, a single-group analysis was conducted to build a baseline model for each gender group. After the baseline models were established for male and female student groups, respectively, multi-group SEM analyses were performed to cross-validate the two models to test the invariance of factor loadings, structural regression coefficients, and factor variances of the baseline model (Byrne, 2011). In previous research, gender differences in reading and strategy use were mainly investigated through t-test (Bügel & Buunk, 1996), factor analysis (Green & Oxford, 1995), and MANOVA (Phakiti, 2003). In addition, language assessment researchers also investigated gender bias issues through different item functioning (Aryadoust, Goh, & Lee, 2011). However, with the exception of the current study, to date, no studies have investigated gender differences through multi-group SEM. Therefore, this study appears to be original in terms of the methodology used to examine gender differences in strategy use and reading test performance.

7.3 Recommendations for Classroom Instruction and Future Research

This study has provided several recommendations for language instruction and research.

7.3.1 Potential Use of the ReTSUQ

In this study, the ReTSUQ was designed as a tool to calibrate test takers' metacognitive awareness and strategy use in the context of reading comprehension tests. The responses obtained from it can be used for test takers to enhance test performance, teachers to improve classroom instruction, and researchers to validate reading tests.

First, the instrument enables readers and test takers to evaluate their metacognitive awareness in reading comprehension tests. Reading is "a powerful means of developing literacy, of developing reading comprehension ability, writing style, vocabulary, grammar, and spelling" (Krashen, 1993, p. 22). In addition, reading comprehension has become one of the most dominant components of a growing number of high-stakes tests in the modern world. How to improve reading test performance has become a primary concern of students and instructors. Employing the ReTSUQ alongside test practice will help students become constructively responsive and strategic readers and test takers (Pressley & Afflerbach, 1995), which in turn may contribute to better performance on reading tests.

Second, teachers and instructors can use the ReTSUQ as a diagnostic tool to assess, monitor, and document students' metacognitive awareness in the process of reading comprehension. The information regarding students' strategy use in reading comprehension can be gleaned from the part on cognitive strategy use, whereas their strategy use on a test can be best derived from the section on metacognitive strategy use. Teachers can examine them separately for a more efficient description of the individual profile and more convenient instruction. Further, the instrument can also be used as a preliminary documentation of students' metacognitive awareness followed by a thorough examination of individuals' think-aloud procedures. This may help keep track of individual performance in portfolios (Henk & Melnick, 1995).

Third, researchers can use the data obtained from the ReTSUQ to investigate the relationships between strategy use and reading test performance. More importantly, test takers' strategy use information can be a good source to examine if the expected processes have been engaged in the reading comprehension test. In other words, will the strategies test takers employ to tackle the items reflect the expected processes required in reading comprehension (Pearson, 2009)? The answer to this question may provide indirect evidence for or against the validity of the test involved (Bachman, 1990; Cohen, 2006). In short, the ReTSUQ provides a tool and platform for students, instructors, and researchers to evaluate and document test takers' metacognitive awareness and strategy use on reading comprehension tests for their specific purposes in the fields of learning, teaching, and research.

7.3.2 Recommendations for Future Research

Although this study made a detailed investigation into the relationships between Chinese college test takers' metacognitive and cognitive strategy use and their reading test performance, several issues which were not addressed in this study warrant further examination.

The first issue concerns the generalization of the current study. Although this study has revealed some interesting findings, it should be stressed that due to the limitations of the sample size and geographical sites of the participants, the generalization of the results to the entire CET-4 population or test takers of other reading tests might be restricted. Furthermore, as only Chinese college test takers were involved in this study, this might also restrict the generalization of this study to other samples from different cultural or educational backgrounds. Therefore, it is suggested that future research in this area be done with a larger CET-4 sample or other reading comprehension tests from different cultural and educational contexts, and with samples of different demographical characteristics. Hopefully, that will provide a broader perspective of test takers' strategy use and reading test performance.

The second issue relates to the operationalization of reading test performance. To investigate the underlying structure of L2 reading test performance, the model of the reading comprehension test was postulated on the basis of relevant literature and the test specifications of the CET-4 Reading. Therefore, it is recommended that future studies be conducted on different reading comprehension tests from different testing situations in order to provide a more complete and balanced view about the construct of L2 reading comprehension tests (Liao, 2009). Additionally, using a retired CET test and giving students a constrained amount of time to work on the test do not necessarily suggest that the test had effectively mimicked a real testing situation, which might otherwise show different patterns of factor loadings and structural parameters in the SEM analysis. It is thus suggested that future research be conducted in a real test situation for a more accurate understanding of test takers' strategy use.

Third, test takers' strategy use for each of the four test sections could be investigated more closely. In this study, the ReTSUQ was used to elicit test takers' general strategy use on the CET-4 Reading subtest. Although this method was useful in examining their pattern of metacognitive and cognitive strategy use on the test, it might over-generalize their specific use of strategies on different sections of the test. Thus, it is suggested that instead of calibrating their strategy use in relation to the overall reading test, further research in this respect could require test takers to report their strategy use in each specific section of the reading comprehension test. In this way, it will not only give a comprehensive and detailed picture of test takers' strategy use, but also have the potential to provide interesting validation information for the test on the basis of the differences in strategy use on different test sections of various test formats.

Furthermore, it is suggested that future research should investigate test takers' strategy use from both quantitative and qualitative perspectives to have a comprehensive picture and perspective of this issue. A quantitative study often has the appearance of rigor because of the statistical procedures, but the results are only as accurate as the information elicited from a questionnaire. Moroney (1956, cited in Cook, 1986) argued that it is a false belief to equate the accuracy of calculation to the accuracy of knowledge. It is recommended that for future studies, researchers collect think-aloud data of how test takers engage in the processes of reading comprehension and test-taking in the CET-4 Reading subtest. Findings from the analysis of think-aloud data can address the issue of how test takers use various metacognitive and cognitive strategies. This will complement and triangulate the findings from the quantitative analyses conducted in this study.

Finally, future studies on gender difference in strategy use are suggested to examine how gender identity rather than biological sex is related to students' reading comprehension performance. Recent research showed that students' psychological and cognitive differences can be better predicted by their gender identity instead of biological sex (e.g., McGeown, Goodwin, Henderson, & Wright, 2012; Pajares & Valiante, 2001). For example, according to McGeown et al. (2012), students can be invited to respond to a survey which measures their traditional masculine, feminine, and neutral traits. That way, comparison can be made between boys' and girls' differences in their gender traits and strategy use and reading test performance. Findings from this type of studies might be more revealing and illuminating.

In conclusion, the purpose of the current study was to investigate the relationships between Chinese college test takers' metacognitive and cognitive strategy use and their test performance on the CET-4 Reading subtest. As a study which made some exploratory attempts in methodology, it has derived some interesting and original findings with regard to Chinese college test takers' strategy use pattern on the test, the factorial structure of L2 reading test performance as measured by the CET-4 Reading subtest, the relationships between test takers' strategy use and reading test performance, the relationships between metacognitive and cognitive strategies in the test context, and the gender differences in strategy use and reading test performance. Finally, it is hoped that future research will address the limitations of the present study and resolve the several unanswered questions mentioned.

7.4 Conclusions

Research on ESL/EFL reading has suggested that comprehension cannot occur without successful operation of lower level processing such as word knowledge, syntactic parsing, and semantic proposition encoding (e.g., Gough & Tunmer, 1986; Grabe, 2009; LaBerge & Samuels, 1974; Samuels & LaBerge, 1983). From a theoretical perspective, this study has provided supporting evidence for the underlying structure of ESL reading test performance. In other words, it lends support to the findings about the theoretical construct of second language reading ability. In addition, it has also given implications for the relationships between metacognitive and cognitive strategies in the test context, which are meaningful in providing empirical support for Bachman and Palmer's (2010) language use framework, especially regarding the role of strategic competence in this model.

In terms of research methodology for ESL/EFL reading research, this study has offered new possibilities for a quantitative approach by using CFA to investigate the factorial structure of the CET-4 Reading subtest. Furthermore, it has demonstrated the value of employing multi-group SEM to examine the relationships between test takers' strategy use and test performance, which can be a point of departure for exploring test-taking processes through a variety of methods. In addition, this study has been exploratory in nature in terms of the methodology used to examine the gender differences in strategy use and reading test performance. It is hoped that it will provide useful information in methodology for further studies in this respect.

Finally, research on ESL/EFL reading should have important implications for pedagogy and our understanding of second language acquisition. This study has several implications for strategy use instructions in test and non-test contexts as well as among different gender groups. In line with the findings from this study, plans for strategy use instructions can be designed specifically for test and non-test contexts. Following an understanding of the differences in strategy use in gender groups, teachers can accommodate different gender groups' needs by means of strategy use awareness training to enhance their performance in test and non-test conditions. In addition, as indicated in the study, the function of strategy use is limited; thus, teachers and students not only need to focus on strategy use practice, but also have to make great efforts to enhance their comprehensive language ability.

In conclusion, it is hoped that this study has contributed to the investigation of L2 learners' strategy use in actual language use contexts, especially in test contexts, both empirically and theoretically.

References

Aryadoust, V. (2012). Differential item functioning in while-listening performance tests: The case of IELTS listening test. *International Journal of Listening, 26*(1), 40–60.

Aryadoust, V. (2013). *Building a validity argument for a listening test of academic proficiency.* Newcastle: Cambridge Scholars Publishing (CSP).

Aryadoust, V., Goh, C., & Lee, O. K. (2011). An investigation of differential item functioning in the MELAB listening test. *Language Assessment Quarterly, 8*(4), 361–385.

Bachman, L. F. (1990). *Fundamental consideration in language testing.* Oxford, England: Oxford University Press.

Bachman, L. F., & Palmer, A. S. (1996). *Language testing in practice.* Oxford, England: Oxford University Press.

Bachman, L. F., & Palmer, A. S. (2010). *Language testing in practice.* Oxford, England: Oxford University Press.

Baker, L. (1991). Metacognition, reading and science education. In C. M. Santa & D. E. Alvermann (Eds.), *Science learning* (pp. 2–13). Newark, DE: International Reading Association.

Bügel, K., & Buunk, B. P. (1996). Sex differences in foreign language text comprehension: The role of interests and prior knowledge. *Modern Language Journal, 80*(1), 15–31.

Byrne, B. M. (2011). *Structural equation modeling with Mplus: Basic concepts, applications, and programming.* New York: Routledge.

Chapelle, C., Grabe, W., & Berns, M. (1997). Communicative language proficiency: Definitions and implications for TOEFL 2000. *TOEFL Monograph Series No. 10.* Princeton, NJ: Educational Testing Service.

Child, J. (1988). Reading proficiency assessment: Section 1: A framework for discussion. In P. Lowe Jr. & C. W. Stansfield (Eds.), *Second language proficiency assessment: Current issues* (pp. 125–135). Englewood Cliffs, NJ: Prentice Hall.

Cohen, A. D. (2006). The coming age of research on test-taking strategies. *Language Assessment Quarterly, 3*(4), 307–331.

Cook, V. (1986). *Experimental approaches to second language learning.* Oxford: Pergamon Press.

Goh, C. (2008). Metacognitive instruction for second language listening development: Theory, practice and research implications. *RELC Journal, 39*(2), 188–213.

Gough, P. B., & Tunmer, W. (1986). Decoding, reading, and reading disability. *Remedial and Special Education, 7,* 6–10.

Grabe, W. (2009). *Reading in a second language: Moving from theory to practice.* Cambridge: Cambridge University Press.

Green, J. M., & Oxford, R. (1995). A closer look at learning strategies, L2 proficiency, and gender. *TESOL Quarterly, 29,* 261–297.

Henk, W. A., & Melnick, S. A. (1995). The Reader Self-Perception Scale (RSPS): A new tool for measuring how children feel about themselves as readers. *The Reading Teacher, 48,* 470–482.

Hyde, J. S. (2005). The gender similarities hypothesis. *American Psychologist, 60*(6), 581–592.

Koda, K. (2007). Reading and language learning: Crosslinguistic constraints on second language reading development. In K. Koda (Ed.), *Reading and language learning* (pp. 1–44). Special issue of *Language Learning Supplement, 57,* 1–44.

Krashen, S. (1993). *The power of reading.* Englewood, CO: Libraries Unlimited.

LaBerge, D., & Samuels, S. J. (1974). Toward a theory of automatic information processing. *Cognitive Psychology, 6*(2), 293–323.

Liao, Y.-F. (2009). *A construct validation study of the GEPT reading and listening sections: Re-examining the model of L2 reading and listening abilities and their relations to lexico-grammatical knowledge.* Unpublished Ph.D. dissertation. USA: Columbia University. *Language Learning, 35,* 423–430.

McGeown, S., Goodwin, H., Henderson, N., & Wright, P. (2012). Gender differences in reading motivation: Does sex or gender identity provide a better account? *Journal of Research in Reading, 35*(3), 328–336.

Moroney, M. J. (1956). *Facts from figures.* Baltimore: Penguin.

O'Malley, J. M., & Chamot, A. U. (1990). *Learning strategies in second language acquisition.* Cambridge: Cambridge University Press.

Oxford, R. L. (1990). *Language learning strategies: What every teacher should know.* New York: Newbury House.

Pajares, F., & Valiante, G. (2001). Gender differences in writing motivation and achievement of middle school students: A function of gender orientation? *Contemporary Educational Psychology, 26,* 366–381.

Paris, S. G., Wasik, B., & Turner, J. (1991). The development of strategic readers. In R. Barr et al. (Eds.), *Handbook of reading research* (pp. 609–640). New York: Longman.

Pearson, P. D. (2009). The roots of reading comprehension instruction. In S. E. Israel & G. Duffy (Eds.), *Handbook of research on reading comprehension* (pp. 3–31). New York: Routledge.

Phakiti, A. (2003). A closer look at gender differences in strategy use in L2 reading. *Language Learning, 53*(4), 649–702.

Phakiti, A. (2008). Construct validation of Bachman and Palmer's (1996) strategic competence model over time in EFL reading tests. *Language Testing, 25*(2), 237–272.

Pressley, M., & Afflerbach, P. (1995). *Verbal protocols of reading: The nature of constructively responsive reading.* Hillsdale, NJ: Erlbaum.

Purpura, J. E. (1997). An analysis of the relationships between test takers' cognitive and metacognitive strategy use and second language test performance. *Language Learning, 47,* 289–325.

Purpura, J. E. (1999). *Learner strategy use and performance on language tests: A structural equation modeling approach.* Cambridge, UK: Cambridge University Press.

Rumelhart, D. (2004). Toward an interactive model of reading. In R. B. Rudell & N. J. Unrau (Eds.), *Theoretical models and processes of reading* (5th ed., pp. 1149–1179). Newark: International Reading Association.

Samuels, S. J., & LaBerge, D. (1983). A critique of 'A theory of automaticity' in reading: Looking back: A retrospective analysis of the LaBerge-Samuels reading model. In L. Gentile, M. L. Kamil, & J. Blanchard (Eds.), *Reading research revisited* (pp. 34–56).

Stanovich, K. E. (1980). Towards an interactive-compensatory model of individual differences in the development of reading fluency. *Reading Research Quarterly, 16,* 32–71.

Vandergrift, L., Goh, C. C. M., Mareschal, C. J., & Tafaghodtari, M. H. (2006). The metacognitive awareness listening questionnaire: Development and validation. *Language Learning, 56*(3), 431–462.

Appendix A
Participant Information Sheet and Consent Form

Dear participants:

I am a research scholar at the English Language and Literature Academic Group, National Institute of Education, Nanyang Technological University, Singapore, pursuing my Doctor of Philosophy studies in Applied Linguistics. The research I am currently conducting is about the relationship between CET−4 test takers' strategy use and their test performance, the results of which is expected to provide some insights into second language reading instructions, CET−4 test preparation instructions, as well as the construct validation of the CET−4 Reading subtest.

Three main research instruments will be used in this study: a new version of the CET−4 Reading subtest, a strategy use questionnaire, and students' verbal report about the process of their completion of the reading test. As a university student, you are cordially invited to participate in this study. However, the strong conviction is that only your voluntary participation can bring benefits to this study. Therefore, you are encouraged to sign on this consent form to indicate that it is of your own volition to involve in this study. Please be assured that all collected data will be kept confidential and anonymous. All information obtained will be used for research purposes only. No participants' name will be identified in any report of the completed study.

Thank you very much for your participation and kind help. It is greatly appreciated.

Sincerely yours
Limei Zhang

© Springer Nature Singapore Pte Ltd. 2018
L. Zhang, *Metacognitive and Cognitive Strategy Use in Reading Comprehension*,
https://doi.org/10.1007/978-981-10-6325-1

Consent Form

I, _____ (Participant name/ Signature), hereby agree to take part in this research voluntarily and I understand all data will be kept confidential and anonymous. All information obtained will be used for research purposes. Participants will not be identified by name in any report of the complete study.

Appendix B
The Reading Test Strategy Use Questionnaire (ReTSUQ)

The purpose of this survey is to collect information about various strategies you use when taking academic reading comprehension tests. Each statement is followed by five numbers, 0, 1, 2, 3, 4, and 5, and each number means the following:

- 0 means that "I **never** do this." (从不)
- 1 means that "I **almost never** do this." (几乎从不)
- 2 means that " I do this **only occasionally**." (偶尔)
- 3 means that "I **sometimes** do this." (about **50%** of the time) (有时:大约50%的机率)
- 4 means that "I **usually** do this." (经常)
- 5 means that "I **always** or almost always do this." (总是).

After reading each statement, circle the number (0, 1, 2, 3, 4, or 5) which applies to you. Note that there is no right or wrong response to any of the items on this survey.

When taking reading comprehension tests

Strategy	Never					Always
1. I plan what to do before I start this reading test. 在开始做阅读测试前我计划要做些什么。	0	1	2	3	4	5
2. I make sure I am clear about the goals of the reading test task. 我确信自己已经明确阅读测试任务的目的。	0	1	2	3	4	5
3. I think over essential steps needed to complete the reading test. 我考虑完成阅读测试所需要的关键步骤。	0	1	2	3	4	5
4. I read the title first and think over what the content of the text is about. 我先阅读文章的题目并猜测文章的内容。	0	1	2	3	4	5
5. Test questions help me establish my purpose in reading. 我利用测试问题确立自己的阅读目的。	0	1	2	3	4	5
6. I know what to do if my plan does not work well when I complete the reading test. 在完成阅读测试时,如果我原定的计划无法有效实施我知道该做什么。	0	1	2	3	4	5

(continued)

© Springer Nature Singapore Pte Ltd. 2018
L. Zhang, *Metacognitive and Cognitive Strategy Use in Reading Comprehension*,
https://doi.org/10.1007/978-981-10-6325-1

(continued)

Strategy	Never					Always
7. I critically evaluate the information presented in the text. 我批判性地评估文中的信息。	0	1	2	3	4	5
8. I evaluate my plan of test completion constantly. 我不断审视自己的阅读计划。	0	1	2	3	4	5
9. I consider whether the content of the text fit my reading purpose. 我考虑文章的内容是否符合我的阅读目的。	0	1	2	3	4	5
10. I am aware of my loss of concentration in reading the text. 在阅读时我知道自己是否注意力涣散。	0	1	2	3	4	5
11. I infer what will happen next when reading the text. 在阅读文章时我思考下面会发生的情节。	0	1	2	3	4	5
12. I make summary of new information to understand the text better. 我总结新的信息以便更好理解文章内容。	0	1	2	3	4	5
13. I take notes to increase my understanding. 我做笔记帮助自己理解。	0	1	2	3	4	5
14. I paraphrase (restate in my own words) to better understand the text better. 我用自己的话重新表述文章的内容以增强理解。	0	1	2	3	4	5
15. I know when I understand something and when I do not. 我很清楚自己是否理解某些内容。	0	1	2	3	4	5
16. I knew when I should complete the test more carefully. 我知道什么时候应该更仔细地完成测试题目。	0	1	2	3	4	5
17. I adjust my reading speed to increase comprehension. 我调整阅读速度以便增强理解。	0	1	2	3	4	5
18. I am aware when and where I am confused in the text. 我注意到自己什么时候以及针对文章的哪些部分不清楚。	0	1	2	3	4	5
19. I know when I should complete the test more quickly. 我知道什么时候应该更快地完成测试题目。	0	1	2	3	4	5
20. I budget my time wisely on this test. 在测试中我有效地安排自己的时间。	0	1	2	3	4	5
21. I adjust pace in answering the questions. 在回答问题时我调整自己的速度。	0	1	2	3	4	5
22. I correct my misunderstanding or mistakes immediately when found. 如果发现理解错误我会立即改正错误。	0	1	2	3	4	5
23. I check my own performance and progress as I complete the test. 在完成测试题目时我审视自己的表现和进展。	0	1	2	3	4	5
24. I use context clues to help me better understand the text. 我利用上下文中的线索帮助自己理解。	0	1	2	3	4	5
25. I overview the text to see what it is about before reading it. 我在阅读文章前浏览文章的大意。	0	1	2	3	4	5
26. I preview the text first by noting its characteristics like length and organization. 我浏览全文并关注文章的长度和结构等特点。	0	1	2	3	4	5
27. I flip through the reading test before I actually start it. 在真正开始完成测试题目前我翻看整个试题册。	0	1	2	3	4	5

(continued)

(continued)

Strategy	Never					Always
28. I read the first sentence of each paragraph for the main idea. 我读每段的第一句话以找到段落大意。	0	1	2	3	4	5
29. I skip unknown words when reading. 在阅读时我跳过不认识的词语。	0	1	2	3	4	5
30. I scan reading materials for specific words or phrases. 我扫读文章以找到特定的词语或短语。	0	1	2	3	4	5
31. I use typographical features like boldface and italics to identify key information. 我利用印刷排版特点,如黑体和斜体识别重要信息。	0	1	2	3	4	5
32. When the text becomes difficult, I reread the problematic part to increase my understanding. 文章变难时,我反复阅读相关部分以便增强理解。	0	1	2	3	4	5
33. If I understand some parts, I would use it as a clue to help me understand other parts. 如果已明白文中的某些部分,我把它当作线索帮助自己理解。	0	1	2	3	4	5
34. I go back and forth in the text to find relationships among ideas in it. 我反复阅读文章寻找文中观点之间的关系。	0	1	2	3	4	5
35. I read the text not only for a surface understanding but also for its implied meaning. 我不光理解文章的表面含义还会推断其隐含的意思。	0	1	2	3	4	5
36. I guess the meanings of new words from the context. 我试图通过上下文猜测文中生词的含义。	0	1	2	3	4	5
37. I make inference beyond the information presented in the text. 我推测文章所提供信息以外的内容。	0	1	2	3	4	5
38. I try to use my prior knowledge to help my understanding. 我试图利用自己以前已有的知识帮助理解文章。	0	1	2	3	4	5

Appendix C
EFA Pattern Matrix of the ReTSUQ

Items	PLA	EVA	MON	INI	IDE	INT	INF
PLA1	**0.665**	0.083	−0.127	0.120	0.005	0.002	0.027
PLA2	**0.573**	0.005	0.107	−0.094	−0.127	0.152	0.131
PLA3	**0.640**	−0.039	0.056	0.147	−0.011	0.028	0.038
PLA4	**0.401**	−0.109	0.067	0.125	0.146	0.004	0.218
PLA5	**0.569**	0.174	−0.148	−0.077	0.039	0.057	−0.107
PLA6	**0.391**	−0.225	0.298	−0.174	0.171	0.002	−0.001
EVA7	−0.061	**0.547**	−0.033	0.160	−0.059	0.201	−0.049
EVA8	0.234	**0.558**	0.224	0.021	−0.060	−0.109	−0.258
EVA9	0.046	**0.704**	0.040	−0.113	0.029	−0.016	−0.010
EVA10	−0.087	**0.712**	−0.064	−0.012	0.114	−0.037	0.157
EVA11	−0.032	**0.674**	−0.070	−0.002	−0.038	−0.024	0.141
EVA12	−0.022	**0.602**	0.055	−0.002	−0.053	0.296	−0.012
EVA13	0.193	**0.594**	0.064	−0.141	0.004	−0.118	0.011
EVA14	−0.055	**0.581**	−0.057	−0.132	0.057	0.036	0.268
MON15	−0.290	0.015	**0.504**	0.235	−0.033	0.033	0.051
MON16	0.025	0.141	**0.740**	−0.144	−0.089	−0.100	−0.049
MON17	0.033	−0.014	**0.491**	0.040	0.148	0.143	−0.109
MON18	−0.102	0.195	**0.616**	−0.125	−0.070	0.017	0.207
MON19	0.034	−0.050	**0.582**	0.032	0.008	−0.141	0.149
MON20	0.174	−0.033	**0.570**	0.047	0.020	−0.186	−0.107
MON21	0.019	−0.091	**0.503**	0.101	0.153	0.125	−0.036
MON22	−0.023	−0.159	**0.488**	−0.086	−0.008	0.150	0.117
MON23	−0.068	0.161	**0.515**	0.188	0.046	−0.171	−0.033
MON24	−0.027	−0.061	**0.433**	−0.038	0.014	0.185	0.248
GEN25	0.137	0.016	−0.126	**0.640**	0.018	0.008	0.110
GEN26	0.204	0.050	−0.098	**0.629**	−0.060	0.004	0.241
GEN27	−0.144	−0.196	0.240	**0.631**	0.041	0.038	−0.001
IDE28	−0.018	0.155	−0.040	0.091	**0.594**	0.056	−0.177
IDE29	−0.012	0.010	−0.149	−0.115	**0.570**	0.150	0.194

(continued)

© Springer Nature Singapore Pte Ltd. 2018
L. Zhang, *Metacognitive and Cognitive Strategy Use in Reading Comprehension*,
https://doi.org/10.1007/978-981-10-6325-1

(continued)

Items	PLA	EVA	MON	INI	IDE	INT	INF
IDE30	0.064	−0.062	0.197	−0.093	**0.552**	−0.049	−0.032
IDE31	0.056	−0.054	0.074	0.117	**0.490**	0.178	−0.132
INT32	0.099	−0.112	0.120	0.039	0.098	**0.585**	0.030
INT33	−0.029	0.088	0.060	−0.135	0.191	**0.438**	0.252
INT34	0.061	0.078	−0.113	−0.031	−0.026	**0.771**	0.008
INT35	0.028	0.030	−0.104	0.087	0.059	**0.801**	−0.120
INF36	−0.039	0.030	0.042	0.086	−0.034	0.018	**0.744**
INF37	0.084	0.005	0.074	0.105	−0.037	−0.059	**0.779**
INF38	0.170	0.278	0.041	0.123	−0.083	−0.077	**0.519**

Printed by Printforce, the Netherlands